Border Walk

Border Walk

Mark J. Hainds

Designed by Vince Pannullo
Printed in the United States of America by RJ Communications.

ISBN: 978-0-578-20170-2

Contents

For my mom and my wife; Betty brought me into this world and Katia is trying to keep me from leaving it prematurely.

1

PROLOGUE

YET another Border Patrol agent stopped in front of us. A middle-aged white guy with captain's bars on his lapel exited the vehicle and approached, asking, "Do you know where you are?" Unspoken, but implied in his tone, *Dumbasses.*

Mike and I laughed, but he wouldn't have it.

"We just had an oil and gas employee and an electrical contractor assaulted out here. This is a very active area." The radio went off in his truck. "Excuse me, they're calling." He walked back to his truck.

Mike and I looked at each other. I said, "We aren't camping here tonight."

"Nope."

The captain returned and pointed down the road. "The pavement ends and past that is no-man's land. You won't have a signal. We can't even use our radios out there. If you get in trouble, you can't call for help. We find an average of fourteen bodies a year down here, and we save countless more. Sometimes their kidneys are shutting down, but we save most of them. The middle of Old Mines is between our sectors. We pretty much don't go there, and you need to be aware of the situation."

Any thoughts of Old Mines not living up to its reputation dissipated.

Asphalt became dirt, and our diligence heightened. If one side of the road was fenced and the other side wasn't, we hugged the fenced side. Anyone with bad intentions would have to cross the road or climb the fence to accost us. I scanned the ground like the Border Patrol, looking for signs of recent human passage.

A truck approached from our front with a crew of roughnecks. The unsmiling driver stopped beside us. "Do you know where you are?"

We didn't laugh the second time.

"We're starting to figure it out," I answered.

"You don't need to be out here after dark," said the driver.

They offered water, shook their heads in disbelief, and drove toward Eagle Pass.

I told Mike, "I only remember being asked that question twice in my life, and both times were today."

The wire had been pulled down at virtually every post. It looked like half of Mexico had crawled over the fence along this road.

Menace hung in the mesquite, like a spider-web laden with morning dew.

The road was straight and dark dots were just visible in the distance. Mike said, "We have pedestrians."

The dots moved toward us.

Mike dropped his gear, pulled his pistol, and chambered a round. He tucked the pistol in the belt behind his back before shouldering his pack.

They were still a couple of hundred yards out.

I snapped a quick picture in their direction, and the phone recorded the time of the photo as 1:22 p.m. I told Mike, "I'll go in front."

2

A FISH IN THE ROAD

"Some writers in the past have thought that living fully meant drinking heavily, experiencing many adventures, having a variety of lovers, and putting themselves in life-threatening danger. A full life, as many viewed it, was found at the extremes. I think of Ernest Hemingway running with the bulls, fighting in a war, deep-sea fishing, hunting big game, and then returning home to use the material as background for his writing."

Tina Welling. *Writing Wild: Forming a Creative Partnership with Nature.* 2014

ANXIETIES, frustrations, uncertainties, and stress: all are channeled so that negative becomes positive, fueling the body further and faster. The sun is glaring, but I wish it were hotter. Were it freezing, I would wish it colder. Physical discomfort, even pain, is desirable. It concentrates the mind on the here and now. Home and work, good and bad, it falls away. Were it not for walking, it would be alcohol or physical tasks that dull the senses and constrain a wandering mind.

I am walking. For the here and now, life narrows to the road before me.

It was hot and dry as I turned the corner at Rome, Alabama, from US 29 onto Lassiter Road; from pavement to dirt.

At one time, Rome had been a large enough community that it bore a name, and a rather grand name at that. Now Rome consists of a barn, an abandoned silo, a bunkhouse (primarily inhabited during Alabama's deer season), a defunct pecan orchard, and surrounding fields and pastures that alternate between corn, peanuts, Bermuda grass, and cotton.

Endurance training had just begun. A trek along the border would require physical and mental fortitude in equal measure.

Carrying a pack, I had put three miles behind me and had another six to the house. Semi-trailers with Mississippi license plates passed regularly as I walked north on Lassiter Road. The trucks carried steel frames, generators, tanks, and other hardware on their way in, and empty flatbeds on their way out.

The surface of the road was damp. Puzzling, considering the absence of thunder or clouds significant enough to produce precipitation.

A half-mile north of US 29, a minnow lay dead in the middle of the road. Ants had found the corpse, and it would be a miniature skeleton before dark.

It didn't take long to work out the how and the why. The stream of big trucks led to an oil or gas rig under construction. Someone paid a contractor to water the road, minimizing dust from continuous comings and goings of big rigs.

Perhaps this minnow was the big fish in his pond, puddle, or stream. Life was good. He would spend the rest of his years in this comfortable setting, consuming small invertebrates, breeding, and keeping a watchful eye for egrets and herons.

Then…catastrophe.

A large, flexible, black pipe splashed into his home and drafted him into a tank, just before he was dumped onto this road, to flop and gasp away his final moments.

Clearly, a sign.

Go to Texas or be sucked up and spit out to die by forces beyond my reckoning.

I picked up the pace.

3

THE TEX-MEX COMPADRES

"The Irish loved being told they were fearless bastards, crazy and unpredictable."

Timothy Egan. *The Immortal Irishman*, 2016

M OST great adventures require significant drudgery on the front end. Who will feed the chickens, dogs, and cat? Which flight? From which airport? How to get to the airport?

Pulling a Cheryl Strayed on the Texas-Mexico Border was out of the question. The author of *Wild* started hiking the Pacific Crest Trail with an overloaded backpack, virtually no physical conditioning, and boots she had never worn... with utterly predictable complications that a hiker could ill afford on the banks of the Rio Grande.

The importance of proper footwear cannot be overemphasized. Speaking as a former Combat Medic who has examined many a tortured foot, it is sometimes said that the first rule for infantrymen is: "Take care of your feet."

It took one hundred miles of hiking and four different pairs of boots before my feet found their home in a pair of Danner Kinetics, a modern version of the Army boots I wore in the eighties and nineties. The boots wore well on short walks, so the route was extended: eight miles, ten miles, fourteen, sixteen, eventually twenty miles, and no sore feet. I purchased an additional pair to wear on alternating days, a technique for minimizing foot fungus.

My confidence grew over the next four hundred miles, humping a pack over dirt roads around Covington County, Alabama, in the heat of the summer with lightning storms, yellow flies, and mosquitoes to spur me on.

To assist in the endeavor, a team of volunteers coalesced. Leading off was Jack, a retired forester from Swainsboro, Georgia. Jack would be followed by a pair of South Carolinians: Dr. Simons Hane, a soon-to-retire emergency room doc; and Simon's good friend—Mfundisi Ronnie, a professional hunter, farmer, and missionary in South Africa. Next up was Bob Larimore, a forester with the Department of Defense. Then Jimmy and Sierra Stiles, dear friends, herpetologists and neighbors from Pleasant Home, Alabama. Then Mike Powell, a best friend, all the way back to my youth on the farm. Following Mike, a hard-drinking, fishing, hunting, biologist friend named John Dickson would fly out for the lower Rio Grande Valley. John had grown up in Texas and Louisiana, and he was the only volunteer somewhat familiar with his section of the route. Rounding out the schedule was Curtis Hainds, my physician assistant brother who lives in Chicago. After some discussion among the lot, we settled on a name for the group: the "Tex-Mex Compadres."

The Compadres would make it to the Texas-Mexico border on their own. If they chose to fly out, my truck would be available for their one-to-two week stints.

We settled on three rules for the Compadres:

#1: Keep Mark alive. (If I ran out of water and perished somewhere in the Chihuahuan Desert, the book wouldn't get written—at least not by me.)

#2: Where Mark finishes one day's walk is where Mark starts the next day's walk.

#3: Mark can't walk past an open bar without taking a drink. (The Tex-Mex Compadres should scout the route accordingly.)

4

El Paso to Socorro

"The first rule of psychogeography is to walk through the streets without preconceived notions; just drift and let the city's underground currents take you where they will."

David Dorado Romo. *Ringside Seat to a Revolution: An Underground Cultural History of El Paso and Juarez: 1893-1923.* 2005

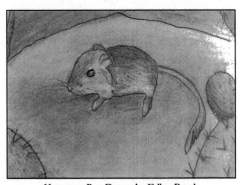

Kangaroo Rat: Drawn by Edlyn Burch

Oct 27–30

THE decision was made where two streams became one.

On the left was time, clear and fast, racing past at speeds unanticipated.

The stream on the right was murkier, its waters bearing unrealized dreams—if not pursued—then to haunt for all time.

I waded to the confluence and currents grabbed hold. Swept away like a buoy, I floated, delivered to a monument that marks the junction of two countries, two cultures, and two languages.

It began.

Rex, Jack, and I rendezvoused at the Hilton Garden Inn in El Paso. There was just enough time to seek out International Mile Marker #1 in the fading light. Nearby, large light banks with generators were strategically placed along the dirt road leading to the monument. Three young Border Patrol agents had followed us down the road.

I asked one, "Is that so you can see the illegals coming across?"

"It's like cockroaches, when the sun goes down…" he answered, while nodding toward the lights. "Sometimes they throw rocks at the lights."

I grimaced at the harsh comparison.

We returned the next morning at 7:15 a.m., on October 27.

Rex, a tall, energetic cinematographer from Hickory, Mississippi, set up his camera and checked a light meter while I paced back and forth, reciting a brief speech to mark the kickoff.

We had met in June while he was in Biloxi researching another film, eventually titled and released as *Longleaf: The Heart of Pine.*

For twenty years, my career centered on the restoration and management of longleaf pine. By the time we met in Biloxi, my resignation was in the works, and word was spreading among my circle of friends and acquaintants about the planned walk along the length of the Texas-Mexico border. When Rex was informed of this upcoming adventure, he asked to follow and film it for his next movie.

I told him, "Hell, yeah! Come on."

It was 7:30 a.m., and Rex had sufficient light.

"My name is Mark Hainds. I am at International Mile Marker #1, marking the border between Texas and Mexico. This is the beginning of a 1,100-mile hike, from El Paso to the Gulf of Mexico. On the front end of this journey, I will be ably assisted by the right honorable Jack of Swainsboro, Georgia, and the soon-to-be famous Tex-Mex Compadres. This journey will be documented by Rex Jones of the Southern Documentary Project at Ole Miss."

Looking into the camera, I continued, "I want to give the beginning of a salute to my two alma maters, and I hope to finish this at the Gulf of Mexico." Now facing the Rio Grande, I gathered my breath and bellowed "M-I-Z." Another breath, another shout, "Waarrr!" before turning back to the camera and saying, "Let's get going."

Jack stood behind Rex during the shoot. We had met up in Sonora, Texas, on the drive out from Alabama. After retiring from an industrial forestry career, Jack worked as a seedling salesman and representative for one of the biggest longleaf pine seedling producers in the country. We got to know each other through frequent encounters at forestry meetings across the Southeast. Whether he knew it or not, Jack was at least partly responsible for my border walk.

Jack once told me, "Now Mark, it doesn't matter how dog tired you are when you come in from the field. If Joseph [my son] says, 'I want to play with you, Daddy,' then you go play with him. Because someday very soon, he is going to tell you, 'Dad, I am leaving for college.' And that is going to break your heart. You will regret all those times you didn't play with him."

Jack's directions were not immediately implemented, but gradually, some portion of my work time became play time: throwing a ball; jumping on the trampoline; playing checkers, chess, and all kinds of games that Joseph invented with his amazing imagination.

Joseph was eight years old, and we'd come to believe he would be our only child. Then, with the able assistance of Dr. Inge, a fertility specialist in Mobile, Alabama, our second one was on the way. We got the news just two months before the scheduled walk. Although the due date was well past my intended return from the border, the pregnancy was further fuel for a fire Katia's friends were stoking. "How can you let Mark leave you all alone? What if he is killed, and you have to raise these children as a widow?"

To them, the walk was selfish indulgence. And I couldn't entirely discount this narrative, but obviously, I had a different perspective.

Too much time had been sequestered for work and other obligations. Job stress and travelling for work became intolerable. A reconfiguration was both necessary and unavoidable.

Besides the stress and exhaustion, inevitable mortality was brought front and center when a surgeon removed a tumor from my side. The doctors said there was little risk associated with the growth, but the word "tumor" carries a lot of baggage.

It was approaching five years since *Year of the Pig* was published, and in that short time, two characters from my first book had passed away.

Pekelo Cosma was a musician from Hana, a town in Maui, Hawaii. My young family had listened to Pekelo play slack-key guitar beneath a famous banyan tree in Lahaina. In a subsequent interview, we talked of the environmental and cultural pressures facing the island and its people. A short time later, Pekelo left the world at age fifty-one.

David Watson was a fellow pig hunter who worked as a professional hunting guide, and as an electrician on the crawler that carried the space shuttle at Cape Canaveral. I stayed in David's house before he guided me through a successful and exciting boar hunt from an airboat in the grassy swamps along the St. John's River. Only four months separated us in age, but David passed away on March 5, 2013, shortly after *Year of the Pig* was published, and one day after my birthday.

Was it my fate to work like a dog until falling dead from a faulty heart or a sudden attack of pneumonia? A fishing trip in Golden Meadow, Louisiana, with John Dickson, was nearly my last one, when my breath wouldn't come and the coughing wouldn't quit. I made it home with a cooler full of fish and went straight to the doctor. A technician chatted me up until she examined my X-Ray and allowed an "Ooohh" to escape before going silent. One lung was full of fluid, but antibiotics saved the day.

Would the dice keep rolling my way?

Dying in the middle of another eighty-hour workweek—the descent to hell would echo with my screams of regret.

Staying with The Longleaf Alliance and Auburn University meant another five years of travel and responsibilities strangling family time. At a minimum, resigning these positions and walking the border would shake things up. *If* I emerged on the other end of the Rio Grande Valley, I would have more time at home, material for a second book, and plenty of adventure along the way.

These considerations weren't fully recognized before the walk. They were pieces of a puzzle that gradually oriented into a picture of my life, as it was, and as it should be. Driving west toward Texas, the picture was framed, but the center was still blank.

After filming the kickoff at International Mile Marker #1, Rex and Jack drove to a bridge just upstream where they explained the situation to a pair of Border Patrol agents, as I walked from the monument.

Rex crossed the bridge to set up his camera while I waited on the west side of the Rio Grande, facing a figurative and literal bridge to the other side. This was it. A pile of sumbitches had predicted my failure or demise. Few were explicit; most betrayed their doubts through their eyes and silence.

For a select group of nonbelievers, my abject failure was preferable to a successful completion. My walking onto Boca Chica beach would disprove their assumption —that Mark was incapable of the task at hand. Now, I could prove them right, or I could prove them wrong.

Everything above the Rio Grande was a mess, but the riverbed provided an idyllic contrast to the industrial wasteland surrounding us. A foot or two of clear water flowed through the channel below. Turtles plied the waters with great egrets, ducks, and other wading birds. A train rumbled over a bridge in the background. My spirit calmed, and confidence flowed.

After a contemplative moment, I looked up and Rex waved me forward. On the other side of the Rio Grande, Jack handed me a beautiful walking stick carved of longleaf heart pine. Staff from the Brosnan Forest in South Carolina made and contributed it specifically for this trek. It was sturdy enough to give the meanest mutt a headache.

There was no established trail to follow. The route was up to me. I walked up a slope, around a chain-link fence, and onto a sidewalk beside a fast moving four-lane highway—the Loop 375 express. My attention turned to the road ahead. Where did this path lead?

Prior to the trek, close friends had issued dire warnings such as, "El Paso will be the most dangerous section of your walk."

But why? Because it was adjacent to Ciudad Juarez, a city widely recognized as one of the most dangerous on the planet?

Another friend had been stationed at nearby Fort Bliss (a misnomer if there ever was) in the late 1980s while I shipped off to the comparatively resort-like Fort Sam Houston in San Antonio. Two and a half decades later, my friend remembered and described El Paso as a "shithole." But knowing the habits of young soldiers in general, and my friend in particular, it's likely that his opinion of El Paso was cultivated at the pawnshops, liquor joints, and strip-clubs that aggregate on the periphery of Army bases. If a person were restricted to a one-mile ring around most military installations, the world would be a dark place indeed.

A cracked sidewalk led west through branches of a feathery green tree that had grown through the fence and over the sidewalk. A branch with sharp thorns hooked my right arm, stopping me in my tracks and drawing blood.

Welcome to Texas.

My attention snapped back to the present. After disentangling myself from the ornery tree, one eye scanned ahead while the other watched for unfamiliar plant life and potential threats in the immediate vicinity.

The highway became an overpass with no sidewalk, forcing me off the road. The way forward led under the highway and through a big construction project. Bobcats and forklifts forced me to maneuver a meandering path around heavy equipment, while skirting what appeared to be a Union Pacific switchyard. Eventually the border fence pinched me back onto the four-lane with no more walking space. I could turn around and walk back through the construction project, searching for an alternate route, or, I could cross the freeway.

Cars ran fast and steady. My pulse increased as I watched for a hole in the traffic, and my fingers went to my forehead, tracing the cross: "In the name of the father, the son, and the holy ghost. Go!"

I jumped the concrete barrier and ran across two lanes of fast moving traffic. A concrete barrier separated me from the next two lanes. I cleared it and paused a moment before dashing across at the next break in traffic. I cleared the third barrier and landed on a sidewalk with a pounding heart and heaving chest. Ten minutes into a months-long journey, with death cheated and blood drawn.

The sidewalk led to a bridge, crossing into downtown El Paso. Below the bridge, an old Santa Fe caboose was covered with an attractive rendition of a naked woman. My father rode a million miles on Santa Fe cabooses, working as a brakeman and fireman in his early years on freight. A mental image formed of Dad hopping onto the caboose with his lantern, coffee thermos, and duffel bag. If Billy Charles Hainds were looking down from heaven, he would have approved of the artist's work, but what would he have thought of this expedition?

Dad was a worrywart, but he was also a dreamer. I sensed his smile above me.

For the last two decades, I'd held dual positions as Research Coordinator with a nonprofit called The Longleaf Alliance, and as a Research Associate within the School of Forestry and Wildlife Sciences at Auburn University. With retirement only five years out, a letter of resignation was tendered, and I had embarked on a journey that might spell my doom.

The fault lay at my own feet—or possibly in my genes. Too many responsibilities both at work and home. My fate was sealed after volunteering for a new position as a liaison between The Longleaf Alliance and twenty new environmental groups that had formed across the range of the longleaf pine. I went from enjoying my job as an instructor and researcher, to hating life.

Dad had been there before me. After decades on the railroad, he only needed a few more years to reach full retirement, but he couldn't take it anymore. A nervous breakdown led to tests revealing hypothyroidism. With treatment, he made it just long enough to retire.

Dad worked through his breakdown in a hospital with therapists and other patients. I would work through my issues alone, on the border.

Lonely walks in the desert lay ahead, but for the time being, my route led through one of Texas's more storied cities.

As toddlers, my sister Billie and I were often tended by Grandma Regina, a devotee of Marty Robbins. The strains from Robbins' megahit "El Paso" were burned straight from the grooves in her old vinyl record to the synapses of a developing brain. Was "wicked Selena" drawing me toward Rose's Cantina?

After the dire warnings from my friends, escaping El Paso alive could be viewed as a major accomplishment. But my initial impressions were difficult, make that impossible, to match with their descriptions.

Rex, Jack, and I had stayed the previous night in the Hilton Garden Inn at the University of Texas El Paso. The hotel was populated with businessmen, totally unconcerned with their surroundings. The streets and buildings around our hotel were clean and well kept, where attractive young college students comprised most of the foot traffic.

My walk continued along Paisano Street, where pedestrians mostly conversed in Spanish. It was an older section of town with plenty of businesses and no graffiti.

Paisano led to Delta and a blue-collar residential district where the streets and yards were manicured, and the typical yard-dog was a Chihuahua.

After the initial mile or two in a construction zone, transiting downtown El Paso had been a peaceful stroll. Maybe the outskirts of El Paso held the tougher areas?

I was more familiar with other big Texas cities like Houston, San Antonio, and Austin. In contrast to those cities, El Paso's police were virtually invisible, especially compared with Houston's police force.

The population of El Paso was overwhelmingly Hispanic, even more so than San Antonio's.

The atmosphere was comfortable, but the hard surfaces of paved roads and concrete sidewalks took a toll. Shin splints developed in my left leg as temperatures climbed above eighty degrees.

My route led to Alameda, where used-car lots stretched for miles.

Shaded park benches and bus stops provided resting places to stop, relax, eat, and drink lots of water.

Now four hours into the hike, only two police cruisers had driven by. From the hundreds of citizens encountered, only one sported a cowboy hat. Taxis were invisible. A large fleet of new buses must have provided a stellar system of public transportation, making cabs superfluous.

I limped along Old Pueblo in the sun and heat before turning left on Socorro Road.

Paved roads in Lower Alabama are heavily traveled by log and chip trucks moving at high velocities, so I traded prep time on hard surfaces, for safer and softer dirt roads around my house, and my country boy legs just weren't up to this much concrete and asphalt.

The first day's walk ended just past the El Paso city limit sign, in the small town of Socorro, where Rex and Jack joined me for a wonderful Mexican meal at the stopping point—El Meson de Onate restaurant at the intersection of Socorro and Winn Streets.

My friends' perceptions of El Paso were way off base. Maybe there are tougher, poorer areas in a city as big as this one, but based upon my seventeen-mile route through town, this west Texas city was cleaner and safer than many, if not most, big cities of the Deep South or Midwest.

A day's walk had disproven my friends' perceptions of El Paso. What else did they have wrong?

Back at the hotel, a quick shower and change of clothing allowed me to relax for the first time in days. A sleep deficit had accumulated over the previous week from: a final conference in Mobile, Alabama, the twelve-hundred-mile drive to Texas, and pre-walk anticipation.

The next day Jack told me, "You went to bed at six, and you were sawing logs before your head hit the pillow."

Pinched in by the Border Wall and César Chavez Highway

A caboose in El Paso: like the ones Dad rode but with a better logo

5

FABENS TO ESPERANZA

"Many of those picturesque towns you whip by on the interstate are small feudal systems ruled by local networks of moneyed families, bankers, developers, lawyers, and merchants."

Joe Bageant, *Deer Hunting with Jesus*. 2008

Gambel's Quail: Drawn by Ava Bailey

REX, Jack, and I left the hotel early on Tuesday morning, October 28. Although it was hitting the eighties by mid-afternoon, early morning temperatures ranged closer to fifty. My attire consisted of jeans, a t-shirt, a short-sleeve shirt, cowboy hat, a back brace, and Danner boots.

My arms grew cold in the morning chill, and the legs protested immediately. The day's goal was a community named Tornillo, but it would be a challenge with sore legs.

Subdivisions gave way to fields of alfalfa and cotton. Pecan groves encroached upon the highway, dropping nuts and shade on the road shoulders. As an opportunistic and determined forager, I flipped the bird at a sign warning, "Harvesting of pecans on road shoulder is prohibited." By squeezing two pecans at a time, I cracked the nuts in my hand, before extracting and eating the meat while walking. Extra nuts went in the backpack.

Walking the softer soil of field edges and berms ameliorated the pain of shin splints, but it was still a hot, thirsty, and hungry approach to Fabens, Texas. In town, a sign for Margarita's identified the first restaurant along my path since El Meson de Onate.

The waitress spoke in English, and I answered in Spanish until the end of the meal when she finally conceded, "*Todo bien?*" My plate was clean of every morsel: *enchiladas con salsa verde, sopa de pollo, arroz, y ensalada.* Two large glasses of iced tea had not quenched my thirst, so I pointed halfway up the glass and requested, "*Medio, vaso más.*"

After downing the tea, I stood to pay another woman. She spoke exclusively in Spanish, asking, "Where are you walking to?"

"Brownsville and the Gulf of Mexico."

"Oh my! You are walking all the way?"

"*Sí, todo el camino. Este es solo mi segundo dia,*" I said, while paying the bill and placing a tip on the table.

The woman behind the register said, "*Por favor, llévalo contigo.*" She kissed a small brown rosary and handed it to me.

"*Muchas gracias señora.*" I thanked her. "*Olvidé traer mi rosario. ¿cuál es su nombre?*"

"Margarita." She smiled.

Ceballos Honey Farm stood a bit east of Fabens and pickup trucks with men in bee-suits plied the highway. Apiaries dotted the fields along Socorro Road.

I called John Sproul of the University of Texas at El Paso (UTEP). Mr. Sproul was a wildlife biologist heading up the restoration efforts at the Rio Bosque Wetland Park, just south of Socorro, and he agreed to give us a quick tour of the park at the conclusion of the day's walk.

It was another six miles to Tornillo, where Jack waited. My mileage improved from 17.5 miles on day one to 21.1 miles on day two, but there were no reserves. My legs almost buckled while covering the last couple of miles.

Jack stopped by Ceballos Honey Farm on the way to Rio Bosque Park. Earlier in the day, he had purchased a quart of their honey and told a young lady named Amanda about our trip. She gave Jack a bag of pomegranates and a bar of their honey soap for my use on the trail. In turn, he gave her a copy of my first book.

After Jack picked me up, he had me stop by Ceballos to sign Amanda's book and thank her for the gifts. From there, I drove west to Rio Bosque where John Sproul met us at the east trailhead gate. John was a thin white man with glasses, looking every bit the botanist. For the next hour, he toured us through the property, identifying some of the more common and notable plants.

A handful of large, planted, honey mesquites stood out because of their size. John said, "These are a non-native variety in the El Paso area. The native western honey mesquites scattered throughout the park are smaller and shrubbier." John also described the native Tornillo or "screw-bean" mesquite. "It's the most common mesquite on this property. It has a characteristic spiraled seedpod."

These trees had been scarce. "Salt cedar covered much of the park," John explained. "In 1997, extensive clearing and grading took place as part of a project to create wetland habitat. Large stands of salt cedar were cleared, but many trees grew right back from surviving roots. Our volunteers spent years cutting them down and treating them with herbicides. After 1997, much of the park was taken over by another invasive species. Our volunteers came out and disappeared into a tumbleweed forest."

The volunteers didn't surrender easily. It took twenty years of battling invasives, but most of Rio Bosque landscape had reverted to native vegetation.

The subtropical tamarisk beetle was another ally (albeit a non-native species) in their restoration efforts. The beetle was introduced downriver near Presidio, Texas, in 2009 to help control the invasive salt cedar. In 2013, the beetle reached El Paso County, and John observed, "It's starting to hit it pretty hard."

Jack and I hopped in John's truck, and he drove while I observed the flora and fauna. John pointed to native herbs and shrubs such as the fourwing saltbush (*Atriplex canescens*), seepwillow (*Baccharis salicifolia*), and wolfberry (*Lycium torreyi*).

John said, "Nature contributed to the restoration through a series of heavy storms in 2006 that stimulated thousands of Tornillo mesquite to germinate and grow."

Local students grew seepwillows and wolfberry to help with the restoration, while John and his staff of volunteers sought out cuttings of coyote and Goodding willows and the Rio Grande cottonwood. The last two species were the largest trees in the park.

Gambel's quail ran, flew, and called from every direction. John said, "This year we had our first visit by a lone javelina. He's been here since early June. The bean of the Tornillo mesquite is an important food for the javelina, as it once was for indigenous tribes of the area. They pounded it into a type of flour."

"What other mammals use the park?"

"There are beaver, desert cottontail, and blacktail jackrabbits."

"Do you have pockets of good habitat remaining as reference sites?"

"It's pretty well gone."

An entire riverine ecosystem had been eliminated. Without a relatively undisturbed reference site, John Sproul and his fellow ecologists lacked an important tool—essentially a blueprint—commonly used to guide restoration efforts.

John pointed to a windmill. "UTEP manages this city park through a long-term agreement with the City of El Paso's Public Service Board. This is the first time since 2002 it held water through the summer. We installed two windmills to maintain a couple of our key wetland spots."

Heavy equipment was at work, digging a trench for a pipeline that would run treated wastewater into the park year-round, allowing for increased water flow and grand improvements in a wetland habitat.

Jack and I thanked John Sproul for touring us through this evolving landscape. After the tour, Jack carried me back to downtown El Paso for another scheduled meeting, this time with a retired administrator from the University of Texas at El Paso.

Wynn Anderson waited at the Chihuahuan Desert Garden, just a few blocks from our hotel. After my arrival, Wynn spent the remaining hour of daylight pointing out species I would encounter along the Rio Grande. They had over seven hundred taxa at the beautiful little two-acre park.

Mr. Anderson mentioned, "The National Champion *Amorpha* grows near Shafter. You should walk near there."

My thoughts turned to my last night in Alabama. Just prior to my departure, my son Joseph spent some of our last hours together carving an elaborate walking stick from *Amorpha*. A pang of sorrow pierced me. It would be weeks before I saw the family again.

Scores of cactus species dotted the garden. Mr. Anderson explained, "The garden became a USDA Plant Rescue Center, so when cacti species were confiscated at border checkpoints, they were often sent here to be replanted."

He pointed to a light green, feathery tree with vicious thorns. "This is a Mexican palo verde."

Immediate recognition! "That tree grabbed me less than five minutes into the walk."

"It's not native to this area. It comes from further south in Mexico, but early Mexican settlers brought it with them and planted it where they settled, probably because the seeds are edible. If they could move a tuber, cutting, or seed, they probably did."

Because of my interest in the subject, Wynn highlighted plants with uses to humans. "Here is a *Euphorbia* species that could be harvested to make candles," Wynn said. "The fruit of this cactus, *Mammallaria macromeris*, is edible."

"Over here," Wynn pointed, "a meal can be made from fourwing salt-bush seed."

John Sproul had highlighted that bush earlier at Rio Bosque.

"This is *Leucophyllum*, also known as 'rain sage," Wynn continued. "*Rhus microphylla* was a staple for the Native Americans. Its seeds were mixed with meat. Barberry (*Berberis trifoliolata*) is also called 'agarito' and is very edible. It was widely used fresh, dried, or made into jams, jellies, or wine."

While the light faded, we discussed the possibility of a visit to a UTEP property south and east of Sierra Blanca, down Green Valley River Road. It wasn't feasible with my current schedule, but with sufficient notice on a return trip, Mr. Anderson could set it up with Dr. Jerry Johnson, the property manager.

It was too dark to identify plants, so I thanked Mr. Anderson and walked back to the Hilton Garden Inn where I showered and fell asleep within minutes.

Jack and I left well before light the following morning. A couple of blocks from the hotel Jack noticed a fast-food restaurant beside the road. "Oh my gosh, there's a Burger King!"

I shook my head and grinned. Two Mexican dinners had stretched Jack's narrow palate to the breaking point.

Jack dropped me off with Wednesday's first light in Tornillo. The landscape grew progressively more rural as the road led east. Irrigation canals, pecan orchards, alfalfa, and cotton lined Texas 20. Houses were more scattered, and dogs became a real issue. Packs of dogs pursued me twice over the day's walk. The first bunch consisted of three mutts in the twenty- pound range. Two were along for fun, but a small red dog wanted a piece of my leg. Measured swings with a walking stick kept the mutt at bay. I didn't want to hurt the dog, and he finally backed off when I walked toward him.

The second pack was bigger in number and size. Six dogs charged from a farmhouse. The bigger dogs stood thigh-high, but they respected the stick and stayed about ten to twenty feet away.

The smallest dog in the pack was a dachshund, and he or she was intent on removing my ankle. I resisted the temptation to crack a canine skull, and swung the walking stick back and forth until the homeowner emerged and called them off.

Green and white Border Patrol vehicles passed every few minutes, mostly at moderate speeds. Then one passed me and gunned his engine while headed south. The next Border Patrol truck came around a bend and slowed to a crawl beside me. The passenger agent eyed me closely before deciding, "This isn't our guy." They sped up and drove south while pulling a horse-trailer. A mile or so down the road Border Patrol vehicles lined the highway. They had unloaded their horses, and two agents on horseback worked a cotton field, along with several other agents on foot.

The day's walk ended a couple of miles past Fort Hancock. Jack had driven ahead to scout the route toward Quitman Pass, so Rex picked me up for a five-minute ride to a fleabag hotel on the north side of Fort Hancock.

At the hotel, I removed my boots and examined my feet. The day started with a pair of thin runner's socks but it took an extra pair of cotton socks to fill my boots. Wearing both pair simultaneously was an unforced error.

After hiking hundreds of miles in lower Alabama without a single blister, poor sock selection on the third day of my Texas walk had led to blisters on both feet.

I showered, toweled off, and started for my luggage. Something sharp punctured my right foot. I hopped to a bed on the least pained foot, and examined the most recent injury. A sandspur, hidden in the carpet, was now impaled in my heel, adding insult to injury.

My stock of bandages was depleting rapidly, so I located the one open store in Fort Hancock and asked the guy behind the register, "Do you have any bandages?"

He looked under the counter, opened a box, and answered, "We only have two left. They're ten cents each."

Abandoned buildings lined the streets of Fort Hancock, advertising decades of declining populations and aspirations. A community that sells and buys individual bandages further illustrates the economics of many small towns in rural west Texas.

I bought their entire stock.

Back at the hotel, I fell asleep while awaiting Jack's return from the scouting mission. He slipped in, showered, and exited the bathroom before exclaiming, "Oh my gosh! What just got me?" Jack hopped to his bed on one foot.

His exclamation woke me. "Dang, Jack. I'm sorry. I should have warned you—there are sandspurs in the carpet."

Jack extracted the offending seed from his foot and said, "These things are vicious."

"How'd the scouting trip go?"

"I drove past a Border Patrol vehicle and kept going until I found Quitman Pass Road. Then I turned around and drove back toward Fort Hancock, passing the same Border Patrol vehicle. A couple of miles down the road, he pulled me over. He got out with an automatic rifle and walked up to the truck."

Jack recounted the conversation for me.

"He asked, 'Sir, are you lost?'"

"No, I know just where I am at."

It made my day, picturing Jack drawling out those words to a stern-faced Border Patrol agent.

"'Sir, we have a lot of trouble with drug smuggling in this area. People go down there, pick the drugs up, and come back, just like you did. Would you mind if I searched your car?'

"Not at all. I have nothing to hide."

"He looked in my car and said, 'You are okay.'"

"I told him, 'We'll be back tomorrow. Mark is walking all the way from El Paso.' Then he looked at my license plates and asked: 'Sir, is this a rental car?'"

"No, I live in Georgia."

"What about the other guy? Is he from El Paso?"

"No, he is from Andalusia, Alabama."

"You all drove all the way from Alabama and Georgia to walk the border?"

"And we have one other guy driving a University of Mississippi vehicle who is videoing Mark for a film on PBS."

"He just shook his head and told me, 'Well, you need to be very careful. The Quitman Pass is an active smuggling route, and you will probably get searched again.'"

It was a short ride from the hotel to my drop-off at Lovelady Park. Rex and Jack drove ahead to check the landscape for good background scenery. Rex liked a spot at the southern base of the Quitman Mountains where the border fence ended, or began. From that point west, three strands of barbed wire stood in the gap until the metal monstrosity picked up again somewhere around El Paso.

Rex and Jack found a Border Patrol vehicle parked at the end of the fence, and an agent wiping out footprints from three drug mules who walked around the fence just the night before. He explained, "We detected them as soon as they rounded the fence and tracked them for fifteen miles up into the Quitman Gap [our route!] where we apprehended them."

Meanwhile, I covered ground along FM (Farm to Market) 192, walking east toward the southern base of the Quitman Mountains. The last community before Quitman Pass was Esperanza. Fort Hancock, with one open store and a restaurant, was booming compared to Esperanza. Broken-down stores and a boarded-up post office were all that remained. Even the fences had given up; rotted wooden posts and rusted wire lay flat along the highway.

Finally, a sign of life. A man stood in his yard with a hoe. When he saw me, he shouted from a distance, "*A donde va?*" (Where are you going?)

I shouted back, "Brownsville and the Gulf of Mexico."

He looked at me quizzically and walked to the road, switching to English. "That's a long way."

I filled him in, and he introduced himself.

"My name is Orlando Carbajal. I thought you were from Mexico."

"Do you get many border crossers here?"

"No, not since 9-11. There used to be many crossers." He pointed toward the border, "But look over there, there, and there." Three Border Patrol vehicles were parked at regular intervals. "Now, I rarely see them [border crossers]."

I shared my background, having also grown up on a farm.

Orlando explained, "We are in a multi-year drought." He pointed to unplanted fields surrounding us. "It has been three years since we could grow a crop."

A herd of free-range goats crossed the road.

"I have some goats, and it rained recently. It's not enough for a crop, but weeds are growing, and they have something to eat."

Orlando told me his daughter attended UTEP and occasionally wrote for the *Hudspeth County Herald*, so we exchanged contact information, in case she was interested in documenting my passage through Hudspeth County.

Two dump trucks filled with soil and tumbleweeds pulled up and stopped while we talked. The first driver conversed with Orlando in Spanish before continuing east. Orlando explained, "The wind piles sand and weeds against the border wall. They are always doing maintenance on the fence. These guys haul the refuse down here."

We talked for another fifteen minutes, and it was time to move along. A few minutes after my conversation with Orlando, I approached three dump trucks and their drivers, parked beside the road. One of them lifted his baseball cap and said, "Hey! I'll trade my hat for your sombrero!" He nodded at my cowboy hat. We all laughed while I declined the offer and kept going until a white truck pulled up beside me. The local mailman introduced himself as "Rudy," before continuing with his route.

I negotiated a dogleg on 192, and a man in a truck pulled out of his driveway and started to drive east. After second thoughts, he stopped and backed up, halting beside me.

I started. "Hello. My name is Mark Hainds. I'm walking from El Paso to the Gulf."

"I'm Jack Bean. I was born and raised here."

"Any relation to Judge Roy Bean?"

He laughed. "Well, my uncle says we are, and Dad says we ain't. I haven't had time to research it."

Jack Bean wished me well and drove east. There wasn't a lot of traffic, but conversations ensued with most everyone on the road.

The paved portion of FM 192 ended at a cattle guard. A mile or two later, the dirt road dipped into a curve where a Border Patrol agent had parked in the low point, concealing his SUV. Because of the geography, his vehicle was invisible at a distance over twenty yards. He lowered his window for yet another conversation.

Officer Gonzales accepted my explanation without question and shared his story. "I am from the Harlingen area, a town called San Benito. I worked down south for a while, and then I got the call."

"What do you see out here?"

"There are lots of snakes," said Officer Gonzales. "I saw one about six feet tall—I mean long—just yesterday."

We conversed awhile, but there had already been too many delays. As I turned to leave, he said, "Be careful. I will be praying for you."

I covered another five miles before Jack picked me up along Esperanza Road. The ride back allowed time for contemplation.

This border walk was an attempt to reclaim my sanity, to prove myself, to reorient my life and career in a direction that allowed more family time. It wasn't the way most people pulled themselves back together, but it might work for me. No one knew just how much was riding on the success of this endeavor. If it failed, it was possible that I would never believe in myself again.

On Quitman Pass

Petroglyphs in Quitman Pass

6

QUITMAN PASS

"Their notion of paradise was modest: a place where the rivers had fish and the woods had game."

Mario Vargas Llosa. *The Storyteller.* 1989

Greater Earless Lizard: Drawn by Edlyn Burch

Oct 31–Nov 1

IT was a beautiful morning along FM 192. The road still more or less paralleled the border fence. The skies were clear and a breeze moderated the effect of climbing temperatures. Wildflowers blessed the desert sand, products of the recent rain.

Peculiar to my interest, road-killed reptiles dotted the road, including three horned lizards and a large snake of an undetermined species. When live animals are invisible, dead ones have a story to tell. Range maps for given species are often expanded based upon the location of road kill specimens.

A vehicle came from behind, slowing and stopping beside me. Rudy, the mailman, checked in before taking my picture and continuing with his route.

Two miles down the road another vehicle approached. It was a Border Patrol agent named Lozano, with a long list of questions including: "Where are you going? Who is with you? What color is your truck? What color is Rex's vehicle? Where are Jack and Rex now?" He had me repeat the whole story again, either because he had gotten the details mixed up or to make sure the story held together. After several minutes, he said, "You will see me on the trail ahead. I am going to relieve another agent."

After a several-mile gap, the border fence reappeared, and not far past that, FM 1111, (aka Quitman Pass Road) headed uphill to the left (north) toward the distant town of Sierra Blanca.

A beautiful lizard lay dead, belly up in the road. It had just been run over, possibly by Agent Lozano. From my photos, Dr. Sean Graham, a herpetologist friend at Sul Ross University, later identified it as a greater earless lizard.

It was about six inches long with a white underside, rough skin, and seven black bars on the tail. The lower portion of the belly, just above the hind legs, sported two black bars coming from the sides and angling toward the head. The area around the black bars glowed with an iridescent blue that would have been equally at home on the wings of a tropical butterfly.

Just up the road from the lizard, a kangaroo mouse had also met its demise beneath a truck tire. The mouse was tan on top and white beneath. The front legs were abbreviated, especially compared with the hind legs, which extended almost the length of the mouse's body. The tail was about twice the length of the body and covered with dark hair that grew longer toward the tip.

The road climbed to a windy plateau where two trucks were parked side by side on the east side of the road. One vehicle held a giant listening device, and the other held Agent Lozano.

I approached the now familiar agent. "How's it going?"

"I'm babysitting this equipment. It's turned off right now."

The spot offered a commanding view of the rugged landscape, where slopes climbed to lofty peaks. The Quitman Mountains topped out thousands of feet above us, to the north and west. My route had skirted the range to the south, before turning on this road, which led north, through a mountain pass to Sierra Blanca. The tan countryside was dotted with cactus, creosote, and yuccas. In general, the plants weren't tall enough to hide behind. Any large animal or person moving across the foothills should be easy to spot.

I asked, "Do you see much wildlife from here?"

"Aoudad, deer, and some donkeys." He pulled out his phone to show pictures of burros, roadrunners, and lots of cattle. The cows of El Paso and Hudspeth counties had been invisible thus far.

"This landscape is pretty barren. It's hard to imagine illegal immigrants coming across here. Do you ever see them from this viewpoint?"

"Not too much from here." He flipped through more images before handing me his phone. On the screen, a line of at least a dozen Mexicans were walking through the desert, flanked by a BP agent on horseback. "This is a big group we caught three days ago."

"A few weeks back we caught another large group, and they told us they had to leave one behind because he wore out and couldn't make it any farther. Our guys went back to look, but they could never locate him. They checked with his family in Mexico, and he hasn't called home in three weeks. So, he is still out there. The area is so vast, it's likely that we will never find him."

Lozano filled one of my empty water bottles with Powerade and wished me well.

Ten months prior to this walk, I attempted a scouting drive along the entire Texas-Mexico border. It kicked off in Andalusia, Alabama, and picked up the border at Boca Chica Beach on the Gulf of Mexico, just outside Brownsville.

After covering almost one thousand miles of the border, I stopped by the Hudspeth County Texas A&M Extension Office, where I explained the purpose of my walk to the local county agent, Cathy. She had just returned to her office after the New Year's Day Holiday.

I told Cathy, "I would like to meet with landowners who are willing to share their stories. If you could introduce me to some characters that have property along my route, I'd love to interview them."

"You need to talk with our sheriff, Arvin West. He's a real character. In the case of landowners, it would be best if you met them in person before the walk."

That was unfeasible. It was a thousand miles from Andalusia to Boca Chica Beach, and about another thousand miles from Boca Chica to Sierra Blanca. And yet another thousand miles lay between Sierra Blanca and home. A return trip prior to the walk simply wasn't in the cards.

Hudspeth County Sheriff's deputies wandered in while we conversed. Cathy introduced us and I inquired, "I was hoping to walk Quitman Pass straight south of here. Is FM 1111 passable?"

A deputy answered, "That's remote country. Most of it doesn't have a cell phone signal. If you climb a mountain and stand on tippy-toe, you may get one bar, but along most of Quitman Pass, you won't be able to call out." He added, "We pick up a lot of bodies down there."

After our conversation, I grabbed lunch in Sierra Blanca while studying my maps. It was another one hundred-plus miles to El Paso. Severe driver and car fatigue ended my westward route. My back was killing me, and the accelerator was stuck wide-open on the little blue Saturn. During the long drive home, I regulated speed with the brake, rather than the gas pedal.

Now, nearly one year after the scouting drive, and I was walking the same road the deputy had warned me about. That county extension office lay directly north of my current position. Luckily, excepting the kangaroo mouse, the only dead bodies had been reptilian.

A decade earlier, another adventurer had traveled the Texas-Mexico border. Keith Bowden, author of *The Tecate Journals*, had canoed the Rio Grande, when he had sufficient water, and bicycled adjoining roads when the water wasn't there. Like me, Keith scouted the route prior to his journey.

Driving south of Sierra Blanca, somewhere near my current position, Keith was flagged down by two Mexican nationals who had been robbed and beaten while skirting a nearby Border Patrol checkpoint on I-10.

The immigrants asked Keith to drive them back to Mexico, saying, "We don't want to stay here. Your country is a dangerous place!"

FM 1111 followed a plateau, offering views of the expansive terrain, with tons of cacti, shrubs, and flowering herbaceous plants. The road gradually gained elevation, offering my first miles on a significant grade. I sat to eat tortillas smothered with peanut butter and Ceballos' honey. A Border Patrol truck drove up from the south and stopped beside me.

The agent on the passenger side asked, "Are you the guy who is walking to the Gulf?"

"Yes, sir."

"Is everything okay?"

"Yes, sir. I am doing pretty well. I just stopped for a bite to eat and rest my legs."

"Let me ask. If you are out here by yourself and get bit by a rattlesnake, how will you get help? There is no cell service up here."

I could have explained that a forester of my age and background would have already spent at least two decades working in the woods by himself—surrounded by venomous snakes. Foresters not adapted to these conditions are selectively removed from the population.

Instead, I offered, "Friends are driving down from Sierra Blanca. They should be waiting on the other side of the washout. If I don't make it, they'll circle around and drive up from the bottom of this road. Every day we plan the route, and they check on me in the morning and at the end of the day's walk."

The answer satisfied them.

By midday, I made the blowout, but Jack and Rex weren't there.

Jack had been particularly effusive about the scenery north of the blowout, prompting Rex to say, "I want to shoot that passage with the camera on the drone."

In addition, someone had told Jack about petroglyphs within a short walk of the blowout.

The landscape was gorgeous, but the route had entered harsh, remote terrain. Exploring for petroglyphs would require energy necessary for covering the many remaining miles to Sierra Blanca.

It was excruciatingly difficult to gauge the risks associated with this walk. The deputy in Sierra Blanca warned of bodies from Quitman Pass. The Border Patrol agents worried about rattlesnakes. Keith (the author) noted the presence of bandits. Rex even had a panic attack, just two days before the trek began. I was still driving west when he called.

"Well, I just talked to a good friend, and he told me some things about the border that really hit me." For the first time, there was uncertainty and fear in Rex's voice. My heart sank. Was Rex backing out? Rex continued, "Just how dangerous is this going to be? My friend shook me up."

How to answer his question, when most of my experience on the border consisted of a three-day drive from Boca Chica to Sierra Blanca?

I reminded Rex of my relatively uneventful tour the previous holiday season, while acknowledging, "I took out a big life insurance policy prior to this trip. But I don't want to put you or any of the Tex-Mex Compadres in a dangerous situation." While the risks were real, I was pretty sure that as the pedestrian, the hazards would be in my court, not his.

Rex seemed somewhat calmed. He normally proceeded with an energetic confidence, and his cold feet caught me off guard, but it shouldn't have been surprising. The border scared just about everyone who didn't live there, and a fair number of those who do!

The shin splints had dissipated, and my strength returned. Progress was better than anticipated, and Rex and Jack were probably on their way. Quitman Pass had a dangerous reputation, but familiarity with an area generally alleviates unfounded fears. Being a novice on the border, there was little experience with which to evaluate the information coming from a hundred directions. Which cautionary tales were based in reality? The answers lay ahead.

Recent rains had created a giant hole in the road. A motorcycle or four-wheeler could have circumvented the obstacle, but a truck or SUV needed an alternate route. What if this wasn't the only wrecked section of the road? Perhaps Rex and Jack were sitting at another blowout, ten miles north. There was too much uncertainty to sit and wait.

The first cattle of the trip wandered through brush and cacti a few hundred yards north of the washout. The black angus were identical to cows we raised on our farm. Their healthy condition was surprising, considering the scarcity of good fodder in the surrounding mountains. And they were tame.

My previous trips to the southwestern United States were elk hunts on public lands in New Mexico, where the occasional cow on or around the Lincoln National Forest ran away faster than the elk.

To my relief, Rex and Jack drove over a ridge. Rex pulled up and asked, "Do you mind if we run you back to the washout? I would like to film you coming through that landscape."

With my nerves calmed, I was ready for anything. "I don't mind at all." I flagged an adjacent bush before hopping in the truck.

"The petroglyphs are supposed to be in an arroyo," said Jack, "uphill to the west of the road."

Back at the washout we set off in search of the ancient artifacts, picking our way through mesquite, cactus, and boulders for a short distance. And we found them, just as reported: petroglyphs on giant boulders and rock faces. The majority were patterns that could have been ancient in origin. Others looked more like brands for ranches, or possibly initials placed by locals.

With the Rio Grande just a few miles distant, life seemed feasible for Native Americans. They would have been tough as nails, foraging food from this landscape, but humans have adapted to extreme lands all over the planet.

The Native Americans were as connected to the environment as the modern American is disconnected from the surrounding world.

The ancient peoples who lived along the Rio Grande provided an example worthy of emulation. Their survival depended upon their ability to make do with resources at hand. If they survived off this land for months or years at a time, surely, I could walk through it. And along the way, I hoped to learn a bit more about the indigenous plants, insects, animals, signs, sights, and sounds that tell the story of a world worthy of preservation.

Jack, Rex and I camped beside a stock tank about two-thirds of the way up Quitman Pass Road. Jack scrounged a piece of tin that he formed into a circle as we made camp. Large mesquite trees with dead branches surrounded the flat campsite, so we collected branches and piled them beside Jack's custom-made fire-ring. While Rex and I erected our tents, Jack built a fire using pieces of fat-lighter I brought from Alabama. Jack had neglected to bring a tent, so Rex offered space in his larger tent, but Jack preferred to sleep beneath the stars. It was windy, but otherwise a beautiful night with clear skies and temperatures around fifty degrees.

November 1, 2014

I arose at 5:00 a.m. to strike my tent and rebuild the fire. The radiant heat warmed my hands as Rex and Jack emerged from their sleeping bags to join me by the flame. The landscape gradually emerged from darkness. When the sun lit the peaks of the Quitman Mountains, it was time to walk.

As FM 1111 continued north toward Sierra Blanca, the road was still dirt, but the surrounding vegetation changed. The brush grew thick, and a vine covered shrubs on the road shoulders. The geography and plant life pointed toward slightly more mesic soils, as compared to the xeric lands further south.

In the distance, a half dozen animals stood in the road, too far away to identify. Perhaps coyotes? The animals ran into the scrub on either side of the road.

In a few minutes, a pack of feral-looking dogs reemerged onto the road. They broke toward me at full speed. I readied the walking stick while thinking, "Here we go again."

The dogs were fast. Though streaking in my direction, they had yet to exhibit any sign of aggression. About twenty yards out, the pack parted. Three dogs angled left, and another three to the right, shooting past me in pursuit of a quarry or destination unseen.

I exhaled.

A few miles north, the road switched from dirt to asphalt.

For all of El Paso County, and much of Hudspeth County, the road shoulders were cleaner than the average country road in the Deep South. The anti-littering campaign, "Don't Mess with Texas!" had grabbed hold out here.

Quitman Pass had been virtually litter free. Admittedly, Quitman Pass didn't get much traffic besides drug smugglers and Border Patrol agents. But sparsely used Alabama roads are often lined with refrigerators, sofas, and piles of construction debris. The primary litter along Hudspeth County's dirt roads was decades old brown bottles. The brands and styles were similar to those from old junk piles in ditches back on the farm. In my grade school days, I'd dig up a dozen bottles at a time, arrange them in a line, and shoot them to pieces with a pump-up BB gun.

A fifty-year-old abandoned car also rested in Quitman Pass, but it just added character.

Along one section, a few yards off FM 1111, plastic blew in every direction from an open pit landfill, covering the landscape with trash. Someone needed to erect a woven-wire fence around the landfill, a simple and inexpensive step that would catch most of the plastic.

The total Halloween traffic along Quitman Pass, besides us, had been two Border Patrol vehicles.

Traffic picked up on the morning of November 1. A ranch truck drove by pulling a trailer with a water tank. Six more Border Patrol vehicles passed me headed north or south. All of them continued on their way without stopping until the last Border Patrol agent, just south of Sierra Blanca.

He slowed to a stop and rolled down his window while holding a burrito in one hand. "Are you trapped, uuuuhhh, lost, errrr, I mean broke down?"

I couldn't help but smile. "None of the above."

"Just hiking?"

"Yes, sir. Headed up to Sierra Blanca."

"Okay, well, let us know if you need any assistance."

"Thank you, sir. I appreciate it."

He rolled up his window while heading south and taking another bite out of his burrito.

The top of the next hill offered a view of Sierra Blanca, including a large detention compound, squatting to the right. For such a sparsely populated county, this was an outsized facility. Reportedly, it holds a collection of detainees arrested at the so-called, "Checkpoint of the Stars."

Walking Quitman Pass allowed me to bypass the installation, but Rex and Jack stopped at the Customs and Border Patrol checkpoint, where agents ticket or arrest anyone unlucky or unwise enough to be in possession of even the smallest amount of controlled substances. Many celebrities had their mug shots taken after getting caught there, and, most famously, Willie Nelson (Dad's country music idol) was busted there for marijuana.

My truck and Rex's SUV were parked in front of a restaurant in Sierra Blanca.

Rex and Jack sat at a table with two North Hudspeth County EMTs. The male EMT had seen the "Andalusia Ford" tag on my truck and introduced himself to Jack. He hailed from a town just north of Birmingham but had relocated to Hudspeth County several years earlier.

The mood was celebratory. We were barely a week into the walk, and I had already traversed a remote section of the trek with a scary reputation, emerging unscathed in Sierra Blanca: no bodies, robbers, bandits, or drug mules, though we hadn't missed the latter group by much.

I dropped my backpack and walking stick in the corner and told the lady at the cash register, "I'll have the biggest breakfast on the menu."

Coffee in hand, I took a seat and asked the EMT, "Do you have many feral dogs in the area? I just saw a pack on Quitman Pass."

"Oh yeah. We put out food for them. They're friendly."

7

SIERRA BLANCA TO THE RED ROCK RANCH

"It had only to do with how it felt to be in the wild. With what it was like to walk for miles for no reason other than to witness the accumulation of trees and meadows, mountains and deserts, streams and rocks, rivers and grasses, sunrises and sunsets. The experience was powerful and fundamental."

Cheryl Strayed. *Wild: Lost to Found on the Pacific Coast Trail.* 2012

Still Life with Grasshopper: Photo by Mark Hainds

November 1–3

AFTER an hour of food, coffee, and conversation, my route took a ninety-degree turn to the east, through the southern portion of Sierra Blanca, to the outskirts of town, where I-10 led to Van Horn. Most of Sierra Blanca's businesses were boarded up. As people and commerce left, nature encroached. During my previous visit, the extension agent in Sierra Blanca told me, "Javelina are coming into town and rooting up gardens."

Barn owls often roost and nest in abandoned buildings and other structures. An on-ramp to I-10 was my exit from Sierra Blanca, and just over the guardrail, a road-killed barn owl lay face-up beside the road. The face, body, and an extended wing were snow white with small dark spots across its belly. Its talons were clenched in death.

To my delight, a good trail paralleled the interstate, running beside a barbed-wire fence on the south side of the road. Walking the well-worn dirt road would draw less scrutiny. I-10 was about the last place I wanted to be, but there was no choice: this was the only route east, with no feasible routes to the south.

One may assume that walking an interstate highway for miles on end would be a mind-numbing experience, but recent rains had fueled a profusion of desert wildflowers and lush green grass on the right-of-way, supporting a tremendous population of grasshoppers. Walking conditions were near ideal on the dirt road, and the diversity slowed me down as I stopped to examine and photograph flowers, insects, and tracks.

A jackrabbit ran into the scrub, followed by the first cottontail rabbit of the trip. The two species were easy to distinguish. Cottontails resemble small, fastballs racing through the brush, while jackrabbits look like two giant ears floating through the scrub.

The landscape abruptly browned on the south side of the fence. Hundreds of acres had been herbicided, killing outright or at least top killing virtually 100 percent of the mesquite, creosote bush, and many of the yuccas. In this case, "ecocide" may have been an appropriate term for the action taken against this landscape. The assumed goal was to favor a few more tufts of grass on a post-herbicide property that would largely consist of bare soil, rocks, and dead stems. It was ugly.

A mile or two down the road, a bright line of green marked the end of the herbicide application, and my mood lifted. Contrary to my expectations, there hadn't been a dull moment along I-10.

I removed my backpack, to journal some thoughts. In the process, I spooked something in a clump of mesquite just feet away. The vegetation shook as a mammal moved through the brush.

A dark animal broke from the mesquite and ran south toward the fence. It looked like a raccoon. I stepped left onto the dirt road to get a better view. Now a big bobcat broke from the bush just five yards out. Both animals disappeared into the creosote and mesquite on the other side of the fence.

Perhaps the raccoon and bobcat had been engaged in a faceoff until I chanced upon their location. Sensing an opportunity for escape, the raccoon broke for freedom while the bobcat was distracted.

Fauna had been fairly scarce south of the Quitman Mountains, but mammalian diversity was picking up along I-10.

Over lunch in Sierra Blanca, Rex expressed a desire to interview some local Libertarian ranchers while I walked the interstate. The following day (November 3), we hoped to meet up with Darice McVay who owned the Red Rock Ranch in Van Horn. The Texas A&M Extension Agent for Culberson County had highly recommended Darice.

Rex picked me up near mile marker 121 on I-10, before driving us to tiny rooms at the Motel 6 in Van Horn. Although cramped (I was still sharing a room with Jack), it was a big step up from the sand-spurred rattrap in Fort Hancock.

The next morning's hike started at first light. Two miles in, a dead western diamondback rattlesnake lay flattened on the dirt road paralleling I-10.

It took three hours and forty-seven minutes to make the ten miles to mile marker #131, with a pace around three miles per hour. If held for eight hours a day, the Gulf of Mexico would appear on schedule. But I couldn't hold the pace for a whole day's walk. There was a consistent trend: fast in the morning while the legs were still fresh; slowest from late morning to early afternoon; and a quicker pace in the late afternoon over the last two or three hours of the walk.

I-10 approached the foothills of a mountain range to the west of Van Horn, and my dirt trail ended as the interstate channeled into a narrow man-made cut through the mountains, forcing me directly onto the road shoulder.

Shin splints returned with a vengeance, while the asphalt radiated heat. My gait slowed and was marked by a pronounced limp: assuredly, a pitiful sight.

Semi-trailers rolled by continuously, and a significant number blew their horns, signals I interpreted as moral support. One eastbound truck was passing at seventy miles per hour when a full box of cereal was flung out the window, landing near my feet. The box broke open and a generic version of Captain Crunch lay scattered over the road shoulder. Had I been truly homeless and hungry, as I assumed they had assumed, it would have been picked up and eaten to the last crumb, but I wasn't quite ready for sandy, crunchy cereal.

The foothills of the mountains had been cut away, exposing steep, nearly sheer rock walls. About twenty feet above me, a complete tire tread was stuck to the rock face. In trucker parlance, they had "blown a cap," throwing the retread at speed. I wondered if a tire retread had ever clocked a pedestrian.

It was still several miles to Van Horn when Rex called, "Jack has a flat tire on Chispa Road. I'm going to try and find him." Like Quitman Pass, Jack had driven ahead to scout the road. Though Quitman had a scary reputation, Chispa took remote and dangerous to a whole other level.

"Oh my God! How far in is he?"

"I'm not sure. He just had enough signal to tell me he was on the road. [Jack's cell was an old school flip-phone with no texting options.] If we aren't back by dark, you have to arrange a rescue."

This was flummoxing. Jack had the truck. I was walking beside I-10. It was the Tex-Mex Compadres' job to support my walk, and now I was in the position of figuring out how to rescue Jack, and possibly Rex too.

My main concern was Jack and Rex's safety, but I was also pissed. The warnings had come one after another: "You can't walk there." "You will be killed." "This is the last we will see of you." "You will be captured and held for ransom."

We had to prove the naysayers wrong: a person could walk the Texas-Mexico border without relying on law enforcement to recover their body or search their last known position. Now we might be forced into asking law enforcement to extricate one- or two-thirds of our team because of a flat tire and no spare.

This situation was partly my fault, but Ford Motor Company also deserved some blame.

The truck was only a year old and it rode great, but it came with the lamest tires. The radials only had twenty thousand miles, and I'd already suffered through half a dozen flats, including a tire that went bad on the drive out to the border.

Jack had driven his truck to the border, but he could use my four-wheel drive pickup as necessary. Jack and Rex had retrieved my F-150 from the Hudspeth County Extension Office while I traipsed Quitman Pass. Jack was now stranded on Chispa because we hadn't gotten around to replacing the worthless tire in my truck bed.

I limped to our room at the Motel 6 in Van Horn. Having made it there safely, it was time to organize a rescue plan for the crew.

Fortunately, before I got started, Rex called. "I have Jack, and we're on our way back to the motel."

We would deal with the truck the following day.

It would have been a disaster if Jack had gotten a flat an hour earlier and further south on Chispa Road. Barring the last mile or two on the north end of Chispa Road, cell phones were useless for communication purposes over the remaining fifty-plus miles to Candelaria. Although Jack was a forester, his active timber cruising days were long past, and a twenty-mile hike through the desert would have been a tall order.

Jack hadn't noticed the leak until he stopped to chat with a Border Patrol agent who was parked at the top or north end of Chispa. The agent pointed out the flattening tire and stayed to make sure help was on the way.

We were damn lucky.

November 3

The three of us arrived early at the Red Rock Ranch's office in Van Horn. Darice wasn't there yet, so I wandered over to a junk store where two old cowboys named Shane and Tinsley were hanging out. They were intimately familiar with Chispa Road. Tinsley had grown up on Chispa and Shane knew the names of the ranches, active and abandoned, along the route.

Later, Darice told me that Tinsley was part of a family that owned a spread of land several times bigger than the Red Rock Ranch, and his family was very influential in the Texas and Southwestern Cattle Ranching Association. According to Darice, the family had disowned Tinsley, owing as they were good Protestants and Tinsley had taken to drink, as a younger man.

I thought, *Dang, I'm glad I grew up Catholic.*

Darice's grandfather established Van Horn's first gas station in 1927, and after that he built Van Horn's first hotel. There weren't many sizable towns in the vicinity. Darice told us, "It's a hundred and twenty miles to a movie theatre or a Wal-Mart."

Darice grew up pumping gas before her father bought Red Rock Ranch in 1967. She toured us through her old gas station where artwork by Jimmy Vaughn Carter covered the walls. "He loved to paint pretty women. I once asked him, 'Do I have to marry you to get a picture of me painted?' He answered, 'Yeah,' so I told him, 'Forget it.'"

She described the cinematographic history of Red Rock, where *Blue Sky* was shot in 1984; *Dead Man's Walk* (prequel to *Lonesome Dove*) in 1994; and *Giant,* which was made in Marfa with James Dean.

"Where did you grow up?" asked Rex.

"Austin, in the sixties."

"You weren't a hippie, were you?"

"Hummm."

Rex laughed.

Darice continued with the history of Red Rock and Van Horn. "We had a talc mine for a long time, but the company in Mexico only paid us for two out of five loads, so we shut it down. If you saw that 'V' on the mountain, that letter was all we could afford. (A giant white V had been constructed of stones on a mountain overlooking the town). The fire department sprays it down every five years, which coincides with our high school reunion that's held every five years because the classes are so small. Another thing that might interest you is we had a six-year drought with only a quarter of an inch of measurable rainfall [in Culberson and Hudspeth counties]. It ended on July 3, 2005."

Much of what Darice told us was interesting, but this was simply shocking. Having grown up on a farm, it was hard to wrap my head around such a calamitous drought.

"We have Wild Horse Creek. It's the only north-flowing creek in Texas. There was a huge flood in 1965. The town was protected, but everything on the other side of the levee was wiped out."

We hopped into Darice's SUV for the ride to Red Rock. On the property, Darice nodded toward a massive red rock. "This is why we're called the Red Rock Ranch. These are Precambrian formations, which means 'before life.'"

Winds shaped the landscape. "We have class three hurricane/sand-storms out here," she explained. "The softer layers are sedimentary sandstone that erode faster. If you think this was made in seven days [she pointed to surrounding mountains], I have some ocean front property to sell you. The funny thing—this *was* ocean front property. Guadalupe Peak is the highest point in Texas, and it was a reef. The deepest part of this sea was around Lobo [a small town just east of Van Horn], where they grew cotton for fifteen years, until they dropped the water table."

A covey of quail ran across the road. "Those were Gambel's quail, but we also have blue or scaled quail."

"I've seen the Gambel's quail," I said.

Darice continued recounting some of the local history. "The Mescalero Apache were the most recent Indian tribes to live in this area. They were nomadic, following the bison. They lived in rock shelters on the Red Rock Ranch. Nine of their middens [refuse heaps] have been recorded on the ranch. They were mostly peaceable until we tried to Christianize and settle them. We have also found pottery from the Anasazi Indians who lived here from about 1000-1200 AD."

Darice probably knew which tribe or tribes had created the petroglyphs along Quitman Pass, but with so much to write down, I neglected to pose the question.

"Wait now. There's that darn bull," Darice said, looking to her right. "It's our neighbor's, and it keeps getting through the fence. We pulled our cattle off in 1992."

"I have seen very few cattle on this walk," I said. "The first and only cows I've come across were some Angus on Quitman Pass Road."

"Angus and Brangus are preferred breeds of cattle out here. By the way, I am glad they are putting cattle back in Quitman Pass. Sheep are so destructive."

"If you don't run cattle, are tours and tourism your only source of income?"

"We sell sand and gravel from one of our creeks to a company in El Paso. That's been a good source of income. And we have guided hunts for mule deer at four hundred and fifty dollars a day."

"How much land do you have?"

"This property consists of twenty-seven sections. My ranch foreman is Julian Fuentes who is eighty-four years old."

To our front, javelina walked into the road while Rex filmed from the window. They weren't spooked by our presence, allowing Darice to drive within a few yards of the animals.

After they crossed the road, she stopped on a steep slope to point out some natural features and plants. While everyone oohed and ahhhed, Rex discovered a small, horned lizard on a rock; it was the first live specimen of the trek. Her property could easily be appropriately renamed the "Red Rock Refuge," based on the amount of wildlife and sign we were encountering.

Darice pointed to a bush with hooked thorns. "That's catclaw acacia, 'The bane of the southwest.' It's also called 'wait a minute.'"

The botanical tour continued. "Tasajillo is the cactus with red berries. It's also known as Christmas cactus."

It was fun, but I found it hard to focus on details while worrying about my truck. Our predicament eventually came up, and I explained, "My pickup is parked on the upper end of Chispa Road."

With a doubtful, sympathetic tone, Darice said, "Maybe your truck is still there."

I panicked. "We need to get my truck—now!"

Darice turned her vehicle around and drove us back to Van Horn. She recommended a tire shop in town where Jack and I purchased a brand-new tire before Jack drove us toward Chispa.

Jack turned south, just past Lobo, driving past scattered ranch houses on FM 2017. Relief swept over me as he approached the intersection with Chispa. The truck was sitting where he had left it. We quickly changed the flat and drove both vehicles back to town. The flat got patched, and we were back in business by lunchtime, meeting Rex and Darice at Papa's Pantry on the east side of Van Horn.

By her own admission, Darice had a cantankerous reputation in the local community. "They call me 'the mean ol' bitch with a 45.'"

She aired her grievances about the community. "Van Horn has the highest per capita teen pregnancy rate in the state."

Jack was equally old school. "When I was a kid and a girl got pregnant, they kicked her out of school."

Rex nodded along. I couldn't tell if he agreed with such draconian policies, or if he was just playing along.

Darice vented. "I can't sell a house for $20,000 in this town. Everyone here is a crook or a drug dealer." If was correct, the majority of the town residents weren't making much for their efforts. Van Horn wasn't exactly booming, although it didn't appear to be in the death spiral gripping Sierra Blanca and Fort Hancock.

She continued, "My dad told me, 'If you go to mixing races and religions it just makes everything more complicated.' I guess that's why I never got married."

I scribbled furiously.

Darice looked at me suspiciously, while posing her question to Rex and Jack. "Is he writing all this down?"

We drove back to the ranch after lunch.

Amongst the incredible geography, geology, plants, and animal life, an incongruous Playboy bunny was stenciled onto a rock outcropping. It had caught my attention during the morning tour, but I had not pursued the topic. This time I asked, "What's up with the bunny?"

It was an obvious sore point. "My father let a church group come here for a weekend retreat, and this is what they did to our property. Dad put a notice in the next newspaper telling the world what had happened and announcing the end of local access to Red Rock Ranch."

On a related note, Darice informed us, "My next book will be called 'Feed the world. Sell the Vatican.'"

Darice drove us to a particularly scenic spot where she parked and led us over rock ledges into a large draw. "This is the X in Texas." She directed our view to a natural rock formation that formed the letter. "God said this is the prettiest place in Texas, so he put a big X right here."

The rock surface had perfectly round holes, several inches in depth. Darice explained, "These holes are man-made. The Apaches ground their mesquite and other hard seeds in the rock. The meal would contain rock fragments so the Indians wore out their teeth by the time they were in their thirties."

She continued, "It's amazing how slowly things deteriorate. I still occasionally find a cow patty out here, and we haven't had cattle since 1992. It's equally incredible how fast things erode with the water moving over stone."

After a bit of exploring, we returned to the vehicles, and Darice said, "Let's go from the sublime to the ridiculous." She drove us to a decrepit movie set from *Dead Man's Walk*. "We tried to fix it up, but movie sets just aren't built to last."

Rex, Jack, and I examined structures built to imitate a Mexican village where the protagonists were incarcerated in Larry McMurtry's bestselling book and movie.

The botanical tour continued with a plethora of cacti: Texas rainbow barrel, eagle claw, ocotillo, hedgehog cactus, the strawberry cactus with edible fruit, and the claret cup cactus, with a bloom the color of claret wine.

Ocotillos were widespread. They are an emblematic species of the desert Southwest, resembling cacti, with upright stems that are barren until it rains, prompting the leaves to emerge.

But not everything was in its natural state. "We don't have big mesquite because they were cut for fence posts." To wrap up the day, Darice drove us to the highest peak on the property, where a talc mine had operated at an elevation of six thousand nine hundred feet. Darice informed us, "We have gained two-thousand, eight hundred feet in elevation since leaving Van Horn, which is only fourteen miles from the talc mine."

From the talc mine, we descended a short distance to big rock ledges where Darice let us each select a "pagoda rock": a small sedimentary formation shaped like a pagoda.

It was dusk and Rex asked Darice, "Would you mind if we sat here quietly and I recorded some sound?"

We spread out on a wide, gentle slope and let the sounds of the desert encompass us. After several minutes, Rex had what he needed, offering, "That was almost a spiritual experience."

Apparently, the ambience and scenery affected people differently, since Darice replied, "People are inclined to get naked and lay on this rock."

Old pump and tank in Quitman Pass

Shane, Tinsley, and Mark in Van Horn

8

VAN HORN TO LOBO

"Having someone who believes in you makes a lot of difference. They don't have to make speeches. Simply believing is usually enough."

Stephen King, *On Writing: A Memoir of the Craft.* 2000

Green Toad: Drawn by Ava Bailey

Nov 4–5

IT was pitch black outside, and my left shin was hurting before the first step was taken. And it was Election Day. The night clerk, whom we'll call "Henry," had the lights on and freshly brewed coffee. He asked, "Are you surveyors?"

"It's a long story."

"For oil and gas?"

After Henry heard our story, he was off and running.

Henry said, "I have an aunt in Crystal City that you should talk to. She lived there during the race riots of the 1950s and '60s. My cousins told me that they would walk to school and see someone lying in an alley—it would be a body."

Henry had grown up in Marfa and Van Horn, and he had worked on the Santa Fe at the same time as my father. Maybe they met somewhere along the million miles of track Dad rode over his career.

"After I got hurt on the railroad, I coached basketball in Presidio. The only game we won that year was against Marfa. I was afraid they would fire me, but the parents said, 'As long as you beat Marfa you can keep your job.'" He explained a long-running antagonism between the primarily Hispanic Presidio and the white Marfa. "Presidio had the courthouse, and they took it away, brick by brick, and rebuilt it in Marfa."

Moving a large building in such a manner sounded incredible. It only took a minute or two of research on the Internet to disprove what may be an urban legend in the area.

The Presidio County Courthouse in Marfa is an impressive structure designed by architect Alfred Giles. It was modeled after a previous courthouse he designed for El Paso County. Marfa's courthouse opened at its current and only location, Marfa, Texas, on January 1, 1887.

Henry's version did hold a grain of truth. The original Presidio County seat was Fort Leaton on the edge of the city of Presidio. The County Seat was moved to Fort Davis in 1875 and moved again to Marfa in 1885.

I explained my intention to turn south and follow Chispa Road to Presidio. Henry thought that was a terrible idea. "If you see someone on the road down there, you need to hide or just keep walking. That's a really dangerous area. Don't talk to anyone on Chispa because the only people you are likely to encounter are dope smugglers and illegals."

The legend of Chispa grew.

We conversed until the skies lightened and it was time to go.

Five minutes after my morning trek began, a cyclist pulled over and introduced himself. Cole had cycled across the center of the country from May through August on the TransAmerica bicycle trail. Now he was working his way across the Southern Tier route.

Several cyclists had ridden by while loaded for long distance trips. Unbeknownst to me, they were following an established bicycle route, much like the Appalachian Trail for hikers.

Cole continued south and west while my route led a few blocks north through Van Horn, before turning right, or east, on US 90. My left leg hurt and the skies had sunk, covering the landscape with a cold, windy blanket of precipitation that alternated between a fog, a light mist, and rain. Perhaps I should have stayed in bed.

From the hotel parking lot, my goal was twenty-three miles away, where FM 2017 turned south off US 90, leading to Chispa Road.

An orange raincoat with a hood over a baseball cap protected my head and upper body from an occasional driving rain. My legs and feet were more exposed to the elements, though pushing forward burned enough calories to maintain my core temperature, despite the cold, wet conditions.

If prompted, I probably would have described the conditions as "miserable." But it wouldn't have been an honest answer. "Miserable" was how I envisioned other people in this situation, given the environmental conditions and location.

Walking into a cold, shrouded, mostly deserted landscape with rain dripping from the bill of my cap and a body soaked from the waist down: I felt joyous. It's not completely clear why extreme environments trigger this euphoric response.

To this day, I hold a comforting memory from growing up on the farm: a young boy climbing a ladder to a barn loft, lying down on a bed of hay, and listening to rain beat against the tin roof, thinking he could stay there forever.

Equally powerful were memories of wading through knee-deep water in freezing rains, pursuing ducks until my thumb was too numb to pull back the hammer on a single-barrel twenty-gauge shotgun, taking joy in the knowledge that 99.9 percent of the population preferred to be inside their houses watching TV. That meant more ducks for me.

Had it had been a sunny day in the central United States, maybe one out of two people, if invited, would have joined me for a walk, because walking requires more effort than sitting in front of a TV.

A much smaller percentage would or could have hung with a twenty-mile hike.

A tiny fraction of these potential walkers would remain if told, "The walk will be along the U.S.-Mexico border."

Yet another tiny fraction of the former tiny fraction would remain if informed, "It will be a twenty-mile hike, along the border, in a cold rain."

That's what made me smile. This was a one-thousand-plus mile hike through heat, cold, rain, wind, and sun. There were roughly three hundred million people in the United States and thirty million people in Texas, and in the history of our country, perhaps a handful of people had ever walked the length of the Texas-Mexico border. If my body held up, I would complete a trek few people ever could or would dream of accomplishing.

Wildlife was sparse and visibility limited, but the road shoulders caught my attention. There had been an occasional chili pepper along I-10 and US 90, but the numbers escalated dramatically as the road led toward Lobo. White cotton balls mixed with red chilies lent a Christmassy feel to the roadside. On the other side of the fence, bright purple cacti from the genus *Opuntia* were appropriate Mardi Gras decorations.

It was cold enough to see my breath, but grasshoppers clung to life. One of the more common species was a giant black and yellow grass-hopper reminiscent of our black and red lubbers in the Deep South. A large, green grasshopper chewed on a red chili just off the road. Maybe the capsaicin would keep his internal juices flowing and the cold at bay a little longer, as the approaching winter signaled his frozen doom.

By midmorning the skies had cleared enough that I couldn't resist stopping for panoramic photos of the landscape. A historical marker just east of the Van Horn Wells provided another stopping point. According to the monument, a natural spring described as "seep wells" had been the only source of reliable water in a very large area. Native Americans drank this water for centuries, but the monument offered no clue as to whether its water still flowed.

According to Darice, water wells had been drilled in the Lobo area in the 1960s, and for a while agriculture had boomed as farmers irrigated their cotton fields. In a very short period of time, perhaps a decade or two, the aquifer was depleted. With the current water table several hundred feet lower than at the time of my birth, farmers continued to raise chilies, cotton, and pecans in the Lobo area, but the irrigation had likely been curtailed dramatically.

Judging by the many abandoned houses and stores that comprised this once thriving but short-lived community, Lobo is an abject lesson in our shortsighted conservation of vital natural resources.

For the space of a couple of hours and a few miles, the pain lessened in my left leg, but it was a temporary respite, and soon enough, the discomfort was worse than ever, necessitating frequent stops, sitting against fence posts to relax the legs. The pain eased during breaks and roared back when hiking resumed.

A large, actively worked pecan orchard stretched for miles on the north side of 90 in Lobo. Workers ran tractors through the trees, blowing or vacuuming leaves and twigs out of the way for the fall harvest. Most of the trees still held their nuts.

To pass the time, I continuously searched the landscape for wildlife, the road for unsafe drivers, and the road shoulders for objects of interest.

I discovered a large, brand name knife lying on the side of the road along the pecan plantation. Did this blade have a story? Had it been used in the commission of a crime and discarded?

It wasn't safe to place it inside my backpack without a scabbard.

Law enforcement and locals already viewed me suspiciously. Carrying a sixteen-inch blade down the road was asking for trouble.

For a while, I carried it behind or in front of my leg, hiding it from oncoming traffic. The next mile marker provided a convenient place to drop the knife, in anticipation of its retrieval later that day.

The pain intensified. It felt as if bolts of electricity were shooting through my leg muscles.

Late in the afternoon, Jack finally checked in. It was only two more miles to the day's goal, and I thought I could make it, so Jack drove ahead to wait at the intersection.

Bending my left knee had become unbearable. As a temporary fix, I shifted my weight to the right side and swung the left leg in an arc while keeping it extended. Yards passed at a snail's pace until the pain became excruciating. Each step forward brought tears to my eyes. I gave up and called Jack. "I can't make it any farther. Let's go back to the hotel."

A bum leg and an unmet goal following a day's rest while touring the Red Rock Ranch on the west side of Van Horn was disheartening.

Jack picked me up, and we stopped to retrieve the found knife. Back at the hotel, it was obvious the leg had been pushed too hard and too long. My left leg and ankle were badly swollen. The only recourse was to lie in bed with bags of ice on the injured extremity. On TV, midterm election returns did nothing to improve my mood, although they made Jack happy.

After my early morning jubilation, it had evolved into an incredibly sucky day.

Before calling it a night, I called Michael Eason, a botanist who had agreed to coach me through some desert flora. Michael would join me along Chispa Road the following day.

November 5

How durable was this body? Walking day after day required pushing through serious pain. It was now apparent that some types of pain could not, or should not, be dominated through sheer grit. Additional damage to muscles or tendons was a cost I could ill afford. If the shooting pains returned, the walking would stop.

By the following morning, the swelling had disappeared. Jack dropped me off on US 90 and promised to check on Michael and me around mid-day.

It was only six-tenths of a mile to the turnoff on County Road 2017, which leads south toward Chispa Road and the Rio Grande. And it was the third consecutive day of precipitation: more rain, wind, and cold.

Fortunately, Highway 2017 is paved. Sadly, it was covered with hundreds of small, spotted, road-killed toads. I collected photos and specimens for Sean at Sul Ross. It only took Dr. Graham a glance to recognize them as green toads.

Green toads are only one and a half to two inches long, making them the smallest member of their genus (*Anaxyrus*) in Texas. True to their name, they are light green in color with small black dots and splotches covering their bodies.

Although hundreds of dead toads littered the highway, not a single live specimen was to be found. The species is nocturnal, hiding by day, and, apparently, moving en masse at night, with the right combination of season, temperature, and precipitation.

Knowing the carnage wrought by each passing vehicle, there are times when I can't stand to drive a vehicle.

Just past the toad massacre were two road-killed horny toads and a small, flattened, western diamondback rattlesnake—one of the most common snakes in west and south Texas.

A few miles south of US 90, County Road 2017 turns right and Chispa Road continues straight south. Chispa is not paved. A dirt surface is generally fine in the desert, but with several inches of rain, Chispa's surface ranged from firm to slick to soupy. This challenging surface would further test my legs.

The blacktop wasn't far behind me when Michael Eason arrived with his dog Roamer. Michael explained that Roamer was a Blue Lacy, a type of dog designated "the official State Dog Breed of Texas."

Michael held a wealth of information on plants, geology, geography, and people. He pointed out the Van Horn Mountains to our right and the Sierra Vieja range to our left.

Michael had studied with an incredible raconteur of a botanist named Dr. Billy Turner, who worked at the University of Texas in Austin. Dr.

Turner was a leading expert on two plant families that comprised much of the diversity in the Chihuahuan Desert: the bean family, *Fabaceae*, and the aster or composite family, *Asteraceae*. The family *Fabaceae* happens to be my specialty in the longleaf ecosystem.

Dr. Turner had discovered and described numerous plant species from the Chihuahuan Desert, including one that he'd tried to grace with the specific epithet "polyorgasmic." But the editor of the scientific journal refused to accept this name in his journal, thus foiling Dr. Turner.

A mutual friend of Michael and Dr. Turner provided this tidbit: "Another pertinent point: I believe his wife at that time was named Polly."

Was she honored or horrified? Randy old scientists present their significant others with unique conundrums.

Michael named one species after another during our slow stroll south on Chispa Road. For virtually every species, he knew the range plus the Latin family, genus, and species. After describing the plant and where it grew, he named similar species a pedestrian may encounter, were they to follow the border south and east. Besides Latin names, Michael typically knew the common names, often in both English and Spanish.

Michael was an atypical botanist in one sense: he was at least somewhat comfortable working with and talking to people.

The botanizing foray continued until we took a seat on the side of Chispa, mostly for the benefit of my sore leg. We ventured into politics and perceptions of the border.

Michael worked solo in very remote areas along the border, and he frequently encountered the Border Patrol.

Many agents asked him, "Don't you know this is a dangerous place?"

In Michael's opinion, rural areas along the border were as safe as most of America. He even went into Mexico on a semi-regular basis. "Four or five times a year, we cross the river to get away. They've got the best grocery store in Ojinaga with the freshest fruit and vegetables. For some of the locals who cross the river on a regular basis, the questioning from the Border Patrol is not an inconvenience, it's an insult."

Michael described two recent cases in the news where undocumented crossers had flagged down the Border Patrol, even though they had made it through the remote stretches and were basically home free. In each case, they had left someone who was incapable of continuing, and they gave themselves up to save a dying colleague.

Michael's assessment was, "The majority of them come for a better life."

Michael knew some ranchers in South Texas who still relied exclusively on undocumented workers. "This one ranch has a guy who crosses the river to work for them. Some days he gets caught, so he phones the ranch to tell them, 'I'll be a little late today. They caught me crossing so I'll have to try again later.'"

High above us a flock of Canada geese flew south. Their calls invariably carried me back to a pit blind with Grandpa Joe Hainds, hunting geese near the Swan Lake National Wildlife Refuge in Missouri. For the last two-plus decades, I had lived in Alabama and Georgia, well outside their migratory route. Fall lacks an essential element without the honks of migrating geese on a brisk November afternoon.

Both Michael and I had spent considerable time advising wealthy landowners, putting us in direct contact with multiple personalities.

Michael described a southwestern example. "They come out here and buy up these huge tracts of land. The next thing they do is fence it and put up signs, 'Don't touch my rocks.' They can be extremists on many issues, but they own and manage the most pristine lands you'll find."

I had seen the same thing a hundred times over in the Southeast. "We may not agree with them on anything else, but we can help them manage their land in ways that benefit the ecosystem and meet their objectives, without judging their prejudices or other shortcomings."

We meandered down the road. Virtually every plant we encountered and discussed was native to the Chihuahuan Desert. Then Michael pointed to a common invasive species and said, "That's the tumbleweed—icon of the American West—from Russia."

While much of the surrounding landscape was free range, there were still plenty of fences between El Paso and Chispa Road, prompting me to ask, "How in the world do they justify cattle ranching in the desert? It can't make economic sense to erect and maintain fences across vast acreages to support one cow per hundred acres."

"It's for tax purposes. But people are switching their land from ranching or agricultural exemptions to wildlife exemptions. These lands grow massive mule deer and wild aoudads."

The sounds of an approaching vehicle drew our attention to the north. Sound traveled well in this barren land. Jack topped a distant horizon in my truck. My leg was shot, and it was a relief to see our ride—even Michael appeared concerned with my painful limp. The truck cut ruts in the soft road as it moved toward us. Michael and I chose a slight rise to mark the end of the day's walk and wait for Jack. The odometer tallied my day's walk at 9.2 miles, the shortest day of the trek. I drove as we turned around, carrying Michael and Romer back to their vehicle. We shook hands and parted, but not before Michael offered to join me for more botanizing down the road.

As a bush-league botanist, I've met my share of hardcore plant people. Many of them have IQs on the trailing tail of the bell curve. Most are even more eccentric than I, which is saying something. A good number of botanists prefer the company of plants to people, yet I have truly enjoyed time in the field with each and every one of them.

The wet, muddy clothing came off at the hotel, exposing white, ice-cold skin. My left leg had swollen to even larger proportions. A warm shower helped to settle the shivers. From there, it was straight to bed with towels and bags of ice packed around the swollen extremity. I awoke at least once an hour to reposition the bags before drifting back to sleep. If the swelling wasn't reduced before the sun came up, the trek would be in jeopardy.

9

VALENTINE TO MARFA

"Those legislators who have fought the huge economic special interests, the racism, and the know-nothingism of Texas are possessed of a special kind of courage."

Molly Ivins. *Molly Ivins Can't Say That, Can She?* 1991

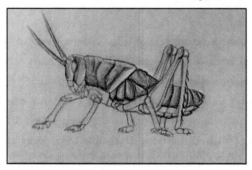

Texas Lubber: Drawn by Ava Bailey

Nov 6–8

BY the next morning, November 6, my leg was back to normal proportions. It was still sore, but at least the pain was bearable.

It had rained through much of the night and into the next morning. After Chispa went soft, we knew it would be difficult to even reach the previous day's stopping point. My leg was a mess. The road was a mess. Local landowners, law enforcement, and virtually everyone familiar with the road encouraged extreme caution along this route. Chispa was a scary, remote run under the best of circumstances, and these were nearly the worst conditions imaginable.

We'd revisit Chispa Road if the weather moderated and everything dried out.

Jack dropped me at the intersection of US 90 and County Road 2017. Instead of turning south, I'd follow US 90 straight east through Valentine and on to Marfa.

It was raining again.

The continuous rain brought a flood of toads. Snakes, in turn, feasted on the abundant prey. The first hour of the walk yielded a road-killed hognose snake, a horned lizard, numerous green toads, and several other snake species. Each new species was photographed, and GPS coordinates were recorded.

Vehicular traffic takes a terrible toll on wildlife, but it made the walk much more interesting. The only live animals along the road were birds and a jackrabbit.

The first tarantula of the trip lay dead on the shoulder. It didn't appear to be traditional road kill since its body was intact. Over the following miles, five dead tarantulas lay on the side of the road.

Tarantulas live in holes in the ground, in a region where it was unusual to receive such prolonged precipitation accompanied by cold weather. Possibly, the rain flushed the large arachnids from their holes where they died from prolonged exposure to the cold, wet conditions.

The outskirts of Valentine appeared mid-afternoon and I hoped to locate the mayor—a man called "Chuy."

While planning my walk, someone passed my name to a guy named BJ Gallego in Alpine, Texas. BJ gave me a call, and through several conversations, he provided names and numbers of suggested contacts across west Texas, including Valentine's mayor.

A car stopped at a house on the western edge of Valentine, and a woman stepped out. I yelled from the edge of US 90, "Hello!" She turned her back to me and walked toward her house. I tried again. "Hola!" She opened her door, stepped inside, and closed the door behind her.

Every restaurant or commercial establishment on the west side of town had long since closed. Most of the buildings had been abandoned for years.

An eastbound, full-size pickup driven by an older, large, white man passed by slowly. He eyed me suspiciously before driving out of sight. Moments later, the same truck appeared in the opposite lane, slowly headed west, with the same old white guy checking me out. I waved him over.

He pulled across to my side of the road and parked his truck with the rear bumper sticking halfway across the eastbound lane. He rolled down his window, and I asked, "Do you need to pull up a bit more?"

"They'll go around me." And they did. While we talked, several vehicles slowed and crossed to the westbound lane to avoid his ass-end.

"Red" lived in Valentine.

I said, "A man named BJ Gallego told me to talk with Chuy." Before adding, "BJ is the cousin of Representative Pete Gallego."

Red smiled. "He got his ass stomped! [Referring to the recent election, in which Rep. Gallego lost to a conservative Republican.] That's a good thing! Right?"

Red had just completed a simple and pernicious equation that's computed millions of times daily in rural Alabama, Georgia, Missouri, and Texas. The unspoken equation goes like this. "You are white. I am white. It's us against them. Long live the GOP."

At the time, I didn't realize that the man who defeated Representative Gallego was a conservative black Republican from San Antonio named William (Will) Hurd, the first black Republican elected to Congress from Texas.

For some cultural background, my boyhood was spent on a family farm about halfway between two small towns: Keytesville and Marceline, Missouri. For a dang close approximation, read about Joe Bageant's hometown of Winchester, Virginia, in *Deer Hunting With Jesus*. My adopted hometown of Andalusia, Alabama, is almost progressive in comparison. Whether in Marceline or Winchester, spend some time with my people—the rural white working class—and you'll figure it out soon enough.

I circumvented Red's question by saying, "I reckon." It was easier than entering a political discourse, and I still needed to locate Chuy.

Red knew Chuy's number by memory. I thanked him for his assistance before dialing the number. Chuy's wife answered. After I provided a short explanation of the walk and my identity, she said, "Chuy will call you when he gets home from his deliveries with FedEx."

Serendipitously, I had stopped in the small town of Valentine during my scouting drive earlier in the year, around January 1. I had noticed the tiny Kay Johnson Public Library on US 90, so I pulled over and entered the establishment. A Hispanic woman tending the library didn't know what to make of me. Nevertheless, I promised to return the following fall or early winter, before signing and donating a copy of my first book, *Year of the Pig*, to the library.

Eleven months had passed, and my promise was kept. I told Chuy's wife about my earlier stop at the library, and she said, "I'll go right over and check out your book!"

It was getting late and Jack was scheduled to pick me up anytime. I took a seat outside the library and reflected on my good fortune, having covered fifteen miles on two good legs with no swelling. It was a good day.

From Valentine, Jack drove us east to the Riata Inn on the east side of Marfa. After the tiny rooms with the Motel 6 in Van Horn, the new living quarters felt more like a hall or a house than a hotel room. All three of us were operating on limited budgets. With more space, we consolidated from two rooms in Van Horn to one room in Marfa. Jack and Rex each took a bed while I volunteered to sleep on the floor.

The day's efforts left me starving. After weeks of granola, jerky, and dried fruits, it was time for a substantial meal, and a restaurant named Cochineal had the best reviews in Marfa.

The Cochineal was a cozy little restaurant tucked into a mostly residential neighborhood, just a few minutes' drive from the Riata. The menu had my mouth watering, though the prices might preclude hikers with limited budgets from eating there on a regular basis.

The bartender recommended a Brooklyn Pilsner that went marvelously with their Chilequitos. Midmeal, Chuy returned my call, scheduling a meeting the next morning with Rex and me at the Valentine Community Center.

Chuy arrived at 8:30 and suggested we follow him to the public school in Valentine where he taught several classes, in addition to being the town mayor and a FedEx deliveryman.

We signed in, and Chuy led us to a classroom to meet his students.

My elementary school in Keytesville, Missouri, was small. During the mid-1970s, there had been a total of two hundred students in the entire school, grades K–12, and the student body at Keytesville was five times larger than Valentine's.

Valentine had a total of thirty-nine students in K-12. Chuy told us, "Valentine had about one hundred students when I was here, with a peak attendance of a hundred and twenty-five students in the 1960s."

Despite challenges unique to small schools, Valentine performed exceptionally well in academics. "We had two seniors graduate last year, and both of them went to college. Four seniors will graduate this year, and they've all been accepted to college."

Several students wore t-shirts from Texas State, having recently visited San Marcos, Texas, where they planned to study after graduation.

Chuy had been Valentine's mayor since 1974. "Sometimes people will tell me, 'Chuy, I am going to run against you this time.' I tell them, 'You don't have to campaign. I will step down, and you can have the job.' They let it go pretty quick."

Two girls, Abbie and Jessie, took notes for the school newspaper. It was a warm and welcoming environment in contrast to my initial impressions of Valentine: the woman who ignored my salutations, and Red's suspicious attention from the day before.

Rex set up his camera and microphone to capture our conversation as Chuy and his students took chairs around a table in front of us.

After graduating from Valentine, Chuy attended a university from 1968 to 1972, achieving a double major in biology and physical education. He returned to Valentine in 1972, where he coached and taught science.

He married his high school sweetheart, became the mayor, and eventually retired from his fulltime teaching job after thirty-seven years. He still taught part-time, with four students in each of his classes: human anatomy and Spanish. Chuy had four students in each class.

After Rex and I explained our projects to the students, a young white kid from a nearby ranch floored us with his first question. "Have you seen any wetbacks?"

Chuy and most of the students in attendance were Hispanic, but at least outwardly they didn't seem the least bit offended.

I turned to the kid and said, "It's interesting that you would use that term because where Rex and I come from that's considered a racial slur. Is this how you all commonly refer to illegal immigrants?"

Chuy took the lead in answering my question. "They [undocumented immigrants] come to town sometimes. It's about thirty miles from here to the border, so we don't see them too often. They mostly come at night. When we see a helicopter southwest of town, we know there are some in the area. They [Border Patrol] drag the roads so they can tell when a group crosses."

Chuy continued, "I once had an Anglo call me a 'wetback.' I told him, 'I'm a freshwater wetback. You are a saltwater wetback.' Unless you are a Native American, you had to get wet on your way to this country."

"In the sixties, the illegals came here looking for work. They were mostly good, hard-working people. Now when most people see an illegal alien with a backpack, they are carrying cocaine or marijuana. It's planned, as there is someone waiting to pick them up."

Chuy offered a positive opinion of the Border Patrol. "Fortunately, we have lots of Border Patrol around. If you stop to urinate more than thirty seconds, the Border Patrol will show up. I think that is a good thing because it keeps this town secure. If the Border Patrol harassed people, I would go directly to the chief of this section in Marfa."

Chuy was rightfully proud of his tenure as mayor. "Since I've been mayor, our budget has never been in the red. Our garbage and water rates are the lowest in the area." Through Chuy's efforts, they had secured grants for "an excellent water system, paved streets, and a state of the art community center. We have economic development and a safe place to live."

Valentine existed because it had been a railroad depot dating back to the 1800s. Chuy described what happened when the railroad quit stopping to exchange crews. "Now the railroad just stops in Alpine. We lost the restaurants and the railroaders. Our population has declined to about a hundred and fifty people."

I went to High School in a small railroad town that depended heavily upon a station and railroad crews. When our railroad station closed, Marceline paid the same economic price as Valentine, though we had other industries to prop up the economy.

Around Valentine, farming had declined because of the lack of willing labor. "There was an onion farm in Presidio that paid five dollars an hour," Chuy said. "That was good money in Mexico. But it went under when they clamped down on undocumented labor."

Chuy gave another example. "There are two tomato farms between Fort Davis and Marfa in greenhouses. They paid ten dollars an hour, but that's not good enough to hire U.S. citizens. They need three hundred workers, but citizens want high-paying jobs, fifteen or twenty an hour."

"What will keep Valentine going in the twenty-first century?"

Chuy answered, "We are not crazy about oil and gas. We have concerns about water quality, fires, and explosions. This is a business and environmentally friendly community. There are lots of ropings in the area, and there is still work for cowboys. Once it gets in their blood, they never want to do anything else."

What about Marfa? It was one of the few towns we had visited since El Paso that did not appear to be in a downward spiral. Chuy was not impressed. "The locals don't like foreigners coming in."

Over the course of my walk, I'd heard similar attitudes toward Marfa. The city might have found a way to survive through arts, literature, and the avant-garde, but outlying communities regarded Marfa as snooty.

A perfect representation of Marfa's influence is positioned along US 90 between Valentine and Marfa. If you are driving this route, watch carefully and you will find a small, cement building with a glass front on the south side of US 90. There are two awnings with "PRADA" in large print, and in smaller print beneath it, "MARFA." Behind the plate glass windows are Prada shoes and purses.

I grew up in Chariton County, Missouri. It was so rural we didn't have a stoplight in a county that covered seven hundred and fifty-one square miles. The county seat has a population of three hundred people. From the family farm, my life progressed through a series of military bases and universities, ending up on a dirt road in south Alabama.

I've watched much of rural America wither away as agricultural mechanization, consolidation, and misguided federal agricultural policies wiped out family farms. Where I grew up, the status quo is death. In Marfa, I saw a potential model for survival. Yet too many country folk prefer the status quo to an infusion of fresh blood, attitudes, and professions.

Chuy's heroic efforts had kept Valentine alive thus far. But it was hard to visualize a bright future for communities like Valentine, Candelaria, and Sierra Blanca.

Before we packed up, the students shared insider information regarding the Prada building east of Valentine. They told us the purses had the bottoms removed and the shoes had been treated similarly, so thieves would gain nothing by breaking into the unmanned art installation. They told us the Prada building had been repeatedly vandalized by unappreciative locals. A female student helped clean the Prada building on occasion. She said, "It fills up with dust and tarantulas." She laughed. "There are scorpions inside the shoes!"

After our interview, we stepped outside to a parking lot filled with sunshine. The change in weather was a welcome relief after several days of rain. Rex dropped me at the Kay Johnson Library for the walk east.

A short distance outside of town, a live tarantula basked on the warm road surface. Fearing it would get run over, I shooed it to the road shoulder where it disappeared into the grass.

Two bicyclists doing the Southern Tier stopped to chat with me. They had seen several live tarantulas in the area and were just as excited to see the big, furry arachnids.

The morning's interview was lengthy, leaving me just enough time to cover fifteen miles, ending on the roadside just across from an observation blimp. Who knew our government still employed blimps? But there it was: a tethered blimp, just down the road from a Prada store stocked with scorpions, in the land of the Marfa Lights.

Jack pulled up in my truck while I flagged the south fence and switched on my GPS app to secure and record the coordinates. Before the process was finished, a loud pop startled me. A young man steered his compact car to the road shoulder, having just blown a tire. A student parking tag from Sul Ross University hung from his rearview mirror, and he held a cell phone. He declined our assistance. "Someone will come pick me up, but thanks for the offer."

The next morning, Rex drove me straight to the Prada installation and filmed from several angles as I repeatedly walked by the fake storefront. It was difficult to keep a straight face, and we broke up several times at the sheer absurdity of the creation. The artist was a genius.

When he finished shooting, Rex dropped me at the blimp. The car with the blown tire was still parked on the side of the road. Apparently, he was as ill-prepared for a flat tire as we'd been on Chispa.

The skies were clear and sunny with temperatures in the thirties. This was my preferred hiking weather.

It was relatively calm early in the morning, but a strong north wind developed, and tumbleweeds raced across US 90 as the wind howled, producing scenes reminiscent of the iconic west that film buffs would recognize from a thousand Hollywood westerns.

According to Chuy, drowsy drivers frequently wrecked along this stretch of road, making the road shoulder a risky proposition. I tried a dirt trail between US 90 and train tracks just to the north of the highway. Open-exposed areas were relatively dry and firm, but dips near culverts turned to sticky mud. It wasn't ideal, but it distanced me from the highway and decreased my odds of becoming road kill.

A Border Patrol agent was parked on the opposite (south) side of US 90. I waved while walking past, but sun glaring off his windshield made it difficult to tell if he saw me or not. Several minutes later he drove past, slowed, did a U-turn, and stopped on my side of the road. He asked, "Where are you headed?"

The same or similar questions had been posed a few dozen times, so I tried a new answer. "Short, medium, or long-term?"

"Whatever." He smiled.

"Short-term, I aim to make it another fifteen miles toward Marfa. Some friends will pick me up around 5:00."

"Intermediate, I hope to make Boca Chica Beach on the Gulf of Mexico before Christmas."

"Long-term, probably Hell, but I intend to have some kind of experiences along the way."

He seemed to get a kick out it.

Shortly thereafter, another Border Patrol agent pulled over to check on me. After the usual Q&A, he added, "If your knees start to swell or you need water or any other type of assistance, don't hesitate to flag us down."

These agents were pretty decent people.

Trudging the endless straightaway, I imagined a bird looking down from high above on six lines stretching from horizon to horizon. The outside lines were barbed-wire fences. From south to north, US 90 was inside the fence, then the dirt trail, and then a line of mesquite trees paralleling a railroad line. After the mesquite hedge were railroad tracks and, finally, the north fence.

Mourning doves held tight in the mesquite trees paralleling the railroad tracks, staying put until I was right beside them, before flushing into the gusting wind. Had I carried a shotgun, I could have shot my limit several times over as this scenario repeated itself hundreds of times.

Apparently, someone passed the word among the Border Patrol that "the hiker is harmless," because the Border Patrol agents were almost as numerous as the mourning doves, but most of them drove by without stopping.

Several miles outside of town, a billboard welcomed me to Marfa. It took another hour of walking for buildings to appear in the distance. Wildlife was scarce in the flat landscape until a large covey of blue quail erupted from a fencerow, before scattering along a shrubby drain.

I finally reached the edge of town, still several miles from the hotel. Tired, sore, and hungry, I stopped at the first non-chain restaurant. Mando's door was open, but it was too late for lunch and the employees were putting chairs on the tables. A waitress approached. "I'm sorry, but the kitchen is closed. Can I get you something to drink?"

"Oh well. A glass of iced-tea would be great."

She returned with a large Styrofoam cup of tea.

"How much do I owe you?"

"Nothing. It's on us."

"Thank you so much." I was smiling again.

The tea and the gesture put a spring in my step, until I came upon a black man sitting on the north side of the road with a three-wheeled cycle and all his belongings. He wasn't cycling the southern tier for sport. He had a broken chain on his ride and a crucifix hanging over his forehead. He said, "That's smart. Carrying it on your back. Are you hiking through?"

"Yes, to the Gulf of Mexico."

"How far is that?"

"About eight hundred miles. Where you headed?"

"Kansas."

"That's a long way. You have people up there?"

"My stepmom. But I don't call her that. I just call her 'Mom'. Yeah, I am going to Alpine, and then I'll turn north to Oklahoma, and then to Kansas." He asked, "Are you okay on food?"

"Yes, sir. I have some."

"How about money?" He pulled his billfold out of his pocket to show some ones and fives.

A sure-enough homeless guy, broke down in Marfa, trying to get to Kansas, offering what little food and money he had to a total stranger. Remembering him still brings tears to my eyes.

"No. I'm okay. Can you use some food? I have some extra granola."

He refused my offer, so we shook hands and wished each other luck.

A few blocks east, a bike shop had the front door open. The store attendant had already talked to the stranded traveler and they didn't have the right size chain. There was little I could do.

A few blocks farther, and a sign pointed to the beer garden at Planet Marfa, thus activating Rule #3.

Conversations halted as I limped in and set my walking stick and backpack beside a picnic table. It was Saturday afternoon, and college football was playing on multiple TVs around the establishment. A waitress took my order and turned to leave. She stopped, hesitated, and turned back. "Do you want to watch the Auburn game?"

My Auburn hoodie (compliments of little brother Curtis) had fortuitously betrayed my allegiance.

"Heck yeah!"

She led me to an unoccupied table in front of a large-screen TV and tuned it to the Auburn–Texas A&M game before leaving to start my tab.

The guys at the Riata answered my call. "I made it to town, but don't expect me before dark. I am hanging at Planet Marfa." Jack drove over and joined me. He bought me a plate of nachos and secretly paid my beer tab, and, apparently, Jack clued the manager into our mission.

Jack took a seat across from me as the manager came over and offered, "Would you like another drink? It's on the house!"

"If you's buying, I'm drinking!"

The manager returned with another beer and stayed long enough to hear my stories from the last few hundred miles. Food and drink were free for the rest of the night. The only down note: Auburn fumbled the ball in the final moments and lost to the inconsistent Aggies. Besides that, it was an absolute blast.

It was dark and cold as hell when I stumbled out of the beer garden with my staff, my backpack, and a mile to go. The temperatures, though very low, weren't bothersome. The grasshopper in Lobo coped by eating a red chili pepper, while free beer functioned as my antifreeze. Luckily, there were no open pits or mean dogs between Planet Marfa and the Riata, because I was blind and defenseless in the dark.

There were twenty-one miles between the tethered blimp and the Riata. This approached the average daily mileage required to reach the Gulf of Mexico by December twenty-third. Somewhere down the road, I had to make up for all the short days east of Van Horn.

I stepped into the room, and Rex said, "Guess who Jack and I saw in Valentine."

"Dang. I don't know."

"Our old buddy Arvin West, the Sheriff from Hudspeth County. He was in town to visit with Red."

At the suggestion of the Hudspeth County Extension Agent in Sierra Blanca, I had called and left messages twice, asking if Sheriff West would be willing to meet for an interview in the Sierra Blanca area. He never returned my call.

"What did they have to say?"

"They flagged us down to shoot the shit. Red had bulldozed an old house before finding out the Border Patrol had hidden thousands of dollars of listening devices inside the house."

The Border Patrol frequently installs sensors in or around structures that may be utilized by undocumented immigrants, such as inside abandoned houses and below bridges.

Rex continued, "All that equipment is buried in the rubble. By the way, Arvin and Red used the shorthand 'wets' to refer to illegal immigrants."

I described my encounter with the homeless guy, and Rex said, "That's how it is. Those with the least to offer are often the most generous with the little they have."

Sierra, the author, and Jimmy in Langtry

Panorama of Quitman Pass

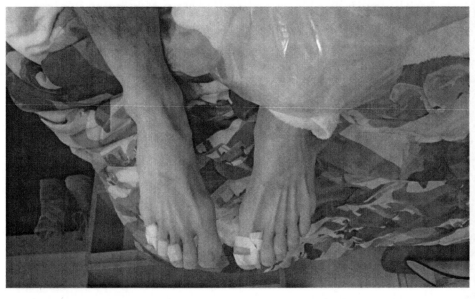

Icing down a leg at the Motel 6 in Van Horn – a vacation dream

10

CHISPA ROAD

"I thought that there were two rules in life—never count the cost, and never do anything unless you can do it wholeheartedly. Now is the time to live."

> Everett Ruess, a 1934 diary entry in *Everett Ruess:*
> *A Vagabond for Beauty.* 1983

Scorpion on Chispa Rd: Photo by author

November 9–11

JACK'S term as a Tex-Mex Compadre was nearly up, and he planned his drive back to Georgia for the next day, Sunday, November 9. Before leaving, Jack offered to drop me at the top of Chispa Road and pick up the incoming Compadres at the El Paso Airport.

Jack had been an incredible asset. Rex immediately adored the slow-talking gentleman from Georgia, and we were continuously entertained with Jack's observations and fascination at the surrounding terrain, people, vegetation, and animals. From the first day in El Paso, Jack had assumed his role with a seriousness and dedication that we couldn't have anticipated. Rex and I hated to see him go.

We were pretty sure that the last few days of sunshine and wind had dried Chispa Road to the point it would be drivable. With much trepidation and against Rex's advice, it was time for another shot at Chispa.

As with Quitman Pass, I planned to camp this section. It was a long run from any hotel to the north end of Chispa. After a day's hike in, it would be too far and difficult for the Compadres to reach me on a daily basis. It was time to test myself against a region too remote for law enforcement.

It was about sixty miles from the Riata to the little ridge on Chispa where Jack had retrieved Michael Eason and me several days earlier. The dirt road had dried out and firmed up. I handed the keys to Jack. As he turned the truck around and left for El Paso, the enormity of the landscape and the situation settled upon me. All the people we had met were scared of Chispa Road, with the exception of Michael the botanist and Tinsley the old cowboy.

My pack was easily double the training weight from Lower Alabama. In addition to water, food, and survival gear, it held a tent, sleeping bag, and other supplies. The pack weight now exceeded forty pounds and was probably closer to fifty.

Chispa led south, toward the Rio Grande.

Two trucks approached from the south at a high rate of speed, before shooting past without slowing down. Flapping tarps revealed partially covered Ocotillo plants in the truck beds—cactus rustlers.

Days earlier, on the northern stretch of Chispa, Michael Eason had told me that much of the property along Chispa Road was held by the General Land Office. It was for sale at very low prices because few people desired property in a relatively inaccessible, deserted, drug-smuggling corridor through the desert.

The cactus smugglers knew that the slow-growing Ocotillo is valued for landscaping, and the odds of getting caught were minuscule.

My first encounter with people on Chispa was interesting, but they weren't the scariest operators in the region.

The bars/reception on my cell phone disappeared. There would be little or no cell service for the duration of Chispa.

An hour or so later and a few miles south, the road forked. Several days earlier, Jack had driven this route before turning around and getting a flat tire on his way out. His notes included the coordinates for this fork with written directions, "Take the good road."

The two roads appeared identical in quality. What type of fucked up advice was this? Eventually, I settled on the left fork.

Approximately two miles down the left fork, a locked gate with a "No Trespassing" sign blocked the road. Jack should have been there, so I could have beaten him with my stick. This diversion had cost time and energy while leading me onto private property—no small deal in Texas, intentional or not. I turned around and walked back up the road as quickly as possible with the heavy pack.

Chispa Road was a quarter mile ahead when the sound of vehicles carried up the road from behind me. I stepped to the side and prepared to face an angry landowner.

The vehicles approached and a convoy of hunters in four trucks emerged from a remote ranch; their truck beds were loaded with gear.

Normally, hunters seeing a hiker in a remote area would stop to offer a ride, talk about the weather, or to question what game was seen or harvested. Not this time.

They eyed me suspiciously as they passed at a distance of ten feet. They had probably received the same advice I had and come to a logical conclusion: a stranger with a backpack on Chispa is a drug smuggler.

At least I didn't have to explain my presence on their road.

The wrong turn cost valuable time and energy, but beautiful weather mitigated these negatives. The road was dry and the scenery incredible. Steep slopes and draws bordered Chispa for much of its length. From high points, the landscape stretched for miles.

In places, barbed wire fences traveled up near vertical cliffs. The men who drove those posts must have been part mountain goat. My mood lightened, with an underlying current of concern mixed with awe.

Chispa wound back and forth, up and down, through long-abandoned ranches, mountains, valleys, draws, and ridges. Besides the dirt road and some fencing, much of this high desert appeared virtually untouched: a tan landscape defined by rock and bare soil. Ocotillos, yuccas, prickly pears, and Christmas cacti colored some areas with light green, and creosote bushes offered a contrasting darker green.

A pile of rocks beside the road was arranged in the same pattern one observes in remote, rural West Texas cemeteries. Lacking a headstone or wooden marker, it was just another resting place for an unidentified person, long dead. An Anglo? A Mexican? An Indian?

I recalled a conversation with a Border Patrol agent further west. Having previously worked on Chispa Road, he told me, "There are lots of old graves down there. Many of them are unmarked, and we have no idea who they are. They may be hundreds of years old."

Someday, anthropologists may find the unmarked graves of Chispa worthy of study and answer these questions.

Private drives left Chispa and disappeared over ridges to camps or houses unseen. Some offshoots had recent tire tracks, but no livestock or horses stood within sight of the road, nor any fresh tracks or manure. The land was largely abandoned with the exception of hunting camps.

Mule deer tracks showed here and there, but the only visible wildlife was an occasional jackrabbit running through the cactus and mesquite.

A heavier backpack and the warm temperature necessitated increased water consumption. I took note of an ephemeral pond, a product of the recent rain, but did not stop. By mid-afternoon, I approached a large Quonset hut with a sign identifying the building as property of the General Land Office. A large, cloudy puddle of water stood near the building.

Cloudy water pointed to suspended clay, but there was a good chance this would be the last water encountered over the day's walk. It was time to employ a water filter.

My filter system consisted of a bag, a filter, and straw. After filling the bag, I attached it to the filter with the straw coming out the other end. By squeezing on the bag, the applied pressure forced the dirty water through the filter, and clear water exited through the straw. The clean water was fed into empty half-liter water bottles.

Clay particles quickly clogged the filter, requiring me to reverse the setup and flush the clay. It was a slow process, but a half hour effort produced two liters of the worst tasting water I'd consumed since drinking Auburn's municipal water as an AU graduate student in the early 1990s.

From the Quonset hut, Chispa wound south and east, descending into the Rio Grande Valley, only a few hundred yards from Mexico.

The first house visible from Chispa Road was in ruins. Adobe walls still stood, but a roof supported by cottonwood trusses had collapsed, with asphalt shingles scattered by ferocious winds.

It was a golden opportunity to search for critters, so I flipped some shingles, revealing several scorpions. Broken doors and windows allowed me to peer into the collapsing house and check for signs of recent use. The floors were cluttered with boards, glass, and other trash. Smart hikers or border crossers would bypass this building for a camping site beneath the stars.

Other, larger pests roamed the landscape around the ruined structure. Fresh hog rooting and tracks covered everything south of the road. The floodplain was eaten up with wild boar.

Discussions of my planned walk always started with, "Why?" Once we got past the reasoning, their next question was, "Will you be carrying?"— meaning a firearm.

A long gun was out of the question. First of all, it would weigh too much. Secondly, I would have felt like a complete idiot carrying a rifle though municipalities. I intended to talk with people along the route, and open carry would intimidate the very people I hoped to meet. Additionally, many stores and restaurants along the way posted notices such as "No Open Carry" or no "No Firearms Allowed." While walking, there wouldn't be a vehicle in which to store a rifle, and it wouldn't make sense to leave a firearm on the sidewalk outside.

The only feasible weapon was a concealed pistol, and I did not own a sidearm. Preferring accuracy over knockdown power, I purchased a Berretta, semi-automatic 22 with a long barrel and started practicing. It was accurate, but heavy.

The Covington County, Alabama, Sheriff's office issued me a concealed carry permit that was reciprocal between Texas and Alabama. Now, I had a pistol and the legal authority to carry a concealed weapon in Texas.

Just before leaving for Texas, I attended my last regional conference as a fulltime employee of The Longleaf Alliance and Auburn University. At an evening reception, a forester and friend reacted in near horror at the notion of my walking the border with a mere .22 caliber pistol. On the spot, he pulled an Air-Weight 38 revolver from his pocket and made me promise to carry his pistol instead.

The .38 weighed half as much as my new .22, and it fit nicely in the bib pocket of my overalls, which I intended to wear while hiking remote areas.

On Chispa Road, I unzipped my bib pocket and positioned the .38 where it could be drawn and fired in a moment's notice. Based upon the abundant sign, there was a good chance of stumbling into a sounder of feral pigs. My mouth watered at a mental image of feral pork sizzling over a mesquite campfire.

Chispa wound along the edge of floodplain, more or less paralleling the nearby Rio Grande. The terrain rose sharply to my left with the elevation peaking hundreds or thousands of feet higher in nearby mountain ranges.

The flat floodplain of the Rio Grande lay slightly below me, to the right, with a backdrop of mountains on the far side of the river.

Mesquite once covered the floodplain, but a recent wildfire had swept through the bottom-ground, top-killing both the native mesquite and the invasive salt cedar. A forest of dead, gray tree skeletons lent a desolate feel to the deserted, post-apocalyptic landscape. No wonder the locals shuddered at the thought of walking Chispa.

While humans were scarce, animals were not. The Rio Grande provided a long-term water source, and animal sign increased exponentially. Besides the omnipresent tracks, scat, rubs, and wallows of feral pigs, there were tracks from mule deer, javelina, raccoon, rabbit, possible aoudad, and mountain lion.

My preparation for the trek had included a phone conversation with the Extension Agent for Presidio County, Texas. Jesse Lee Snider offered valuable suggestions on hiking the area, from a credible background. Jesse said, "I grew up on a ranch along the Rio Grande. Half my family works for the Border Patrol."

We discussed the challenges before me. She cautioned, "There will be rattlesnakes, bears, and plenty of mountain lions."

"Rattlesnakes are a dime a dozen in my neighborhood," I replied. "Bears are few and far between in Alabama, but I am the least familiar with mountain lions."

"Generally the lions aren't a problem, but occasionally a hungry female will go after hikers, particularly when the lion is above her target. Realistically, the biggest risk you face is stumbling upon something that you were not supposed to see, like a major drug transfer. You'd just be an innocent bystander, but they'd know that you are isolated and exposed. I'm not trying to be too dramatic, but that's a real risk."

This scenario had already played itself out in my head with a dozen different variations, so she only confirmed my second greatest worry. My greatest fear was running out of water.

I reflected out loud, "If I watch *No Country for Old Men* again, I just might rethink this whole walk."

The panther tracks recalled her warning, but they were just as quickly forgotten. The landscape was too dramatic, so I soaked up the surrounding views, animal sign, and sounds that enveloped me.

A mile past the abandoned house, a flat, open space provided an ideal campsite between the cacti and mesquite. There appeared to be occupied houses on the distant Mexican side of the Rio Grande, but everything on the U.S. side was abandoned.

I erected the tent, unrolled the sleeping bag, and gathered a pile of dry mesquite while considering the pros and cons of a campfire.

Without illumination, the campsite would be invisible from Chispa Road. A campfire, on the other hand, would produce light and smoke, potentially calling the attention of nefarious forces.

On the positive side, a campfire emits radiant heat and positive energy in equal parts. And if, by chance, the Border Patrol drove by at night, which was very doubtful, a campfire should indicate that the camper was not hiding. Drug smugglers probably don't roast marshmallows and hotdogs on Chispa.

The positives outweighed the negatives, and a fire was soon crackling in front of the tent. The skies were clear, and the temperature dropped with the setting sun. After a quick supper, I crawled into the tent. Mindful of scorpions, I placed my boots inside the tent beside me.

The sleeping bag and tent weren't sufficient to ward off the chill, and I awoke, shivering, at 3:00 a.m. Temperatures in the thirties prompted me to crawl outside and rebuild the campfire from mesquite embers.

A family of coyotes took umbrage at the invader in their stomping grounds. They barked, yipped, howled, and growled. One coyote circled my campsite and barked from the hilltop behind my tent, only sixty to eighty yards away.

Quitman Pass had provided an extremely remote, rugged landscape to test my abilities. My trek south of Sierra Blanca had offered solitude in stretches of a few hours at a time. Chispa Road took these aspects to another level, and I loved it. There was no place I'd rather have been than lying beside that campfire, a few hundred yards from Mexico, in a smuggling corridor, cussed by coyotes while recording my thoughts and feelings in a small yellow journal.

The coyotes tired of their lecture as the surrounding black lightened to gray. I struck camp and starting hiking well before dawn. There were zero bars on my phone, yet, inexplicably, a text message from Rex mysteriously appeared.

The new Compadres had made it to the Riata. They were on their way from Marfa to Chispa with an estimated arrival time of 10:00 to 10:30 a.m.

A few hours later, Chispa Road left the floodplain, climbing into the hills above. The sounds of an approaching vehicle reached me on a straightaway. I unzipped the bib pocket of my overalls and positioned the grip of the .38 facing upward, before turning to face the oncoming vehicle. It was my truck.

Jack had picked up Simons and Mfundisi Ronnie at the El Paso airport. Rather than leaving for Georgia, he had stayed another night with Rex at the hotel. Earlier that morning, Jack handed Simons the keys to my pickup and guided them back to Chispa Road, while riding in the back seat.

Simons was an ER doctor who had just retired a month before the walk began. We became acquainted while he attended three different courses offered by my employer, The Longleaf Alliance. Simons was a landowner, conservationist, and a serious hunter. When he read my first book on pig hunting, he purchased an extra copy and mailed it to Ronnie, who sidelines as a professional hunter in South Africa.

After Ronnie read *Year of the Pig*, he and Simons had me installed as an honorary member of The Order of the Warthog. They also arranged a gift in the form of a custom-made lock-blade knife. The blade was Damascus steel, and the body was constructed from warthog ivory. It is one of the most beautiful and thoughtful gifts I have ever received.

After Simons volunteered as a Tex-Mex Compadre, Ronnie offered to join Simons and split the task of keeping me alive on the border (Rule #1). Ronnie's offer was conditional: no walking on his part. Having received said guarantee, Ronnie purchased plane tickets from Johannesburg, South Africa to New York, then JFK to Charleston, South Carolina, where Ronnie had family. Ronnie joined Simons in South Carolina, and the pair flew from Columbia to El Paso. After many thousands of miles, the well-traveled team now joined us on Chispa.

Their timing was wonderful. All that remained of my water supplies was a last half liter of disgusting puddle water. Had they arrived much later, my thirst would have required filtering water straight from the Rio Grande.

Simons was driving, and Ronnie rode shotgun. Simons stopped the truck and stepped out with a big smile. He was taller than I with a dark mustache and glasses. Simons was more reserved by himself, but he was seldom without a smile in the company of the shorter, more gregarious Ronnie. When they got together, the world was a wondrous place. They laughed, looked for good places to eat, cooked great food, or sipped brown liquor well outside my price range.

The crew provided more food, water, and an extra layer of clothing. They would drive approximately ten miles farther down Chispa to flag a potential campsite by the road, where they would stash water and the sleeping bag. Then they would continue on through Chispa for a rendezvous the following afternoon in Candelaria.

They drove east. My pack wasn't quite as full, but it was still heavy. An hour later, my truck rounded a bend with the Compadres coming back west. They had left supplies as planned, but Chispa Road was blown out about one mile past the campsite.

Jack estimated that Candelaria was another eight or nine miles past the blowout. Instead of a short drive through Candelaria to our reservations at Chinati Hot Springs, they had a four-hour drive ahead of them: north on Chispa, east on US 90, south to Presidio, and west through Ruidosa.

The road led to a T-intersection. Jack had stopped at this junction where he recorded the coordinates and wrote, "Take the good road."

I cursed out my frustration, swinging my walking stick at an imaginary Jack, before dropping my pack and considering the evidence. There was ongoing human activity in the area. A generator was running along with distant sounds of construction. The sound appeared to be coming from the right. More than likely, the right fork was a driveway leading to an active construction project. I turned left.

This time my intuition proved correct. The road looped around a peninsula before dropping back into the Rio Grande floodplain, where Chispa Road tracked south along the main channel of the river.

I traipsed along Chispa, alert for animals or humans.

"Ting, ting, ting." Having grown up building and tending fences on a cattle farm, I recognized the distinctive and familiar tone of someone driving steel fence posts into the ground. The sound stopped, and a puff of white smoke rose into the air. The laborer was enjoying a smoke break.

I cleared a rise and spied a Mexican cowboy standing beside the fence to my right.

His eyes widened in surprise. Seeking to relieve his suspicions, I smiled and called out, "¡*Buenas tardes!*" He replied in Spanish, and the conversation stayed there.

"*Voy a Candelaria.*" (I am going to Candelaria.)

He replied in a serious tone, "*Candelaria es muy lejos. Muy lejos. (Candelaria is very far.)*"

I inquired, "¿*Esta bueno el camino?* (Is the road good?)"

"*Si, esta bien.* (Yes, it is.)"

That was a relief, although it was somewhat questionable to call the road "good" when I already knew it was blown out a few miles ahead.

He wished me "*Buen viaje,*" and I continued south.

Perhaps a mile or two past the cowboy, there was a gate with a sign: "El Rancho Alvarado: Milares, Texas."

Recalling my conversation with the old cowboys by the Red Rock Office in Van Horn, I had asked them if Chispa Road was passable to Candelaria.

Shane had turned to Tinsley and asked, "What's the road like past Alvarado's?"

Tinsley answered, "It's a good road."

Shane explained, "He says it's good, but Tinsley has walked or ridden a horse his whole life. A good road for Tinsley means the mesquite is less than chest-high."

So far the road had been rough and meandering, but easy enough to follow (no thanks to Jack).

Unfortunately, the pack was whipping my butt.

A firm trail is great. Good weather is awesome. But nothing factors as much as the weight in one's backpack.

Nine hours of hiking had my muscles screaming for relief. I dropped the pack and took a seat facing north toward a mountain range running east and west between Chispa and the distant US 90. A brown and green walking stick insect took this opportunity to amble up my boot, over my pants, and rest on my knee. It was about six inches long. After surveying its surroundings from knee mountain, it continued down my leg, with a gentle, swaying pace, like a stick in a breeze, onto the soil, and east on Chispa.

I pictured the young adventurer, Everett Ruess, wandering the landscapes of the desert Southwest alone, the mountains beckoning. A coworker at The Longleaf Alliance had recommended Ruess's diary, which I read while preparing for the trek. Now, Everett's ghost guided my steps.

With so much to explore and land this big, it's easy to imagine you are the first human to see this fossil, to climb a particular ledge, or to fish that stream.

In his drawings, block prints, and letters home, Ruess went large, depicting mountains, skies, and landscapes. Everything was bigger in the west.

For my part, the small was equally fascinating: the earless lizard, the kangaroo mouse, and the walking stick.

After numerous rest stops, I made it to the drop site at 4:00 p.m. with no strength to spare.

I pitched the tent just off the road and gathered dry mesquite for a warming fire. Supper consisted of dried fruits, nuts, and granola bars.

No wonder the Border Patrol didn't work Chispa. It was safer and more effective for them to stop smugglers and undocumented immigrants on the highway thirty miles north. If trouble arose on US 90, they could summon backups that would arrive in minutes, perhaps even seconds. On Chispa, their radios might not work. If their truck broke down, no one would find them for an extended period of time.

There were no obvious signs of active smuggling, though several Border Patrol officers had assured us that this was a hot zone. Smart smugglers would avoid creating visible trails, varying their routes through the mesquite and cactus. They would know how to find their way through the boulders, cliffs, and slopes in the mountains, not so distant. They probably walked this harsh country at night, carrying packs that weighed as much or more than mine. Their line of work required some sure-enough tough *hombres.*

The next morning found me at the washout, almost exactly a mile past the campsite.

Presumably, the arroyo was passable until recent rains washed the soil from beneath a cement slab that had stretched across the drain. The slab collapsed, leaving a sheer drop to broken concrete in the arroyo below. Some of the remaining slab was suspended with nothing but air beneath.

Recent tire tracks from vehicles, including my truck, approached from the west but not from the other side of the arroyo. The lack of traffic from the east implied more blowouts or obstructions further down the road.

I had studied online images or maps of the area along Chispa Road, trying to piece together a route from US 90 to Candelaria. Each time, the effort was frustrated by a maze of pig trails on the satellite photos. Could a person find his way on foot, along a route he could not untangle online?

The Right Honorable Jack also attempted to find a route online but had gotten no further than I. Jack's best guess was another eight or nine miles between the washout and Candelaria. It should work out to three or four hours of walking at the most, even with a heavy pack. After finishing Chispa, I intended to lunch in Candelaria, drop camping supplies, and log some additional miles before dark.

Chispa had mostly followed high, open ground, occasionally dropping into the floodplain where it hugged tight to open slopes with low growing vegetation. This changed as Chispa entered the floodplain and a mature mesquite forest, untouched by wildfire. Now the road was a green tunnel lined with thorns that could rip the skin off an unwary pedestrian.

The road forked. Fresh four-wheeler tracks on both forks prompted an immediate switch from nature watcher to wary pedestrian. The tracks may have been left by a local landowner, the Border Patrol, or smugglers; there was no way to know.

On the other side of Candelaria, the first sizable town was Presidio. Rex and I had been in touch with a local landowner and historian from

Presidio who had warned us off Chispa Road, strongly suggesting we circle around this portion of the border.

He accurately described how the mesquite closed on the road, telling us, "It's way too dangerous. I wouldn't go anywhere near there at night. I wouldn't even walk it during the day."

I started down the left fork and almost immediately realized that the road led to an abandoned ranch. If the tracks belonged to smugglers, my health and welfare could be adversely affected at the end of this road. I hightailed it back to the fork and proceeded through the mesquite tunnel on the right.

Eventually, the terrain opened up as the road approached a creek flowing from left to right, toward the Rio Grande. The four-wheeler tracks peeled right, following the rocky bed downstream to the Rio Grande and Mexico. The ATVs had crossed from Mexico, so those were smuggler's tracks.

On the other side of the creek, there were no additional signs of recent human activity, to my great relief.

Staying on track was tricky. The road meandered in and out of mesquite and salt cedar forests, mud flats, up to high ground, and back down to the floodplain. Up. Down. Left. Right. No signs, no recent wheeled traffic, and multiple trails in every direction with nothing to go on except intuition.

Trails close to the Rio Grande were hot and humid. On higher ground, winds dissipated the clouds of mosquitoes dogging my every step. It was four hours into the walk, and I should have covered a minimum of ten miles, well beyond Jack's estimate for Candelaria.

Then, disaster.

A fence blocked the road with a sign, "No Trespassing." I sat down in despair.

A public road wouldn't have a permanent fence across it, would it?

Had there been a wrong turn? The desert went forever, and I simply didn't have food or strength for a fifty-mile hike back to US 90. The situation was so disheartening that I composed a note, enclosed it in a bag, and hung it from the fence. "Mark J. Hainds was here at 11:53 a.m., Nov

11, 2014. Coordinates 30° 15', 7.5" N, 104° 43', 24.7" W. There is a 'No Trespassing' sign. I have no choice but to go ahead. Love to my wife and son."

Would this note be my last correspondence with the family?

Was this even the right road?

Candelaria was somewhere to the south, but the compass was useless in this terrain. Choosing and walking a cardinal direction would be an exercise in futility. Much of the landscape was impassable with sheer cliffs, steep gorges, and almost impenetrable brush dictating the course.

It was a low point, but no one was giving up. I switched to survival mode and slid beneath the gate.

A mental checklist formed as clothing and equipment were prioritized by weight and utility.

Feral pig sign was ubiquitous, and I was armed. One pig equaled many calories, so food shouldn't be a limiting factor.

The Rio Grande was only a few hundred yards distant. Under no circumstances could I afford to get lost in the mountains without water. Who knew what polluting chemicals would remain in water filtered from the Rio Grande? However, pollutants were a minor concern compared to doing without H2O.

The mosquitoes were brutal in the floodplain, so campsites should be situated on slopes above the river where a tent and campfire would be more visible from the air.

If the road reached a dead end in a box canyon or at some type of precipice, then I had indeed made a wrong turn. Backtracking through the network of pig trails and smuggler's paths to Chispa Road was a daunting proposition. If I didn't get lost and dropped half my pack weight, it was possible to make Alvarado's ranch in half a day, perhaps longer. The time and distance would increase the farther I proceeded in my current direction.

As my water supply dwindled, I dropped my backpack and crawled through the mesquite and mud to a fast-flowing, steep-banked ditch that appeared to be the Rio Grande, though nothing was certain at this point.

The water was just fifteen feet away, but the slick, muddy, nearly vertical banks stymied its retrieval. Sliding down the steep banks and then clawing my way back out of the channel was a challenge for which I wasn't quite ready. I returned to my backpack empty-handed, hoping for easier access downstream.

Mud covered my boots and jeans as the trail wound through the floodplains. Mosquitoes attacked every inch of exposed skin, while sweat soaked my torso, and my shoulders ached in protest at the weight they carried. This was utter misery.

Just when the combination of stresses had me on the edge of despair, a man rode into sight on a paint horse with a dog beside him. The *caballero* was an older, Hispanic gentleman with a welcoming smile. I greeted him with obvious relief and inquired, "*¿Es Usted de Candelaria?*" (Are you from Candelaria?)

"*Sí. De Candelaria.*" (Yes)

"*¿Estamos lejos de Candelaria?*" (Is it far?)

"*No, no. Una milla, más o menos.*" (No, one mile, more or less.)

I could have cried in relief, but I just stroked the horse's neck.

His name was "Antonio," and he continued in Spanish, "People will be scared of you." He held out his arm, as if to keep me at bay. "Because there are many bad people around." He explained how to allay their fears. "*Solo díles que eres amigo de Antonio.*" (Just tell them you are Antonio's friend.)

I asked if there was a phone in Candelaria since there was still no reception with mine. He provided the name of a woman in town with a telephone, while explaining that the road would go through some water and eventually turn up "*alto, alto, alto*" as he pointed toward the sky.

I thanked him profusely and continued down the trail. An hour and approximately three miles later, I was still wading through mud and gritting my teeth as mosquitoes attempted to collapse my veins.

There were two potential explanations. Either this was the correct route and the mounted cowboy had no grasp of distance, or I had missed the trail to Candelaria.

I paused to look up at the clear skies above me, and a migrating monarch flew over. We were going the same direction. For some reason it was reassuring.

Two weeks earlier, during my drive to El Paso, I had been sitting in my truck on I-10, just east of Baton Rouge, where traffic had slowed to a crawl around the Acadian Throughway.

Stalled in traffic I watched as a monarch flew over stopped cars in the westbound lanes. Seconds later, yet another monarch followed the same path. The two butterflies crossed into the

eastbound lanes, gaining altitude while making their ways south and west as cars zipped beneath. I had wondered then if we'd meet again on the border.

Had it not been for the merciless mosquitoes pursuing me along the Rio Grande, I would have crashed by a mesquite tree to rest my aching shoulders and count migrating monarchs, but the bloodsuckers pushed me forward.

I rounded a bend and saw people in the distance. Simons, Ronnie, and Rex were standing in the trail at a distance of a few hundred yards.

My relief bordered on indescribable. From lost to found. From failure to success. Quitman Pass had been a jog in the park compared to the marathon that was Chispa. The border trek would continue, with strong legs and my confidence restored.

Simons and Ronnie waved for me to stop by some deep, water-filled ruts. The last vehicle to attempt Chispa from the south had ceased forward progress at this point. Judging by other tracks in the area, it had required a tracked vehicle like a bulldozer to extricate the unfortunate vehicle. This explained the lack of wheeled traffic between Candelaria and the blownout road near my previous campsite.

They waved me forward. I slogged through the final hundred yards of mud and mosquitoes with Rex filming my progress.

Reaching the group, I dropped the pack while a smiling Ronnie handed me a cold beer. The guys were exuberant.

"You can't imagine how relieved we are," said Rex. "We had just decided that in fifteen minutes we were calling in the Border Patrol, the

State Patrol, the Sheriff, and the National Guard. We were about ready to give up on you!"

"It's a lot longer than the eight or nine miles we estimated. I've been walking hard since about 7:00 a.m. this morning."

"I hate to tell you, but you aren't done," Rex added. "I want to shoot you walking by the 'BFR' [big fucking rock]. That's what the Border Patrol and English-speaking locals call the formation in front of you."

I looked up. "*Alto, alto, alto*" as *mi amigo* Señor Antonio had described the road. "No problem, as long as I dump this extra weight. I would rather knock out the BFR now than start with that climb in the morning."

Rex drove to the top of the BFR with Ronnie. Once the video camera was set up, they blew the horn and I started climbing. It was the steepest section of road or trail for the entire trip. My breath came in gasps, but I finished the incline without stopping, my spirits buoyed from surviving Chispa.

Candelaria was not at the top of the hill. The town was several miles farther down the road. The distance between my last campsite and Candelaria was about twice as far as we had been led to believe, and Señor Antonio's "one mile, more or less" was closer to five miles distant.

It was about an hour's drive to Chinati Hot Springs, a resort and base of operations for the Tex-Mex Compadres. Simons parked the truck, and we stepped out to a familiar and depressing sight. The rear driver's side tire was rapidly deflating. Simons and Ronnie told me to settle in while they changed the tire. At least, we had a spare.

The owner/manager of Chinati Hot Springs was a local girl. Dianna was excited to host us for this section of the trip, going so far as to comp the room I shared with Rex.

After a change of clothing, I eased my aching body into their famous spring water. The small pool was continuously filled by a natural hot spring. Twenty minutes later, Rex took a seat across from me, and before long, the remaining spots were filled by a young couple from Austin. Rex was a former Austinite, so they discussed Austin doings while I soaked in complete bliss.

Simons and Ronnie sat down at a nearby table and graciously handed me another cold beer.

From slogging through the mud, heat, and mosquitoes, while wondering, "Where in the hell am I?" to a relaxing soak at Chinati Hot Springs, with a cold one in my hand—that was a contrast for the ages.

Michael Eason on Chispa

Walking in the Rain on US 90

11

CANDELARIA TO PRESIDIO

"There were roads, of course, leading in a dozen directions out of Nairobi. They started out boldly enough, but grew narrow and rough after a few miles and dwindled into the rock-studded hills, or lost themselves in a morass of red muram mud or black cotton soil, in the flat country and valleys."

Beryl Markham. *West with the Night*. 1942

Aoudad: Drawn by Ava Bailey

November 12–14

DIANNA suggested that Rex and I interview two brothers who owned a large remote ranch north of Candelaria. They'd been busted running horse trailers loaded with marijuana, done their time, and were back working the ranch. It would have been exciting to interview former smugglers, but when Dianna finally reached them by phone, they had no interest in sharing their stories.

She then suggested a lifelong Candelaria resident named René. René's family had lived in Candelaria for generations, and Dianna's son had gone to school with him.

Dianna held a wealth of information. She described an incident involving her son and other kids from Candelaria. They were herding some Mexican cattle back across the narrow Rio Grande when several armed Border Patrol agents jumped from the bushes with automatic rifles. The agents pointed their rifles at the kids and made them lie prone. The boys were then searched for nonexistent contraband before being released.

After the incident, Dianna complained to the section chief of the Border Patrol, and the agents backed off from Candelaria.

Rex and I were up well before first light, making coffee in the communal kitchen and microwaving a half-dozen homemade tamales left by previous guests. The tamales were so good I placed another half dozen in my backpack before loading into Rex's truck for the ride toward the BFR west of Candelaria.

Rabbits scampered everywhere in the dark, with equal numbers of jackrabbits and cottontails darting across the road. While fairly similar in appearance, they couldn't taste more different. Against everyone's advice, I once shot, cleaned, and fried a jackrabbit from New Mexico. One bite proved them right. But that's my nature, to learn from experience.

The road was paved in town, but it turned to rock and dirt on the west side of Candelaria. About a half mile out of town, a pair of coyotes loped down the road in front of us. We expected them to turn aside, but they stayed on Chispa, as Rex slowed his vehicle, following them for several minutes. They would occasionally stop to look back before loping farther down the road. Eventually, one of the coyotes stopped to communicate his or her displeasure and simultaneously mark its territory by urinating on a rock.

It took about two hours to walk back to Candelaria after the pissed-rock episode. The scenery above the BFR was nearly as breathtaking as the country around Pilares: steep mountains, arroyos, giant rocks, cacti, and wildflowers.

We located René and his father pulling weeds for an out-of-town homeowner. Rex set up his camera while I wandered over to photograph aoudad skulls on a barn gate in the background.

"Ranchers in this area get good money for hunting leases," René told me. "They hunt mule deer, aoudad, and some whitetail deer."

René was a young man who had witnessed significant changes to the landscape and population.

René nodded to a salt cedar covered floodplain below. "I remember when we grew cotton, watermelon, and alfalfa on the same ground."

Over time, the invasive, non-native salt cedar colonized the fallow fields, displacing cultivated crops.

The decline in agriculture paralleled the town's population. The school closed and Candelaria's students now boarded the bus at 5:30 a.m. for a ride to Presidio.

René lamented, "We had a lot more time to study and play after school. Mrs. Johnny Chambers was one of the best teachers I ever had. She taught most of the people in Candelaria. Now the school is closed, and the Border Patrol leases the building for a few months out of the year."

The Mexican town of San Antonio del Bravo was visible in the distance, across the Rio Grande.

René continued, "There was a footbridge that was important to both towns. Everyone has relatives on both sides of the river, but the footbridge was torn down after the attacks on September 11, 2001."

Again, and again, as we journeyed the Rio Grande, people divided eras as before or after September 11.

"There was no phone or mail service on the Mexican side, so they would come over here to send mail or make phone calls, and we walked across the footbridge to visit a medical clinic and buy groceries; now we have to drive fifty miles to Presidio."

For centuries, the fabrics of these towns were woven together as one cloth. Faceless bureaucrats and craven politicians care little about the residents of Candelaria and San Antonio del Bravo, but history will harshly judge those who tear down bridges and replace them with walls.

These policies led to friction between the locals and the Border Patrol. René also touched on the incident that Dianna had previously described, offering his version. "There were some seventeen-year-old kids here from San Antonio. They tried to push some cattle back across the river, and the Border Patrol pointed their guns at them."

Candelaria had been in the Marfa sector of the Border Patrol. Apparently, the aforementioned incident occurred when the Presidio Sector assumed control over Candelaria.

René offered his assessment of the Presidio Sector. "For some reason, most of them are assholes."

According to René, after the much-maligned incident, Candelaria switched back to the Marfa Sector, and things settled down.

Months later, I called Dianna at Chinati Hot Springs to verify some details. Referring to the Border Patrol agents from Presidio, she said, "They have transferred new agents in from El Paso and New Mexico, and they are wonderful! The situation has changed completely. René and I talked about this the other day. The earlier Presidio agents were young and new at the job. The problem is that nothing happens in this area, so they ended up hassling us. The new agents are more experienced, more professional, and we couldn't be happier."

Continuing the interview, I asked René, "What jobs are available for the locals?"

"There are good ranching jobs in the area. In dry times, we have to haul water to keep the cows alive."

Ranching jobs in the desert did not impress me as sustainable occupations. "Do you think Candelaria will still be here in a hundred years?"

"Yes, I think it has a future."

After the interview, Rex and I drove a few hundred yards to the Rio Grande. The footbridge was long gone, but a beaten path testified to regular and ongoing foot traffic through the knee-deep water. After taking some photos and video, we wandered back through Candelaria. The stores were boarded up and many houses were empty or falling down. We visited an abandoned schoolhouse and a cemetery on the east side of town, where I stopped to photograph a small Catholic Church. Our Lady of Peace was classified as a "mission," meaning services were few and far between.

The stores were closed. The school was closed. Mass was no longer held on a regular basis. René saw a bright future that I could not visualize.

A woman in a Baylor University t-shirt walked to her mailbox. She asked, "Why are you taking photos?"

"It reminds me of our little parish back at the farm."

"It's ugly. Everything here is ugly."

"No! It's simple."

She shook her head. "It's ugly. I want to go to Abilene."

With Candelaria behind us, it would be a long run to Presidio. Chinati Hot Springs suited me perfectly, but the resort had limited Wi-Fi, and Rex, Ronnie, and Simons wanted access to modern amenities, so the crew moved my luggage and supplies to another hotel in Presidio with the same name as our earlier lodging in Marfa—the Riata.

Rex left me to walk from Candelaria. Around lunchtime, a Border Patrol vehicle approached from the east. He was the first agent I had seen in four days, and he promptly pulled over to check me out. Manny had heard about my Chispa Road adventure. He told me that Chispa was "a huge drug area." He seemed impressed that I had made it through.

He also had a different take on Candelaria. "Most of them are Mexican citizens. We don't mess with them as long as they aren't involved with smuggling."

The next community up the road was Ruidosa. "There are just a handful of people who live there. You should talk to the Bloombergs. They stood up to the smugglers in the area."

"You're in an area that was controlled by Pablo Escobar. He used to run Ojinaga [the city across the Rio Grande from Presidio] when it was the cocaine capital of the world."

Manny was born in El Paso, and he had worked several sectors as a Border Patrol agent before transferring from Eagle Pass to Presidio. "I haven't recovered any bodies here, but we used to recover ten or more annually in my previous sector. Almost every one of them [the deceased] would be naked or maybe just had on their underwear. They'd be sitting against a mesquite tree or anything that provided a little shade. Something about dying of dehydration causes people to feel very hot—so they strip off their clothes."

Manny warned, "Be very careful around Rio Grande City and McAllen. That's the hottest area [for smuggling] on the border."

"Do you cross over to Mexico?" I asked.

"Never."

We were leaning against Manny's truck when Simons and Ronnie pulled up with lunch. They handed me a sandwich, and I introduced everyone. Manny shared more stories and fielded questions from the Tex-Mex Compadres until it was time for me to go.

Traffic on FM 170 was minimal. Fewer than ten vehicles passed over eight-plus hours of walking. One was the postman. One was Dianna from Chinati Hot Springs. One was Manny. A couple trucks had placards identifying them as property of Presidio County.

With such limited traffic, a strange vehicle and occupants would stand out like a sore thumb.

FM 170 was a relatively new blacktop, running southeast from its terminus in Candelaria, through Presidio, and east into Big Bend. The highway paralleled the Rio Grande, so a traveler was seldom out of sight of the floodplain and the hills, mountains, and villages of Mexico.

The river was all but invisible. Along this section of the Rio Grande, the water was confined to a small channel that could easily be confused with a drainage ditch. Mesquite and salt cedar covered the floodplain, except where the forest had been burnt back by farmers trying to increase grazing for their sheep, cattle, or goats.

By dusk, my legs were aching, and I was dang happy to see Simons and Ronnie roll up the road. Simons parked the truck, exited, and took my pack, while Ronnie opened and handed me a cold bottle of beer. Rex should have come along to film the completion of the day's walk as required viewing for all incoming Compadres. Suggested title: "SOP for Tex-Mex Compadres."

The following morning started with my usual routine. Was there enough water to make it through the day without resupply? Drink as much water as the belly would hold, then fill three liters to carry.

Caloric consumption was off the charts, so pack dried fruits, granola bars, jerky, and tortillas smothered with peanut butter and honey.

The feet were taking a severe beating. Wrap gauze or bandages around each big toe and other problematic spots, to minimize rubbing, blisters, and painful corns.

As a caffeine addict, consume several cups of coffee during prep time, and more on the ride out.

Ronnie, Simons, and I left the Riata with jackrabbits and cottontails seemingly darting from every bush. A beatific vision formed: I was retired and in possession of a full section of bottom ground, hunting rabbits with beagles, quail with setters, and ducks with retrievers, but someone else fed and housed the hunting dogs. How to make that happen?

They dropped me at a cattle guard on FM 170, just west of the tiny community of Ruidosa. The sun wouldn't be up for another half hour, but there was plenty of light for walking.

The sun was up as I walked into the outskirts of Ruidosa. A large house stood on the left, and my heart nearly stopped as three Rottweilers charged the fence. The .38 was packed in the luggage with Rex. If the dogs escaped the yard together, my minutes were numbered. The dogs ran up and down the fence, but they couldn't get at me. Packs of small- to medium-sized dogs were one thing. But an unchecked attack by three of those beasts would have meant near certain death.

In town, one of Ruidosa's landmarks was in severe disrepair. Little remained of an ancient Catholic church except walls and a roof. The structure was open on both ends, inviting me to stroll through. Adobe blocks were stacked inside, evidence of an intended renovation that had come to a standstill.

Ruidosa's only store stood on a street corner with a "For Sale" sign in the window. Although it appeared empty, a woman swept off the front porch while refusing to acknowledge my presence.

East of Ruidosa, a Border Patrol vehicle drove toward me on the south side of the road, pulling tires with a chain over a dragline paralleling FM 170. The driver saw me and gunned the vehicle, while still dragging the tires. It looked like the two agents were going to bounce out of the truck on the rough trail. They stopped at about fifty yards, and the driver stepped out while keeping the door between us, exhibiting considerably more caution than agents from previous encounters.

I identified myself, and he waved me forward. Like Manny, the two young agents had heard the same reports of someone walking Chispa Road. After our conversation, other Border Patrol vehicles slowed, looked, recognized me, waved, and continued on their way.

While I was researching the area around Presidio, an interesting blog post turned up from a young couple who had bicycled the entire U.S.-Mexico border. They described a visit with Enrique and Ruby Madrid in Redford, a small community east of Presidio. Their photos and commentary piqued my interest in the Madrids. I emailed the young lady, Katy Brandes, a couple weeks before leaving Alabama but didn't hear back from her until I checked my email at the Motel 6 in Van Horn, Texas. Katy was living in El Paso, where she offered lodging and a phone number for Ruby and Enrique's while warning, "They aren't big fans of the telephone."

No one answered the Madrid's phone on the first, second, or third attempt, so I hoped to find them while passing through Redford.

The next vehicle to stop was a jeep with a decal for "Angell Expeditions: River Rafting, Hiking, Biking, and Jeep Tours." Charles Angell introduced himself and apologized for not getting me a four-wheeler earlier in the week. I had no idea what he was talking about, but assumed that Dianna and Rex had been looking for some type of ATV to locate or rescue me when I was late coming off Chispa Road.

"I've got a place on the other side of Presidio near a little town called Redford," Charles said. "You are welcome to stay there. Watch for my sign on the side of the road. There is a water hydrant on the property."

"Thank you. By the way, do you know Enrique Madrid in Redford?"

"Sure. He lives across the road from my river access. To be honest, his place is kind of a dump. Look for the plywood Indian in front of their house." Charlie gave me his card and said, "Give me a call if you need anything."

The rest of the day was uneventful. Though the body protested mightily each morning, the legs grew stronger.

Back at the Riata, there was good news on two fronts. First, the Right Honorable Jack had not driven straight back to Georgia. After leaving Chinati Hot Springs, he traveled River Road through Big Bend State Park and up to Lajitas. At the general store in Lajitas he employed his southern charm and regaled two ladies with stories of our journey. Debbie and Vickie were so impressed that they offered to host a "Welcome to Lajitas Day" for us.

Jack had been an admirable Compadre on the trail. Now he was an ongoing advocate spreading the Gospel in communities we had yet to reach.

Simons and Ronnie were no slackers in the public relations department. While eating at a restaurant in Presidio called The Bean, they enlightened officials from the Presidio city government who were anxious to meet me after learning of the trek.

Finally, Simons and Ronnie destroyed my expectations of camp food when they prepared grilled steaks, potatoes, and a salad at the Riata. Where Rex had been disappointed by Jack's absence, he now recognized that the gentlemen from South Carolina and South Africa had their charms. I counted my lucky stars before falling into a near comatose, sated sleep.

Simons and Ronnie dropped me off for my third day on FM 170. I planned to cover a few miles in the morning and meet a local historian, before pushing through Presidio, and possibly make the town of Redford.

In the meantime, Rex checked out of the Riata so he could drive to El Paso and pick up his wife who was flying in from Mississippi for a week with Rex. My conjugal visit would have to wait until I logged two additional days of walking before my flight from El Paso to Fort Walton Beach,

Florida. I was scheduled to lecture at my last Longleaf Academy as a full-time employee of The Alliance and Auburn University. The course would take place at Fort Benning, Georgia, and the itinerary allowed one night at home with the family, both before and after the academy. A return flight to El Paso was scheduled for November 21, and the trek would resume on the twenty-second.

Midmorning found me at the entrance to "La Junta," the ranch at the junction of the Rio Grande and the Rio Conchos, which flowed north out of Mexico. I wandered up a private road that led to a barn and some very old adobe structures. Ten minutes later, Terry Bishop drove up in his pickup truck. He dropped the tailgate and fixed a ramp so an old dog and an ancient wolf could limp their way down.

Both Gracie the dog and Wizard the wolf had been companions of A. Kelly Pruitt, a western artist who owned and lived on the property, La Junta, until his death in 1999. "Mr. Pruitt used to wander all over this country. One day he happened upon a female wolf that had been shot along with her litter of pups. Somehow, they missed Wizard, and the pup ran right up to A. Kelly." Terry explained that Wizard was eighteen years old.

Mr. Pruitt's online obituary revealed an astounding range. He was an artist, painting in oil and sculpting in bronze. He wrote two books of poetry and five novels. Terry said, "His works were collected by LBJ and most of the cast of *Gunsmoke*."

Mr. Pruitt had served in the U.S. Cavalry during World War II, where he deployed to the Burmese theatre in what was almost certainly one of the last wartime actions by U.S. horse and mule Cavalry. Terry suspected that Mr. Pruitt was wounded both physically and mentally during his service, and never completely recovered from his wartime trauma.

Terry led me to Mr. Pruitt's grave. "He once told me, 'There's too much suffering in this world for people to keep their money.' So, he gave away almost everything he owned."

Right up to his death, Mr. Pruitt had been cowboy-tough. "A. Kelley was shoeing a horse when he had a heart attack. He wouldn't let us take him to the doctor, and it took about a week for him to die. He said, 'I don't want anyone cutting on me.' He asked me to bury him here. He died at 5:15 a.m. We rolled him in his bedroll, and put him in this grave."

"Women loved this guy, but A. Kelley once told me, 'You know, Terry, I am not gay, but I sleep with stuffed rabbits for pillows, because they speak to my feminine side.'"

Many other graves dotted the area. Most were unmarked piles of stone. Terry said, "I'd like to know who these other people are. Many of them died when this was part of Mexico, so I've considered trying to research their [Mexican] archives."

From the graves, we wandered back to the adobe structures. One had been a general store and another served as a garrison.

Terry looked out over the recently cleared floodplain. He said, "La Junta has been continuously inhabited for over ten thousand years. This ground is littered with artifacts."

I promised to mail Terry a copy of my book once it was finished. He gave me a physical address and said, "I don't own a computer. I refuse to completely move into this century."

After the fascinating tour, Terry suggested an alternative route east. "Why don't you walk the levee rather than the highway? It will lead you beneath the international bridge to Ojinaga."

The levee was property of the U.S. Boundary and Water Commission, and permission was required before entering the area; but Terry said his sister was the local judge and they could get me out of any sticky situations that arose. I threw caution to the wind and followed his advice.

Across the Rio Grande, another levee protected the town of Ojinaga. Between the levees, a large herd of Mexican cattle grazed the verdant Bermuda grass as a cowherd surveyed the idyllic setting from the top of the opposing berm.

It wasn't quite as pretty on the U.S. side, where the bottom ground had been farmed, abandoned, and grown up in salt cedar and mesquite, just like in Candelaria. However, Terry Bishop now managed this property on the U.S. side. Terry had piled all the woody brush, prepping the ground for a return to agriculture. Terry had told me that he used to operate one of the five biggest vegetable farms in Texas. "We mailed out a thousand W2s annually. Eventually it became too difficult to secure manual labor." He was ready to farm again but hadn't settled on what to grow or how to grow it.

The piles of mesquite and salt cedar were perfect habitat for cottontail rabbits. Even though it was the middle of the day, when they normally hide, numerous rabbits broke and ran along the levee.

Rabbits are highly sought prey for many predators, and it wasn't surprising to see two bobcats break cover and run into nearby brush.

It didn't take long before a Border Patrol vehicle approached from the south. It held a good-natured Anglo who laughed repeatedly at my adventures thus far.

The levee ended and the road split. I went left. After a bend or two, the dirt trail wound through an unofficial dump. After hundreds of miles of epic, natural scenery, I felt out of place, like an intruder, wandering through this mix of scrub and abandoned household appliances.

Eventually the trail dumped me onto the backstreets of Presidio. The earlier left turn meant a missed opportunity to walk beneath the International Bridge. Maybe it was a lucky break. Even if Terry's sister was a local judge, I pictured myself sitting in a holding cell for an extended period of time before my predicament was brought to her benevolent attention.

A few blocks into town, two men stood in the street, staring at me. It was somewhat intimidating until one of the two said, "You're Mark Hainds."

I answered, "Yes, I am."

They were the city officials who had met Simons and Ronnie at the Bean.

One of the pair was an Anglo named Brad Newton. He told me to call him "Border Brad."

The other was Mr. Carlos Nieto.

Mr. Nieto asked for a synopsis of the walk. Once provided, Mr. Nieto asked, "There is so much bullshit about the border. When you finish this walk, will you be kind to us? Will you be able to come back and look us in the eye?"

I interpreted his question this way: "Are you going to tell the truth about what you see and experience? Or are you going to sensationalize your story to sell your book and push a political agenda?"

I would not do that which he feared, and when I returned, we would look each other in the eye, as friends.

"Yes, I will tell the truth."

They insisted that we ride to the Bean for lunch and discussion of politics and border issues. Mr. Nieto described a serious problem with undocumented border crossers. "Every night, about a thousand undocumented immigrants move from the U.S. to Mexico. These feral pigs cross the Rio Grande and raid the farmers' fields around Ojinaga, Mexico. It's a real problem!"

Why wasn't this issue in the national news? Having written a whole book on the subject of killing feral pigs, I took this anecdote as a virtual invitation to a professional pig-killer: in the name of international relations, come back and kill these pigs. It was my MacArthur on the Philippine beach moment. "I shall return!"

"Presidio is a safe city," said Border Brad. "Everyone thinks the border is a war zone, but the front door of my house is unlocked, and I leave the keys in my car each night."

Border Brad was describing conditions at our farm in Missouri, or my home on a dirt road in rural Alabama.

Border Brad said, "I am going to Mexico City to meet with my Mexican counterpart. We are going to discuss sharing resources and cross-border cooperation."

"Are you fluent in Spanish?"

Border Brad shook his head and said, "It's amazing how far a smile and a gracious attitude will get you."

Mr. Nieto described a major flood in 2008. "It almost wiped away Presidio. We pulled together as a community to fill sandbags and save the town. We called the governor, and Rick Perry sent helicopters to reinforce the levee."

After that close call, Presidio had secured funding to raise the levee I had walked earlier that day.

A young waitress brought menus and asked if she could have her photo taken with me: a flattering request.

Border Brad pointed to the menu where he was immortalized with the "Brad Burger," which I immediately ordered.

Presidio was overwhelmingly Latino but completely integrated.

Mr. Carlos Nieto said, "We are a very patriotic community. We served in all them damn wars. And you can tell a lot by the cemeteries around towns. Our dead are integrated, but they are still segregated in Alpine, Marfa, and Fort Davis."

The Brad Burger, fries, and a wonderful dessert called *tres leches* made for a pleasant lunch.

Brad and Carlos introduced me to most everyone who came in the restaurant, including a young doctor from Langtry. The doctor took my contact information and said, "When you get to Langtry you have to meet my parents and stay at their place on the river."

After an extended lunch, I tore away and followed FM 170 out the east side of town. The Big Bend State Park (not to be confused with the National Park) was headquartered at the historic Fort Leaton, east of Presidio on FM 170—also referred to as "River Road."

I entered the old fort to examine a map inside. There were no shortcuts to Lajitas, the next town east. Any detour required huge gains and losses in elevation while adding mileage before various park roads rejoined River Road. Stunning scenery from my New Year's scouting drive was still fresh in my memory, so it wasn't a disappointment to stick with River Road/FM 170.

Late that afternoon, Simons and Ronnie picked me up a short distance past Fort Leaton. They offered floor space in their hotel room. The Riata wasn't expensive, but there were no funds for a room to myself.

Rex had already left Presidio to pick up his wife at the El Paso airport,

and I needed another day of walking before flying home for my last
Longleaf Academy.

Rex and abandoned lockers in Candelaria

Climbing hill by BFR on Chispa

12

FORT LEATON TO REDFORD

"For eleven thousand years, at least, people have lived here, first those we call natives because they were not European, as I am. They did not arrive by boat, as most Europeans did. They arrived by foot or by horse; and we, of course, have a strange and conflicted belief that the person who arrives by the most complicated conveyance gets to be boss."

Janisse Ray. *Drifting Into Darien*. 2011

Jackrabbit: Drawn by Ava Bailey

November 15–21

I T was a short early morning run from the Riata on the north end of town to my starting point just east of Fort Leaton and Presidio. We probably arrived a little too early. I didn't mind walking in the dark, but getting hit by a car would unnecessarily complicate the trek.

Traffic was limited to a handful of vehicles, all headed toward Presidio. The first westbound vehicle was the good-natured Border Patrol agent from the levee along the Rio Grande. He was laughing again when he said, "Someone called in to report a guy with a backpack on River Road. I figured it was you."

Apparently, the word got around, and the next agent on River Road pulled over and asked if he could take my photo. "I want to show my family the guy who hiked Chispa! And all the way from El Paso!"

It was relatively quiet from that point forward.

The first section of high fence tracked along River Road.

Normal barbed wire or woven wire fences are about chest high. This is sufficient for traditional livestock like horses, cattle, pigs, and sheep.

High fences, on the other hand, are designed to hold deer and other large game animals that can jump regular stock fences. It's common for high-fence operations to stock exotic animals from foreign countries like fallow deer, sika deer, nilgai, and scores of other expensive "trophies."

High fences are very expensive to erect. They require maintenance, and as is often the case, extraordinary stocking levels require landowners to provide supplemental feed.

If the fence is well maintained, it keeps exotics in and native big game species out. But high fences have the potential to shut down the movement or migration of every big game species in North America. If the fence is between native deer or elk and their water source, then the animals have to find another water source or a different route.

During storms, or when absentee landowners do not tend their fences, gaps may develop in the fence from flood waters, falling trees, or cars running off the road and through the fence. Poorly maintained high fences have led to the establishment of several exotic species in Texas, the most notable an Egyptian goat named the aoudad. It is believed there are more aoudad in Texas than exist across their native range in North Africa. The same is true of the ibex, which escaped high-fence operations and now wander the deserts of New Mexico and Arizona.

By late morning, I was approaching Redford, where a family sat in their car on the western outskirts of town. A young man with a tie exited the driver's side and opened the back door to retrieve something. My suspicions were justified when he handed me the *Watchtower*. As always, the Jehovah's Witnesses were friendly and outgoing. After learning my mission, the young wife and mother handed me a homemade burrito.

A building in Redford matched Charlie Angell's description of Enrique and Ruby Madrid's house, but it almost looked abandoned. Meanwhile, numerous Redford dogs took offense at my presence. Their barking drew the attention of a nearby resident who assured me that I had found the Madrids' house. With no luck at the front door, I cautiously circled around back. Several more dogs emerged from the house and proceeded to raise Cain. I tightened my grip on the walking stick but kept it by my side. It would be bad form to whoop dogs belonging to the very people I hoped to meet.

The back door opened, and an elderly Hispanic man slowly walked out. He had a mustache, graying hair, and the pained stoop of arthritis. He motioned to a couple of chairs. "Never mind the dogs. They are not mean. They are just doing their job," he said.

We sat down, and I briefly introduced myself. Enrique didn't ask for further explanation; he just started talking. I took notes and occasionally asked for clarification while Enrique expounded.

After a few minutes, Enrique's smiling wife, Ruby, emerged and invited us in for tea and empanadas.

Inside, the house was comparatively clean but completely cluttered. By this time, the dogs had accepted me and begged to be petted. Enrique and I sat down in a dark living room across from each other over a fossil-covered coffee table. Books covered the furniture and lined shelves on surrounding walls.

Enrique took my glance at the fossils for a cue. Jumping into evolution, he said, "DNA is the blueprint for life. The shape is mutable. The DNA is immutable."

Enrique shared theories on the evolution of religion and how belief in God shaped our politics, laws, and societies—mostly to our detriment.

"My brother was a seminarian in Concepción," Enrique said. "He went on to become a priest, much to my chagrin. If you have a couple of hours, you will touch, feel, and see what God looks like."

He looked at me while feigning suspicion. "You are aware that most of the world's great religions originated in the desert, aren't you? You will understand, I must be cautious of a man walking through the desert with a pack and a staff."

I chuckled.

Enrique looked me in the eye. "Don't you dare stop here and meditate! You may discover a new religion and off we go again."

"You have to become God to see God," said Enrique. He referred to a Johns Hopkins paper on Psilocybin. "We now know most of the neuroscience of God. You understand, I am trying to keep you from creating another religion."

"I have no such intention," I promised.

Enrique periodically arose from his seat to retrieve a replica of a human skull, a fossil, or another prop that illustrated his point. He showed me "God" in the form of drawings and patterns created from Euclidian geometry.

At one point, a dog jumped into his seat. Enrique asked Ruby to bring him another chair. "The dogs have human rights in our house."

Enrique held little regard for our governments. "Who is running the show? It's a Southern Baptist-Fundamentalist worldview. At one time, half the country's population was rural. But they moved to town and brought their philosophy with them."

Ruby brought a tray of hot tea and a freshly baked empanada. I helped clean a spot on the coffee table, and Enrique switched to the environment. "In Arizona, they protect their forests by law. So they come to Texas and take away our ocotillos by the semi-trailer."

I recalled the cactus rustlers on Chispa.

"This has been going on for forty years. Those cacti won't survive the trip to Arizona. They used to pay fifty cents for an ocotillo. People sell the rocks. They sell the cactus. They would sell their grandmother if someone would buy her."

Ruby joined us in the living room, and between topics, I complimented Ruby on the fine tea and empanada.

Ruby and Enrique had moved to Redford in 1969—the year of my birth.

While he did not mention it, I later discovered that Enrique Madrid is featured in a book titled, *Authentic Texas, People of the Big Bend.*

Enrique spoke in a soft tone, but the words had a harsh edge. "You consider yourself an American? Let me challenge you on the one thing that separates you from Africans and Native Americans."

Enrique retrieved a book, *Europe, the Struggle for Supremacy, from 1453 to the Present,* by Brendan Simms.

"Americans are not European. Why do white people come here and destroy everything? It is because they still regard America as a European colony. Christianity is a European religion. My mom was never accepted because they will never accept Native Americans and blacks. That is why they were able to come here and kill our children."

I had just enough background information to understand where he was going.

Redford is a tiny, isolated community on the banks of the Rio Grande. Nondescript. Poor. Forgotten. Tragic. Most of the world failed to notice when this community paid a horrific price for our misguided efforts at policing the border.

Someone had the bright idea of sending U.S. Marines to patrol our border with Mexico.

On May 20, 1997, a small squad of Marines wore ghillie suits and hid in the brush near Redford while an eighteen-year-old Redford resident named Esequiel Hernández Jr. herded his goats, while carrying a .22 rifle. At some point, the Marines claimed Esequiel shot at them from a distance of two hundred yards.

For those of us who know firearms—this caliber and this distance— the Marines were not under mortal threat. But that didn't stop the squad leader, twenty minutes later, when he followed and executed the eighteen-year old American citizen, high school student, and goat herder.

Charges were never leveled against the Marine with blood on his hands. His unit was withdrawn, and for a brief time, people realized just how bad an idea it was to send active duty military to the U.S. Mexico border.

The incident rises to the level of a Greek Tragedy when it was revealed that Esequiel had been talking to a Marine recruiter about enlistment following graduation from high school.

This should be taught in our schools. Every American citizen should know the potential consequences of using our military in a law enforcement role within our borders.

Politicians score points with certain audiences when they promise to enforce the border by any and all means. And in the process, a young American citizen is shot down for the crime of herding goats on his own property.

I took my leave of the Madrids when the Compadres arrived. It was the final day before our flights back to Alabama and South Carolina.

Katy Brandes, the young bicyclist, had invited me to stay at Casa Puente in El Paso. I left Ronnie and Simons at their hotel and drove a few miles to Katy's place. Her cycling partner, Eric, was away, traveling in Central America.

Casa Puente was an older house in a clean, working-class neighborhood of El Paso, just a few minutes from the El Paso International Airport. With multiple bedrooms and a good-sized kitchen, Casa Puente served as temporary housing for undocumented youth with nowhere to stay. House rules in English and Spanish were taped to bedroom doors, and more lists on kitchen etiquette were posted on the refrigerator.

Katy was a young, idealistic twenty-something with a fit build, brown hair, and serious eyes. Once I settled in, she described their twenty-two-hundred mile journey along the U.S.-Mexico border.

Katy and Eric started on the California coast and cycled east, crossing back and forth from the U.S. to Mexico while visiting every major city on the border. They spent the first third of their trip on the Mexican side of the border, cycling through Baja and Sonora.

Katy said, "We spent a while in Altar, Sonora. It serves as a major kickoff point for undocumented immigrants. Seventy percent of the economy is based upon providing services to these immigrants.

"We interviewed a driver who transported undocumented immigrants through Sonora. He told us the cartel charged one price for Mexicans and another price for Central Americans. The driver told us, 'We are required to call ahead to a contact within the cartel that operates checkpoints along the road. When we get there, if the numbers are different from what we called in, they will beat us.'"

Katy and Eric had no altercations with criminal elements on either side of the border, but they were warned off one road in Mexico that was solely for cartel use. Judging by where they had been and what they had seen, Eric and Katy bordered on fearless.

Katy and Eric had planned to stay for two hours in Redford, but they ended up staying two days with Enrique and Ruby. Eventually, they got away and rode east, finishing the entire trip on February 12th, 2012, at Boca Chica Beach.

"Where did you start your walk?" asked Katy.

"I started at International Mile Marker #1. I used a private bridge to cross the Rio Grande, and the border fence choked me back onto a fast-moving four-lane highway. It was a scary road to cross."

Katy said, "A lot of undocumented immigrants are hit and killed while trying to cross that section of Cesar Chavez Highway."

From Casa Puente, Katy drove us to an establishment named L&J's. Katy told me, "It's the oldest restaurant in El Paso." Katy's friend Shali, another young female immigration activist, joined us for a fabulous meal.

Katy refused any money for lodging. "We often stayed for free during our trip. We'll spend the rest of our lives paying it forward."

I spent the rest of the evening at Casa Puente sorting gear and packing unneeded clothing for the flight home.

The next morning, I drove to the airport and left the truck in long-term parking. After checking my bags and clearing security, Simons, Ronnie, and I found an open bar where we reflected on our experiences, while Simons treated me to free drinks and lunch and rain fell upon the windows and baggage handlers outside.

From the bar, I wandered down to the gate area where windows allowed an unrestricted view of a glorious rainbow spanning El Paso International: like the fish in the road, another sign. Katia and Joseph awaited my return in Andalusia, but the message was loud and clear: "Come back quickly. You were meant to walk this trail."

Though we had booked our flights independently, Simons, Ronnie, and I boarded the plane and took our seats directly adjacent to each other.

The world turned upside down, from the unpopulated trail to the packed confines of a commercial airliner. From working the same dual positions—with Auburn University and The Longleaf Alliance—for nineteen and a half years, to the ranks of the unemployed on November twentieth.

To this point, my life and career were highly structured, proceeding along a predetermined and steady path. Now, plans didn't stretch beyond finishing this trek, and an author in residence position for the month of February. But having chosen this path, I interpreted the uncertain future as unlimited opportunities.

For the last morning of the Longleaf Academy, we toured management scenario sites on Fort Benning, Georgia. After the final stop in the field, we convoyed toward the hotel in Columbus. We were still on Fort Benning when I felt the characteristic pull and shimmy of a flat tire. I pulled to the side of a dirt road while students jumped out to change the tire. Meanwhile, Humvees and troop transports passed on their way to and from maneuvers and firing ranges.

Back at the hotel, I packed up and started the three-and-a-half hour drive from Columbus, Georgia, to Andalusia, Alabama. I was making seventy-five miles an hour between Auburn and Montgomery on I-85 when the Expedition started wobbling. I just managed to keep it on the road while steering the stricken vehicle to the shoulder. I had another flat tire and no spare.

Over a two-decade career with The Longleaf Alliance and Auburn University, I recalled two or three flat tires while on the road with a University vehicle. My last day of employment yielded two more and a clear message: "Drive less. Walk more."

Rex and René in Candelaria (Ocotillo between them)

Candelaria Cemetery

Terry Bishop, Wizard the Wolf, and A. Kelly Pruitt's grave

13

LAJITAS TO STUDY BUTTE

"Terlingua is the most godforsaken place in the United States."
Jefferson Morganthaler.
The River Has Never Divided Us. 2004

Western Diamondback: Photo by Mark Hainds

November 22–24

THE flight back to El Paso was uneventful. I left a pile of clothing in Alabama, filling that luggage space with food. Priorities had changed: satisfying an appetite and maintaining body weight were paramount.

The next Tex-Mex Compadre to join us was Bob Larimore. We became acquainted in the early 1990s while he worked as the Base Forester at Fort Benning.

Fifteen years earlier, Bob had attended a meeting for DoD foresters at the Solon Dixon Center in Andalusia, where The Longleaf Alliance was based. After a day in the classroom, I invited Bob to join me for a coon hunt on the fifty-three-hundred-acre Dixon Center. My crackerjack bluetick hounds treed two raccoons that night. Although Bob is a Southerner, that may have been his first coon hunt.

Bob was promoted up through the Department of Defense to his current position at Fort Sam Houston in San Antonio where he presided over DoD environmental staff on many millions of acres across the country.

During the Longleaf Academy I'd just left, several of Fort Benning's current forestry and wildlife personnel had asked me to pass on their greetings and encourage Bob to come back to Fort Benning.

Cell phone signals stopped at Redford, so I texted Bob on the drive from El Paso. "I'll be somewhere on River Road east of Presidio and Redford."

Rex was waiting east of Presidio at the Arenosa campsite along River Road in Big Bend State Park. I made it to the campsite with just enough time to erect my tent before dark. Rex was in fine spirits after the week with his wife, despite a lingering headache that had developed during her visit.

Rex and Cara had enjoyed an in-depth tour of the Red Rock Ranch, where Darice guided them to petroglyphs we had missed on our previous tour. The week off left Rex invigorated and ready for the hundreds of miles ahead.

Our tents were only yards from the Rio Grande. Because we were downstream from La Junta (the junction), the river was bigger and faster than the ditch by Candelaria. The Rio Grande provided a constant, soft, background noise as the water tumbled over and through the boulder-strewn riverbed.

We agreed to get up very early so Rex could drop me in front of Enrique and Ruby Madrid's house, hopefully, before they awoke. They were a thoroughly enjoyable couple, but our schedule required more walking and less talking.

Our plan worked, and I was covering ground on River Road well before sunrise. River Road was every bit as gorgeous as I remembered, and the further east we went, the less traffic we encountered. This section of River Road only saw one or two vehicles per hour.

The Border Patrol was invisible for good reason. The Mexican side of the Rio Grande was mountainous. If an undocumented alien or a smuggler successfully navigated the terrain south of the Rio Grande and crossed the river, he or she faced scores of additional miles through harsh mountains and deserts on the U.S. side.

If through some unadulterated miracle, an undocumented immigrant or a smuggler achieved this feat, he was still stuck. Almost all roads north filtered through permanent Border Patrol checkpoints.

Illicit border crossing doesn't appear to be a significant issue below Big Bend National Park. That's not to say smuggling was at a standstill. On my return trip from El Paso, I witnessed the Border Patrol dismantling a truck and trailer at their checkpoint south of Marfa, just prior to my rendezvous with Rex.

In his book, *Contrabando: Confessions of a Drug-Smuggling Texas Cowboy*, Don Henry Ford Jr. describes his years running dope across the river and over dirt roads through this country to points north, but that was well before the Border Patrol installed its checkpoints along all north-south routes.

River Road repeatedly gained and lost elevation as it wound toward Big Bend National Park. I walked at a good pace until Bob appeared in his rental car around mid-afternoon. From there, he drove ahead to scout the next campsite

Eventually, there was a hill like no other. The distant summit was visible but unobtainable with shooting pains in both legs. The pain eased during rest stops and returned as soon I re-shouldered the pack and started the climb.

The rainy days east of Van Horn were fresh in my mind, where the pain and swelling had almost incapacitated me. I limped to the road shoulder and dropped the pack. I had covered twenty miles from the morning's starting point to this overlook on the verge of a precipice.

Hundreds of feet below, the Rio Grande ran swiftly through a channel lined with near vertical cliffs on both the U.S. and Mexican sides of the river.

Bob picked me up at 4:00 p.m. and drove us to another state park campground farther east on River Road. After we erected our tents, the three of us drove to Lajitas for sandwiches at the General Store.

I wondered if the woman tending the store in Lajitas was half of the pair that Jack had conversed with. I explained that I had stopped there during the New Year's scouting drive ten months earlier for a sandwich and beer. She found it interesting, but she didn't break out the party hats.

We stepped onto the front porch with our sandwiches and drinks. Rex said, "This isn't happening."

Jack had stoked our hopes of a grand reception in Lajitas. Now it appeared that it would be just the three of us drinking a beer on the front porch before heading back to the campsite.

"Let's just hang out and see what develops," I suggested.

Jack had met someone who was enthusiastic about our trek, and it didn't appear to be the woman inside.

We finished our sandwiches while I nursed my beer. Another lady pulled up, climbed the porch, and introduced herself. Debbie quickly recognized us from her conversation with Jack, and her excitement boiled over.

Debbie made some calls before introducing us to the Mayor of Lajitas (a goat named Henry) and leading us to a swanky hotel adjacent to the Lajitas golf resort. Through Debbie's intervention, we were booked into three-hundred-dollar-a-night rooms at the golf resort, at no cost to us.

After checking in and securing our hotel keys, we drove back to the campsite, struck our tents by the headlights of our trucks, and returned to Lajitas.

Rex took one room while Bob and I shared another. My bed felt like a cloud.

The following morning, Bob drove us out River Road, cresting the peak of the mountain that had bested me the day before.

It was still dark as Bob drove back to Lajitas, and I completed the climb to the highest point on River Road. Now the steepest decline of the journey lay ahead. I started down the slope in a straight line but switched to a zigzag pattern, trying to ease the descent. Without a pack, it wouldn't have been too bad. With a pack, each step was a blow to my joints. I pictured the cartilage in my knees being ground away like medicine in a mortar and pestle.

The uphill portion was the easier side of the mountain.

Partway down the slope, a wooden cross marked the spot where someone's life journey had ended. Brakes had failed, and a motor vehicle had left the road, plunging over the side. I stopped to rest my knees and peer over the repaired railing into the gorge below. A clear skid trail marked the final descent, with a crumpled ball of steel resting at the bottom of the canyon.

I finished the grade, limping in pain. Visions of big miles faded as I swallowed two ibuprofen and re-shouldered the pack.

A woodcock flew overhead. Minutes later, the sun's first golden rays lit mountain peaks in Mexico. The road turned east and then north as sunlight moved down the slopes. Eventually the fiery globe rose above mountains protruding from a silent landscape. The road was mine alone, and an hour ticked off before a passing vehicle broke the spell.

After the ibuprofen kicked in, my gait steadied and miles seemed to pass more quickly. Charlie Angell—the outfitter I'd met between Candelaria and Presidio—stopped to check on my progress. Several vans headed west, carrying river rafters bound for Coronado Canyon.

River Road took a turn north, looping around a large private inholding. Periodically, coveys of bobwhite quail erupted from the grass or brush. West of Presidio, most of the quail had been blues or scaled quail. Further west yet, Gambel's quail populated the scrub around El Paso.

Rex filmed my entry to Lajitas before setting up one more time to shoot me walking along a guardrail with the river to my right. Pointing toward the water, Rex said, "There's the Mexican Military." Two Humvees were parked beside the river, and troops in camouflage lounged around the vehicles. One of the troops looked straight at us through a pair of binoculars. They were the first non-civilians (military or police) Rex or I had seen on the other side of the border.

"Let's meet up again at the General Store," I suggested. "I am ready for lunch, and it won't take me long to get there."

Everybody rendezvoused at the store where Debbie and Vickie (another employee or part-owner of the store) treated us like royalty, comping our sandwiches and beer. While we ate on the front porch, a Brewster County Deputy idled by, and Debbie waved him over. Before he exited the car, Debbie said, "Sheriff H. will sometimes pull you over just to talk." (Although Debbie called him "Sheriff," he was actually a deputy,) She hugged the deputy as he stepped onto the porch.

At the same time, Vickie had to leave. "I wish you the best of luck on your trip," she said to me. "We are honored to have you."

"It's been my pleasure."

"There are a lot of good people here," said Vickie. "I'm sure you know this, but some places just concentrate good people."

"I can see it."

Deputy H. took a seat and joined in the conversation. Someone brought up the survivalist/end of times folks. The deputy said, "You got some people that are ready to make it fifty years. One guy by Alpine had a whole shipping container of canned tuna delivered. It lasts forever. Then there was this other fellow who lived by himself. He eventually died of natural causes. When they were cleaning out his place, they saw that he had shooting ports in all directions with the yardage marked on the wall to each fence post or rock."

Although it had to be a tired subject for the locals, Deputy H. readily offered his thoughts on illegal immigration. "I'd bring in the National Guard to back up the Border Patrol."

The Deputy seemed like a decent guy, but the conversation with Ruby and Enrique Madrid was still ringing in my ears. This wasn't a job for the military, and requiring locals to maneuver through one more layer of security—the National Guard—sounded pretty silly to me.

The deputy opined on lots of issues. "The only reason the President is doing that amnesty [for the Dreamers] is to get another four million Democratic votes. Many of them are just coming over to have their anchor babies." This was nothing new for me. If you hang around enough rural white men, you're bound to ingest a steady diet of soul-rotting Limbaugh and Hannity.

Rex changed the subject. "We saw the Mexican military down by the river. Do they operate much around here?"

"They might have been military," H. explained. "Or they might have been with a cartel, posing as the military. Nothing is for sure on the other side of the border."

The same could be said of this side of the border. Lajitas was located on the Presidio-Brewster County line. A couple of decades earlier, Presidio County Sheriff Rick Thompson had been busted while helping move a ton of cocaine across the border. At that time (Dec, 1991), it was the biggest drug bust in West Texas history.

When labeling undocumented immigrants, Deputy H. fell back on "wetbacks" or the abbreviated version "wets."

Debbie asked him, "Isn't that considered offensive?"

"No. That's not an insult. They consider 'beaner' offensive because it implies they only have enough money for beans. Sometimes you can tell they just crossed over because their shoes are still wet."

I needed more miles, and the day was getting away from us. Debbie wanted to get together and watch the sunset from her favorite overlook, so Bob would pick me up in a few hours for a rendezvous at the golf course.

I stepped off the porch and turned left on FM 170. If my legs held up, I'd make it halfway to Terlingua.

A bit north of Lajitas, highway crews had just finished pouring a concrete anchor with a metal receiver for a yet to be mounted traffic sign. The wet concrete was too tempting to pass without leaving my mark. For posterity, I scratched, "MJH 11/23/2014."

I had just left the scene of the crime when an older model vehicle pulled over and a woman rolled down her window to offer a ride (which was kind) and a couch to crash on (amazing!). Sandy worked in Lajitas but lived in Terlingua. She explained, "The desert eats people. Everyone around here stops—not tourists, because they are afraid—but the locals will."

Not long after I declined that ride, another car pulled over. This one was driven by a young man, "You want a ride, bro?" Glancing at my backpack he added, "Or you good?"

"I'm good. Thanks for the offer."

"Take care." He gave me a thumbs up and drove toward Terlingua.

I limped north until Bob picked me up for the ride back to Lajitas where we joined Rex, Debbie, and Debbie's husband, Tim. We hopped into a convoy of three golf carts and wound our way through the golf course to the Upper 7 and Box 14. From the elevated green, Big Bend National Park was visible to the South, Mexico to the west, Lajitas to the north, and in the distance behind Lajitas, Big Bend State Park.

Debbie placed a cooler of wine and beer on the grass. I selected a Montejo, a Mexican import that was new to me. Most of us reclined on the green while Tim drove a few balls into the valley below. Rex set up his video camera to capture the sunset.

Debbie and Tim described a festival that took place just below us called "Voices From Both Sides." Tim said, "Bands set up on both sides of the river. They always have a better sound system than we do. It starts with Frisbees flying back and forth across the river. There is free food—no one accepts payment. Eventually it's a free flow of people back and forth."

This wasn't the only festival in the area. Debbie was instrumental in organizing another Lajitas original: Goatstock, a celebration of Peace, Love, and Goats.

If the sun weren't setting and the temperature weren't dropping, I could have stayed at Box 14 for a long time. The further we traveled, the more amazing the terrain and its inhabitants.

Debbie and Tim weren't done with us. Our next stop was the Thirsty Goat, a local bar where I recall clearing a plate of delicious food and my second bourbon on the rocks. The conversation was brilliant, I am sure, but the details are evasive because I promptly fell asleep in a comfortable chair.

The following day, I approached Terlingua around midmorning. Piles of tailings and a disturbed landscape pointed to long-abandoned mines beneath the surface. Vegetation had yet to reclaim the spoils. Despite the forbidding terrain, small communities of tenacious desert people persisted in the valleys and above sheer cliffs.

Roadside placards told the history of mines in this area, which mainly sought a mineral called cinnabar, which in turn yielded quicksilver, or, as it is known today, mercury.

Aboveground, the unrelenting sun, wind, and lack of water sucked life from all but the strongest. Those who hoped for a slightly better existence below ground, the miners long gone, were crushed in cave-ins or poisoned by the minerals they extracted. This was the harshest, most inhospitable land of the trek.

I took a road left, uphill to Terlingua, winding through the community past an old cemetery and funky sculptures to a café named *Espresso...y poco mas* (and a little more).

Lajitas tourists were invisible, but Terlingua was chock full of out-of-towners. Where I attracted considerable attention in every other small town along the route, no one batted an eye in Terlingua. After breakfast and coffee, I asked the cooks if they knew "Cynta" whom Debbie in Lajitas had referred to as, "the spiritual guru for Terlingua."

They pointed downhill, and I walked back toward the highway. Their directions didn't match with the description of Cynta's abode, so I rejoined the highway and continued toward Study Butte.

An hour of walking led me past La Kiva on the right. The bar had been closed since February 4, when La Kiva's owner, Glenn Felts, was killed by a friend, patron, and local river guide named Tony Flint.

Flint claimed self-defense, and in the subsequent trial, Flint was acquitted of first-degree murder charges by a Hudspeth County jury.

Debbie from Lajitas had known the victim and the perpetrator. She told me, "None of us understand what happened." Beyond Debbie's brief explanation, the crime went unmentioned in my Lajitas and Terlingua conversations. It was still a fresh trauma for a rural community unaccustomed to violence.

Just before noon, a white Ford F150 pulled over, and two Hispanic guys pointed down the road, offering a ride. The passenger had an opened Coors Lite between his legs.

"No thanks. I am walking to Brownsville."

"Wow. That's a long way."

"I walked here from El Paso."

"Why?"

I told my story, thanked them again, and kept going.

In the first three hundred and fifty plus miles of my trek, not a single vehicle had pulled over to offer me a seat. With less than thirty miles between Lajitas and Study Butte, I had already declined three rides.

FM 170 joined FM 118 with a large convenience store standing at the intersection. After stopping for a light lunch, I walked out the door and noticed Bob talking to a guy in the parking lot. It was an assistant professor from Sul Ross University in Alpine. I joined their conversation.

Dr. Doug Luna said, "People want to know, 'Why don't I have quail?' and they don't have nesting habitat. They want to know, 'Why don't I have pronghorn or mule deer?' and they don't have forbs."

It had been about seventy-five years since sheep had cleared out the groundcover, and the effects were still evident. He explained that their department head at Sul Ross, Dr. Bonnie Warnock, established prescribed burn demonstrations in the area, mostly to reduce shrubs and increase herbaceous cover, thereby reclaiming areas dominated by mesquite.

"Are they doing any direct seeding out here?" I asked.

"There are some ranches working with Texas A&M around Kingsville. They're working with buffalo grass, side oats, and blue grama, around twenty or thirty different varieties through a native seed project."

Dr. Ryan Luna had confirmed my suspicions and reinforced what I learned from Michael Eason back on Chispa. Yes, this was desert, but much of the landscape should've had more native bunchgrasses, more forbs, and less brush. The barren soils were relics of overgrazing, past and present, and the absence of fire.

Choices in land management had reduced the grass and increased the shrubs. If these conditions were corrected (overgrazing and lack of fire), the landscape would revert back to herbaceous cover, and the wildlife would return. In other words, "Build it, and they will come."

It was just a few more miles to the small community of Study Butte (pronounced "stoody-bute"), where an abandoned gas station marked the end of this leg.

The original plan was to walk all the way through Big Bend National Park. From the intersection of FM 170, I could continue to the right on Panther Junction Road, all the way to Marathon. Alternatively, I could turn left and walk north to Alpine.

We were already several days behind owing to the detour on US 90 while waiting for Chispa to dry. That, and a forty-five-year-old body that wasn't quite up to task, at least in the early days.

I decided to continue the previous route on US 90: returning to the Riata Inn on the east side of Marfa, where I had stopped just before the epic Chispa Road section. From there it would be a straight shot east to Alpine, Marathon, and onward.

Before heading north, we drove south to Terlingua for a late lunch at the High Sierra, taking our seats at 3:00 p.m. on an open-air deck. Debbie had provided Cynta's phone number, so I tried it again. This time Cynta answered, and she agreed to meet us at the High Sierra. Rex joined Bob and me on the deck, and a few minutes later, Cynta climbed the stairs and took a seat at our table. She was a tall, thin, middle-aged woman with long, wind-tossed hair, sun-weathered skin, and a direct gaze. Whatever her origin, she was now a creature of the desert.

Cynta said, "I saw you on the side of the road. I could tell you were on a mission. And I could see you were in pain."

It had been eighteen years since Cynta left Manhattan, moving to Terlingua to work as a river guide. Eventually, a medical condition curtailed her physical activities, and Cynta now devoted much of her time to bettering life on both sides of the border.

Cynta served as the Vice President of Albargue Casa Hogar, an orphanage across the river in Ojinaga. She said, "No one adopts in Mexico for the same reasons we used to let our kids go here." By this, I believe she meant that many poor families in Mexico were stretched to their financial limits supporting their own children, and there just weren't enough resources to support orphaned children from outside the immediate family.

As I had imagined, smuggling and immigration were nonfactors in the area. "We call them the 'Boredom Patrol,'" said Cynta. "I am the liaison between Terlingua and the Border Patrol. I called them up and said, 'You aren't doing anything for the people of this area.' So they secured some ambulances to help us out, and now we have excellent relations."

Cynta described life in Terlingua. "Our keys are in our cars. We never lock our doors. Look at our dogs. No one has Rottweilers [unlike Ruidosa]. Four of the safest cities in America are border towns or are in border states: El Paso, San Diego, Phoenix, and Austin. People talk about 'spillover' from the gang wars in Mexico. But it has never happened!"

"And we have taken a vow of poverty," Cynta added, referring to several people in the Terlingua community.

We were kindred spirits, since living as an author virtually guarantees a lack of sufficient income.

Cynta continued, "This is a tight-knit community with very few children. Most of us are single, so when someone does have a child, the whole community adopts him or her. You can't live this far outside the wall and not live with your heart."

She said, "As soon as you get to the state park, you see a river that is allowed to recover. People are not sucking it dry. You can breathe."

"Where we live, it's the scenery. We don't have a Wal-Mart. We don't even have a radio station, though we had a pirate station until the FCC shut it down."

Cynta was in the process of walking the Camino del Santiago in Spain, with only seventy-one more miles to go. "It's another world when you are walking and everything is clicking like it should be."

I said, "There were days like that when I trained on the dirt roads back in Alabama. And there have been some places and times on my border walk when I felt that way. But right now, as you observed, I am mostly in pain."

I asked Cynta about the remainder of my route. "We've been told that things will heat up along the lower Rio Grande."

"We're past the harvest season so the smuggling will have slowed down. September and October would have been more weird."

"Harvest season?"

"Marijuana."

On the subject of dope, I expected the hippies of Terlingua to be more understanding. Cynta didn't take that route, "If you smoke cheap Mexican weed, you are responsible for the raping and the killing in Mexico."

As Cynta rose to leave, I asked, "What books would you recommend about the border?"

"The best book on the border is *The River Has Never Divided Us*. Feel free to call me if you have any more questions."

Rainbow over El Paso Airport

Simons and Ronnie on flight to Atlanta

14

MARFA TO SANDERSON

"But wasn't that what bars were—churches for people who'd lost their faith?"

Benjamin Alire Sáenz. *Everything Begins and Ends at the Kentucky Club.* 2012

Javelina: Drawn by Edlyn Burch

November 25–29

FROM the High Sierra, we retrieved my truck in Lajitas and drove north. This time we turned left at the junction of FM 118 and FM 170, taking the road to Alpine. The road gained elevation as the sun lost altitude and the temperature dropped. The surrounding hills and mountains reflected more color than previous landscapes, appearing purple in the fading light.

The private properties north of Big Bend National Park held more deer, presumably whitetails and mule deer, than I had seen in the last four hundred miles. A group of javelinas crossed the road just yards in front of my bumper.

It was blustery as we checked into the Alpine Holiday Inn Express. Although Alpine was a relatively short distance north of the Rio Grande, temperatures were twenty to thirty degrees cooler than in Lajitas. Rex, Bob, and I moved our stuff into one room, and I took the floor.

Bob and I were up early, hanging around just long enough to eat a free breakfast before heading west where Bob dropped me in the Riata's parking lot on the east edge of Marfa. After a series of tough days and sore, stiff mornings, my legs felt good and it was time to book.

Temperatures in the low thirties accelerated my pace. Somewhere along the line, I had started using two walking sticks instead of one. With the heavy backpack, two sticks provided much needed stability when climbing or walking steep road banks or other challenging topography.

Besides the longleaf walking stick, I now carried a sturdy and attractive walking stick made from sweetgum. It was also a gift, carved for my use on the border by a customer named "Decie" from the Palafox Market in Pensacola. It was ironic that my new stick came from a tree that many foresters spend decades trying to reduce or eliminate from their stands or plantations in favor of more preferred species.

The temperature quickly rose to the fifties, prompting me to strip layers of clothing as the sun rose.

The Marfa Grasslands stretched from horizon to horizon, supporting numerous herds of cattle on a landscape with softer edges than Big Bend National Park.

US 90 stayed busy between Marfa and Alpine, and it was loaded with Border Patrol agents. The first vehicle to stop was an unmarked Chevy Tahoe driven by Agent Acosta. He identified himself as "Border Patrol Intelligence." We talked for a bit, and he let me continue walking.

The second agent drove a green and white sedan. These are the traditional colors for the Border Patrol, but virtually all my previous encounters involved agents in vehicles suited for rough terrain. It was another brief conversation.

There were so many interviews that I've forgotten the order, but it might have been the next agent who asked, "What are you up to?"

"I am attempting to set the world record for the greatest number of Border Patrol interviews in a twenty-four-hour period."

He took it in stride.

Yet another agent stopped in an unmarked sedan, and although he didn't say so, I assumed he was also in Border Patrol Intelligence. He was easily the tallest agent of the trip, and for the first time he required my documents, which pissed me off, although it probably shouldn't have.

I was surprised at my own reaction. Before starting this trip, I had expected to show my ID on a regular basis, but that hadn't proven the case. His request for identification came across as an attack on my credibility. I considered the border people who deal with these situations on a daily basis and remembered Michael Eason's words from the top of Chispa Road: "The questioning from the Border Patrol is not an inconvenience, it is an insult."

I waited impatiently behind his car while other BP agents pulled over to monitor the situation, providing a show for passing motorists. Eventually, the tall agent returned with my ID, having confirmed that the hiker was indeed, Mark J. Hainds, with no outstanding warrants. The crowd of agents was now in a jovial mood, which helped dissipate my anger. The agent who had run my ID even asked to take my photo, to which I acquiesced.

I hoped to make Alpine, but it would be difficult with a Border Patrol interview every half hour.

Over the course of my walk, there had been scores of roadside memorials erected for travelers who had lost their lives on both busy and desolate highways.

A particularly poignant memorial was situated about ten miles west of Alpine. Four crosses stood with a plaque attached to a Siberian elm. It read:

In loving memory:

Maria Magdalena Ortega, July 21, 1961–Dec 24, 2000.

Heber Ortega, Aug 7, 1988–Dec 24, 2000

Lynette Ortega, Oct 2, 1992–Dec 24, 2000

Elizabeth Ortega, May 4, 1994–Dec 24, 2000

"We will always remember you."

"McDonald's Restaurant Staff, Alpine, Texas."

I forgot all about the Border Patrol.

A family was lost the day before Christmas and two days after my mother's birthday. One of the young victims, Lynette, bore the same name as my sister. I considered visiting the McDonalds Restaurant in Alpine to see if the staff remembered the Ortegas and December 24th, 2000. Assuming a typical fast-food employee turnover rate, the mission would have been fruitless.

Months later, I located an archived article about the crash from a border newspaper.

According to the January 4, 2001 edition of the *Big Bend Sentinel*, Señora Ortega was driving her family to Ojinaga to meet her husband for Christmas. A child in the back seat distracted her, and she veered off the road and struck a tree. There were five occupants of the car, and only one wore a seat belt. Eleven-year old Juan Jose Ortega, Jr. was buckled into the backseat, and he was the sole survivor.

Around lunchtime, another unmarked car pulled over. I thought, "Here we go again." But this time it was a Hispanic civilian.

"I saw you earlier. I am from Marfa, and I was driving to Alpine. I bought a lunch for me and you. Here!" He handed me a cold Coca-Cola, a yogurt and a warm hamburger from McDonalds. Conveniently, a roadside park with picnic tables was in view, just to the east.

I felt guilty but moved. His obvious assumption was, "Here is a poor homeless guy." It was a kind gesture, and it would be cruel to refuse such generosity. "Thank you, Señor. *Muchas gracias.*"

"*De nada.* Be safe and good luck!"

Like Katy Brandes, the bicyclist who provided lodging in El Paso, I resolved to pay this forward. The mechanism was determined months later. After wrapping up at the Palafox Market, we distributed unsold blueberries and other edibles to the homeless who wander Pensacola's streets. It was an easy way to forward the generosity shown to me by strangers on the border.

It took a while to make the connection, but the Good Samaritan's lunch came from the same McDonalds where the late Señora Ortega had worked, and whose staff had erected the memorial I had visited moments before. This was more than chance. The connections were too intricate. Elements of Karma were playing out over time and geography, but I couldn't tease out the grand scheme.

What good could come, all these years later, from a car accident that destroyed a family on the day before Christmas? And how did I fit into the equation?

Or it was all circumstance, and my mental expenditures were in vain.

I was one month into the trek, and my muscles had finally adapted to hikes equivalent to a daily marathon, although my left knee felt a little wobbly. If everything held together, the day's walk would end at the hotel.

The pastures along the highway were subject to variable stocking levels. Some were grazed to stubble, while others were thick with grass. Eastern red cedar had invaded much of the landscape, but occasional wildfires jumped off the road and ran into the hills, leaving lush grass and the black skeletons of dead cedar trees in the fire's wake. With the obvious benefits of wildfire, why weren't they using more prescribed fire out here?

The sun was still up as I entered Alpine, and I realized why so many Border Patrol agents had stopped to check me: their sector station stood on the west end of town, and dozens of green and white vehicles passed by as the shift changed.

In Alpine, US 90 split with a city block of buildings between the east- and westbound traffic. I stayed on the right (eastbound) side as US 90 entered the city. It didn't take long to locate an open bar.

Rule #3.

There was an empty table near the front. I dropped the pack and walking sticks before sidling up to the bar. They had local beers on tap, and after I introduced myself, a local rancher named James filled me in. "We can run forty cows to the section around here." This compared with six cows to the section around El Paso. Although Marfa had more grass and beef prices were up, the ranchers weren't investing in their infrastructure. James said, "All the fences around here are about a hundred years old."

"Do you see many immigrants pass through the area?"

"The quality of the people who come through ain't worth a shit."

I took that to mean they wouldn't work for room and board or less than minimum wage. I had heard the same complaint from many industries in the Southeast. If they didn't pay a decent wage, undocumented workers would leave for better paying jobs in the city.

The owner of the bar walked in, a German named Harry Mois. Harry had left Germany after his wife had passed away from lung cancer. He settled in Alpine and set up a brewery, whose products I was quaffing. Later, Harry bought the bar that had arrested my eastward march.

Harry had asthma, and he frequently used an inhaler while touring me around the establishment and instructing the bartenders to provide free beer for the rest of my stay.

It was difficult to keep up with all of Harry's stories because he spoke with an accent and I can't hear worth a damn. We moved from room to room, inside and outside the establishment, meeting patrons while the waitresses plied me with free beer. It was a hell of a good time.

Several hours passed before I left Harry's. Luckily, it was a straight but very brisk shot to the hotel. The guys were more impressed with my mileage than my bar stories. It was 26.8 miles from the starting point in Marfa to the end point at the Holiday Inn Express in Alpine, and my legs held up well. I felt like a thick-furred puppy experiencing the first cold snap after a long, hot summer. The environment was changing in my favor, and I couldn't be held back.

The next morning, as usual, I was up around 5:00 a.m., taping my toes, filling my pack with water, getting dressed, and eating breakfast. Just across the street from the hotel, a herd of deer browsed their way through Alpine.

In the first five minutes of walking, more deer showed themselves than had in the first two counties (El Paso and Hudspeth) of my trek.

More ungulates browsed on the east end of town. A small herd of pronghorn antelope and mule deer moved through the brush just north of US 90. Three immature mule deer bucks—two and three points, using western scoring—walked through the grass and shrubs: some of the first antlered deer of my walk.

I stopped for a drink of water, and a Brewster County deputy sheriff pulled up. He stepped halfway out of his patrol car while calling in his location on the radio. Then he asked, "Are you hoofing it into Alpine?"

"No. I stayed there last night. I'm coming from El Paso and headed for the Gulf."

He accepted this without further explanation. As long as I was leaving town, I wasn't a threat worthy of investigation.

Late morning found me at a roadside park, at the junction of 90 and 67. US 90 continued east, and US 67 peeled north to Fort Stockton, the next closest town of any size. My route would follow 90 west, another two hundred miles to Del Rio, the next town approximating the size of an Alpine or Fort Stockton: one hell of a long, barren stretch.

The park was still in range of Alpine's cellular towers, so I called the local newspaper, the *Alpine Avalanche* and talked with the editor. Jim invited me to stop by for an interview later that afternoon.

Union Pacific trains passed on my right, their tracks paralleling US 90 to the south. Most of the vehicular traffic from Alpine and Marfa turned north on US 67, affording a quieter and safer hike past the rest stop and intersection. Even Border Patrol agents were few and far between on this stretch. It was sunny and breezy, with temperatures in the sixties. After lunch, the road shoulder looked pretty comfortable, but I pushed on despite a strong nap temptation, needing extra miles on the road to Del Rio. Bob picked me up at 4:00 p.m. and drove to Alpine where he parked by Front Street Books, one of very few independent bookstores in West Texas. We strolled around the block and located a building holding the *Alpine Avalanche*. Two or three people worked inside, including the editor.

Jim interviewed us about our trip thus far, at one point asking if I had seen any *mojados*. My Spanish was good enough to translate this to "wet ones." There were many terms for undocumented Mexicans who crossed the border.

From the building housing the *Alpine Avalanche*, we walked a couple of blocks to a plaza on US 90, where Jim photographed me walking in front of murals celebrating the Anglo and Mexican heritage of the Alpine area.

With the interview and photo-session complete, Bob drove me to a pharmacy where I purchased gauze, tape, and a knee-brace. My muscles steadily strengthened, but my left knee had yet to fully recover from the grueling grades on River Road.

The next day was Thanksgiving, and people kept asking, "How are you going to celebrate? Are you going to spend it with your family?"

I answered, "My family is a thousand miles away, and I need another twenty-plus miles."

Rex wasn't quite as pragmatic. He had previously stayed with his wife at a historic hotel in the tiny town of Marathon. The Gage Hotel and its accompanying restaurant offered a Thanksgiving feast unparalleled on the U.S. side of the border, so Rex made lunch reservations for the three of us.

I started walking well before sunrise, with beautiful weather and multiple deer crossing the road in front of me.

From Marathon, US 385 peeled north at another junction. After that intersection, traffic diminished from a slow to negligible trickle on US 90. But wildlife was abundant: deer, antelope, and quail thrived in the arid environment. I made a few more miles before Bob and Rex picked me up for our much-anticipated lunch.

We took our seats outside beneath a bright sun whose rays weren't sufficient to fight off the chilly air. The restaurant had placed gas heaters by the tables to radiate heat onto the patio. After we ordered our drinks and the buffet, we moved inside where I piled my plate to its maximum capacity with some of the most attractive foods I've ever witnessed in a buffet line: shrimp, elk, steaks cooked to order, caviar, and a fresh salad bar. The dessert bar didn't stop: fresh tarts, brownies, pies, cakes, and ice cream and many other offerings. For the first time on the trek I had alcohol with lunch, sipping a sublime margarita.

When the bill finally came, I almost fell out of my seat. The meal had been delicious, but it cost more than any single meal in my prior forty-five years of existence. And it was worth it, as long as my wife didn't find out how much was spent on a Thanksgiving meal.

After lunch, Rex and Bob dropped me east of Marathon, amidst flat grasslands that had received its share of recent precipitation. A depression on the south side of the road held a solitary coot, unalarmed by my presence. Further down the road, a pond to the north held a dozen big ducks that took flight at my intrusion.

The week before leaving Alabama for the long drive to Texas, I attended my last Regional Conference for The Longleaf Alliance in Mobile, Alabama, where I was responsible for organizing several sessions. One such session was dedicated to local implementation teams—groups that formed across the southeast to further local longleaf restoration efforts.

Kent Evans walked to the front of the room to speak for the Texas-Louisiana Longleaf Task Force. Kent had grown up on a ranch north of Fort Worth and he addressed the crowd. "Mark is leaving us for the Texas-Mexico border." He turned to me and continue, "When you are walking the border, you should start and end each day by looking to the horizon and saying:

The sun is riz,

the sun is set.

Here I is,

in Texas yet."

Kent's little poem was particularly fitting on US 90 where it seemed like the road went forever. I finished the day's walk with 24.4 miles, and there I was, in Texas yet. After dragging ass for the first several weeks, the conditioning took hold and my left knee steadied. I also remembered Cynta's words from the High Sierra in Terlingua. "There's nothing like it when your body resembles a well-oiled machine, and you cover that ground."

The following day was Bob's last full one as a Tex-Mex Compadre, and he wanted to walk with me.

Bob did his best to prepare for this walk, jogging up to fourteen miles a day in San Antonio. And he wasn't impressed with my footwear. He trained with and wore light hiking shoes instead of boots. Now we could test his conditioning and shoes against mine.

From the Sanderson Budget Inn, we crossed the road in the fading afternoon light to eat at one of two open restaurants in town. After supper we walked back to the hotel where two cyclists sat outside their room, having a drink. I was curious as to their experiences, but the motel floor had my name on it, and sleep had priority.

The next morning, Rex drove, and the equally long-legged Bob rode shotgun. Both of them had at least four inches of height on me. Rex was lean while Bob was a little more rounded. We hadn't cleared Sanderson when they saw a ring-tailed cat (a cousin of the raccoon) crossing the road to our front. I leaned forward from the backseat, hoping for a glimpse, but the elusive ringtail had already escaped into the darkness.

Rex dropped us forty miles west of Sanderson. The miles passed quickly as Bob and I discussed intractable issues facing land managers and environmentalists across the south. We saw eye to eye on the big picture, but Bob was becoming jaded. He was certain his policies would be abandoned when he retired from his current position atop a sprawling DoD bureaucracy.

In the not so distant past, Bob had served as the Base Forester for Fort Benning, where his guidance had proven instrumental in the restoration of fire and healthy longleaf ecosystems across tens of thousands of acres. But many of the foresters he and I work with are incapable of grasping the larger goal. They are too focused on growing wood, often at the expense of diversity, aesthetics, and wildlife.

We worked through issue after issue, and the miles flew by. After a month of walking solo, I had grown accustomed to arguing with me, myself, and I, and this was a lot more fun.

We reached the Pecos County line, marking the end of my trek through

Brewster County—the largest county by area in Texas. Brewster County covers over five hundred square miles, but the population just exceeded nine thousand people during the 2010 census.

Our pace was compatible. Neither of us struggled in the morning hours, but as the day progressed, Bob started to limp. He said, "It feels like a water balloon on the bottom of my right foot. I can feel it rolling."

About an hour later he said, "I felt it [the blister] break."

"Do you want to stop and bandage it? I have gauze and tape in my pack."

"No, I'm afraid to look at it."

Without cell phone reception, Rex was concerned about Bob's conditioning and our inability to call for help, so he drove out twice to check the situation. On the second trip, he brought burritos from the Stripes convenience store in Sanderson. We ate and relaxed on the side of the road as cyclists approached from the east, before stopping beside us. It was the pair that had lodged next door at the Budget Inn in Sanderson.

They were pedaling the Southern Tier and one of the two hailed from Switzerland. While studying the route, he discovered a Swiss coffee store just ahead in Alpine. Further research revealed that the family who ran the store in Alpine also had a café at his hometown in Switzerland, so he planned to stop in to surprise them.

After they critiqued my clothing, they kept going west while Bob and I prepared to walk east. For the second time Rex offered Bob a ride. "I can carry you back with me."

"No, I am going to make it." Bob had grit.

It was particularly hard for Bob to start moving after a rest. He stiffened up during breaks, so stoppages were minimized for the remainder of the hike.

Bob and Rex had seen elk the day before, and the ringtail cat in the morning. I was jealous for having missed both species. Bob and I jumped an occasional jackrabbit, but mostly, we encountered road kill, including coyotes and Bob's first sighting of a porcupine, albeit a flat one.

We reached the Terrell County Line. Of the sixteen counties on my route, I would spend the most time in Brewster and the least in Pecos. A small triangle of Pecos crossed US 90, and we had just finished walking completely across it.

At dusk, we reached our final destination—a small roadside park, where Rex was waiting. Bob and I walked to a picnic table where Rex asked Bob, "How did it go?"

"My injuries are myriad."

We had covered 25.6 miles, my second-best day of the trek thus far.

Back at the hotel, Rex organized his gear outside while Bob limped in and took a seat on the motel bed. He had avoided looking at his feet all day, and I was curious as to the damage.

Bob gingerly removed his right shoe. He took hold of the sock and gently pulled it down. As he did so, much of the skin on his foot came with the sock. I gasped. His skin had separated midway down the sole of his foot, revealing the pink flesh beneath. The skin resembled a loose fitting sock all the way to the tips of his toes. I said, "Oh my God. Let me get Rex."

I ran outside and said, "You have to get your camera. This is gruesome."

Rex was equally floored, and a tad bit amused by the carnage. Rex videoed the stoic hiker, and Bob took it all in stride.

With the imagery safely recorded, I told Bob, "Do not let that foot touch the floor." The carpet looked to be decades old. I could just imagine gangrene taking his foot.

I found my medical bag and offered to doctor his foot. Bob said he could handle it, so he went to work with my supplies: antibiotic ointment, pads, and tape.

Bob had hung tough for twenty-five miles, despite his physical duress. He told us, "I will probably never walk that far again. But I am still glad I did it." He looked over at me. "Whatever shoes and clothing you've been wearing—stick with it."

The day's walk had been one of the most enjoyable of my trip, and as with Jack, Simons, and Ronnie, we hated to see him go, but Bob was due at work in San Antonio the following day.

We rose before dawn, and Bob dropped me at the picnic tables. My friends continued to amaze me. Bob had sacrificed a week of vacation and his feet, and just before he left, he handed me two, sorely needed, hundred-dollar bills to help with expenses.

It was hard to imagine how I could ever repay the Tex-Mex Compadres.

For the first time since International Mile Marker #1, the trek was unsupported by a Compadre. After Bob's slot, another filmmaker, whom we will call "Sally," had volunteered to drive out and support me for the first week of December.

Sally and I had met earlier that year while she developed a short film on invasive species, including feral pigs. She was referred to me because of my first book, *Year of the Pig*, which documents my experiences in 2007, when I spent the year studying, chasing, and killing feral pigs from Alabama to Hawaii and back.

After our interview, I told her about my upcoming walk. She asked if she could follow and assist Rex in the filming, but Rex declined her offer. "I am a one-person operation."

Sally was still excited about the trek, and she volunteered to drive out and provide logistical support. Of the Tex-Mex Compadres, she and Ronnie (who had accompanied Simons) were the two people I was least familiar with prior to this journey.

Sally's slot was approaching, and she was not responding to the regular updates emailed to all the Tex-Mex Compadres. A week or so before her scheduled arrival, Sally told me, "Work and family life are crazy, but I will make it out anyway."

Rex didn't believe her. "Dude, she ain't coming."

Other friends had promised to come but had not committed to specific dates. As Sally's slot approached, I encouraged them to drive out in case Sally didn't make it. My good friends and neighbors, Jimmy and Sierra, packed their stuff and started the long drive from Alabama.

Bob's time drew to a close, and Sally confirmed Rex's doubts, canceling her trip just days before her scheduled slot. I was disappointed, but Rex seemed happy. He was sure she was just coming to learn more about filming documentaries.

It was a Saturday, and huge football games were scheduled for both of our teams. Rex was employed by the University of Mississippi ("Ole Miss"), but he was a Mississippi State University ("State") graduate. State and Ole Miss were scheduled to play in the Egg Bowl later that afternoon. Just in case his allegiances weren't clear, Rex reminded me, "Nothing is sweeter than the taste of Ole Miss tears."

State came in with a 10-1 record and a shot at the SEC West title, which could in turn lead to a shot at the National Championship.

Ole Miss came in with a respectable national ranking of #19, but Rex was confident that State would pull it off.

Rex stayed at the motel to catch up on numerous chores, and I walked toward Sanderson.

Rex and I shared similar positions. After the Egg Bowl, an eight and three Auburn University team would take on the one loss Tide (University of Alabama) in the Iron Bowl. Although the University of Alabama Press published my first book, I had no mixed feelings that Saturday. With the SEC West still in play, Rex was also rooting for my Tigers. If Alabama lost and State won, Starkville could claim the division title for the SEC West.

I entered town, and a Terrell County Deputy Sheriff's vehicle drove past. A little later it drove past me again, and yet again. I expected to be stopped and questioned, but they just kept driving back and forth, keeping an eye on the suspicious guy with a backpack.

By late morning, I made it to the Budget Inn on the east side of town, where I dropped unneeded clothing in the room and took a seat outside. Rex worked on his gear while I retaped some problematic toes.

The manager of the hotel, a thin wisp of a man named Dalipseth from India, walked over to chat. He asked, "This is the walker?"

Rex said, "He is the man. I am just a boy."

Dalipseth said, "I can make you some Indian tea and bring it in the morning. Would you like? What time do you get up?"

"That would be great. I am up at 6:00 and we leave about 6:30."

Dalipseth grimaced, "Oh no! That's way too early."

Rex and I both started laughing. I reassured him, "That's okay. I understand."

But Dalipseth continued, "I can bring you some now?"

"Sure."

While Dalipseth's mother prepared the tea, Rex asked, "How did you get here?"

Dalipseth explained that it was a combination of ill winds, including a divorce and big losses in the stock market.

Waiting for the tea led to an extended break, but it was completely worth the wait. The tea and scones were delicious.

Taped up and rejuvenated, I exited town to the east, walking past the deputies' vehicle one more time. They had safely fended off the Deep South Gangster.

A low bridge crossed Sanderson Canyon on the east side of town. From the bridge railing, I gazed into a dry, rock-strewn channel covered with a blanket of prickly pear cactus.

Sanderson Canyon wound back and forth for many miles leading into town. Bob and I had crossed it many times over the previous two days of walking on US 90. Looking at this dry riverbed filled with cactus, it was hard to imagine the events of June 11, 1965, when a night of heavy rain produced a wall of water that washed away much of Sanderson, leaving twenty-six people dead or missing. Newspapers reported bodies up to five hundred miles downstream in the Rio Grande.

The road climbed in elevation as US 90 led east. At the top of a high hill, I dropped my pack and selected a spot to sit and journal. After a few minutes of rest, I stood up and lifted the pack onto my back, riddling my ass with cactus spines.

Smart enough to thoroughly check the spot where I sat down, but not bright enough to check the backpack. The pack had picked up several cactus pads, and the weight of the pack drove the spines deep into my backside.

I dropped the pack again, in a cactus-free spot, and extracted the spines one by one. After a close inspection of my backpack, I tentatively resumed the journey.

The town of Sanderson wasn't far behind, when an eastbound truck pulled to the side of the road. A woman remained in the passenger seat while the driver exited the vehicle and crossed the road with a smile on his face. He extended his hand and asked, "How's the trip going?"

"Pretty good." I shook his hand, struggling to place the face.

He assisted me. "I am Adrian Billings' dad—Warren."

The dots connected. Adrian was the young doctor from the Bean in Presidio. "Oh. Okay! It's great to meet you."

We crossed the road so Warren could introduce his wife, Ann. They assured me of a place to stay in Langtry, where I also hoped to meet Adrian's grandfather, Pete Billings.

At some point after Presidio, I had figured out Adrian's grandfather was a good friend of Keith Bowden, who wrote *The Tecate Journals*. As far as I was concerned, *The Tecate Journals* is the best description of the Rio Grande and its inhabitants. For that matter, Keith knows the river better than any living person. Possibly, Keith knows more about the river than anyone who has ever lived.

I called Adrian from Sanderson. He got in touch with his parents and they offered to host us in Langtry, the next town of any size on US 90.

I had gotten off on the wrong foot with Terrell County. The suspicious, circling deputies had irked me. Then I realized that the road shoulders were every bit as trashed as our roads back in LA (lower Alabama). Then the landscape went to hell!

The terrain I had walked previously—to the west of Sanderson—was just as rugged and dry, but it had diverse groundcover, and there were even some trees along US 90 and Sanderson Canyon.

But east of town something had devastated the landscape. On the hills and ridges east of Sanderson, thousands of acres appeared to have been mechanically manipulated in some devastating manner. The mostly bare soil supported a near monoculture of creosote bush. Virtually all the wildflowers, grasses, yuccas, and cacti were missing.

As a forester/ecologist who appreciates diversity, this was depressing as all hell.

Without Bob to distract me, the miles dragged by. Eventually Rex called. "Should I come get you? It's halftime."

I'd had enough of this monotonous landscape; it was time for football. I secured my coordinates, and Rex arrived shortly thereafter.

Mississippi State had held tough through halftime, and Rex was upbeat during the drive back to the motel. But State folded in the second half, and his hopes of a post-season miracle evaporated. Rex was pissed at the world.

I felt bad for Rex, but despite predictions to the contrary, I was hoping Auburn could pull off an upset similar to the previous Iron Bowl.

Auburn made a good show for three quarters, but the dominant Tide pulled away in the fourth.

Now the entire crew was disconsolate, the world having turned against us. How could fate be so cruel?

I removed my socks and compared my battered but intact feet to a mental image of Bob's mangled lower extremities. Well, maybe life wasn't so bad after all.

The Rio Grande along River Road

Rex on Precambrian Formation at Red Rock Ranch

15

DRYDEN TO LANGTRY

"But the old shadows, the old names and customs, persist, and they keep drawing us back to the original inclination of these landscapes, to the surprising possibilities for discovery and recovery embedded in this abused earth."

Bill Finch, et. al. *Longleaf, Far as the Eye Can See.* 2012

Tarantula near Valentine

November 30–December 2

JIMMY and Sierra Stiles were on the way, but it would take them two days to cover the thousand miles between Andalusia, Alabama, and Langtry. Their drive would be shorter than my foot route along the border.

Jimmy and Sierra were neighbors and longtime friends from the Pleasant Home Community near Andalusia. Since they are herpetologists and I am a plant person, we are equally weird, in our own biological proclivities. All three of us received our advanced degrees from the Auburn University School of Forestry and Wildlife Sciences, where I graduated with an MS in Forest Biology two decades prior. Jimmy and Sierra's degrees were less dated and their graduate projects centered on the reintroduction of North America's largest native snake to a portion of its former range. The Eastern indigo snake had been absent from Alabama for many decades until Jimmy and Sierra loosed several dozen onto the Conecuh National Forest, which borders my property in the Pleasant Home Community.

Jimmy and I were similar in height, but his beard outdid mine by a long shot.

Sierra was shorter with a long ponytail and a youthful face that was seldom without a smile.

Whenever and wherever we got together there would be good food, hunting and fishing stories, and relatively constant laughter.

Yet another friend and Honorary Tex-Mex Compadre (Roger Reid) had produced and directed a one-hour TV episode about the Eastern indigo, featuring Jimmy and Sierra, for the TV series, *Discovering Alabama*. Roger was hoping to join me further south along the border, as another Tex-Mex Compadre.

Rex dropped me ten miles from Sanderson, with another fifty to Langtry.

Stars still lit the sky, but they winked out as a heavy fog rolled in blanketing the landscape. I walked a Border Patrol dragline on the south side of the road, beside fences that alternated between traditional barbed wire and newer, woven wire-high fences. The transitioning fence styles signaled a change in the ranches' management objectives, from beef with the former to antlers with the latter.

Although the gravel path was an uneven, somewhat challenging surface to walk, it was safer than the highway. Visibility was limited to a few yards, and I would have been a nervous wreck walking the road shoulder in the dense fog. Another trail benefit: numerous animal tracks to study when the dragline was sand or dirt.

Exposing tracks was the whole purpose for the Border Patrol dragging tires beside the highway. Undocumented immigrants or smugglers who walked across the exposed soil would leave fresh tracks, although it wasn't foolproof. One agent told me that some border crossers wore bags over their feet to obscure their tracks.

As long as a person had a trail or a fence to follow, as I did, he could probably pass unseen in the heavy fog. Smugglers surely pay keen attention to weather forecasts and attempt to move their cargo, people or narcotics on days like this one.

By midmorning, the fog began to dissipate and visibility increased to a few hundred yards. Two objects hung from the fence ahead: a brace of grey foxes tied by their hind paws with their tails cut off. Their carcasses had yet to bloat, and there was no smell. I stopped to take a picture, and a Border Patrol agent pulled over. After a short Q&A, we went our separate ways.

I came upon a collection of abandoned buildings and corrals with a sign that read: "Indio Calzada Stockyards." I was tempted to climb the fence or crawl beneath the gate and look around, but resisted the impulse.

Some of my earliest and fondest recollections from the farm were loading our cattle or pigs onto trailers and riding with Grandpa, Joe Hainds, to the local livestock auctions. The sights, sounds, and smells are still imprinted in my memory.

I stared through the fence. No cattle lowing. No farmers lounged by the fences. No aromas of manure or fresh hay. A vibrant farming community had once supported these stockyards. Now the wind and the sun slowly ground the structures to ruin.

US 90 passed through another tiny community at the intersection of 349 and 90. Dryden looked to follow the path of the Indio Calzada Stockyards. A scattering of inhabited houses and trailers lined the road, but all the stores had closed, excepting one small building that carried livestock feed and corn for the hunters. Even this establishment was closed midday.

The landscape moderated its harsher edges: no mountains, cliffs, or deep valleys. Hilltops offered views of a gently rolling landscape with distant horizons.

Corn feeders and shooting houses were ubiquitous. These hills held thousands of tripods supporting barrels or buckets full of corn. At the bottom of each container, a spinner stood ready to scatter corn. The feeders were hooked to battery packs or solar units. Feeders are typically set to spin near sunrise and sunset when game is most active. Some feeders are filled and operated year around, and larger game ranches may run through tons of corn on a weekly basis.

Deer, pigs, javelinas, and many other animals locate the "free" food. If game species are fed and unmolested for long periods of time, the sound of corn kernels flying from the spinner and bouncing off the legs of the tripod and surrounding brush triggers a Pavlovian response, and the critters come running.

Hunters sit in shooting houses stationed on high points overlooking the feeders. The distance between the shooting house and feeder depends upon the weapon employed. Bowhunters may sit as close as twenty yards from the corn, while shooters with centerfire rifles may be a hundred or more yards distant.

This was another topic that Bob and I discussed while walking west of Sanderson.

Bob told me, "Hunters should be environmentalists. They should be our natural allies in restoring longleaf ecosystems."

As organizations like my former employer, The Longleaf Alliance, train more professionals and landowners about maintaining and restoring our native ecosystems, more people use fire to restore native ecosystems. In the southeastern US, we convert dense, shady loblolly plantations to open fire-maintained longleaf forests, thereby transforming the landscape. Turkeys and quail get bugging and nesting habitat. Deer grow fat and increase their reproduction with more browse. The diversity that was lost through intensive site preparation treatments and short rotation forestry begins to return.

The same could be true in Texas, where reducing grazing pressure and prescribed fire could restore native habitats on which wildlife depends.

Many hunters take offense at the liberal connotations of the word "environmentalist" yet their record shows a history of environmental activism. Were it not for duck hunters, the US would retain a much smaller fraction of our vital wetlands. Were it not for trout fishermen, even more of our pristine rivers would be dammed and polluted.

To the detriment of our land and our knowledge of the natural world, many hunters no longer have any concept of the traditional skills involved in harvesting game.

They no longer need the ability to scout the land or read sign such as tracks, scrapes, rubs, or hair caught in fences. Instead, they mount automatic cameras beside feeders. The cameras record the images of the animals and the precise time of the day they come to feed.

I spent the whole day walking past feeders, before Rex picked me up to retrieve our gear from the Budget Inn, in Sanderson, where the manager, Dalipseth, awaited. After getting to know us, he told us to call him "Dalip."

He was fascinated with my story and Rex's position as a cinematographer. Dalip volunteered his mother's cooking again. Rex and I told him we appreciated the offer, but Langtry was waiting. Dalip looked so pitiful that we quickly relented.

We took advantage of the downtime and phone reception to make some calls. Adrian had previously cautioned me, "You won't have signal in Langtry."

Dalip's mother prepared a feast fit for a maharajah. It was an amazing spread, and they refused any compensation. I wasn't familiar enough with Indian food to recognize the foods beyond dishes with rice, curry, breads, and sweets. They packed the food in paper and styrofoam containers. Before leaving we took photos of Dalip and his mother, and we posed in front of the Budget Inn sign with Dalip. The meal alone was worth more than the cost of a night's lodging at the Budget Inn - Sanderson.

Technically we stayed in a motel, but Dalip and his mother did their best to make it feel like a home.

From Sanderson, it was a sixty-mile run to Langtry and the Billings residence, where their new house sat on a ridge overlooking the Rio Grande. We drove down a gravel driveway and Warren stepped out to greet us. He led us to the three-bedroom, original Billings residence where we unpacked our gear. Warren, Ann, and Warren's brother Aaron were staying in the new house.

We hoped to see their view of the Rio Grande Valley, but because of the delay in Sanderson, it was dark by the time we made Langtry. Warren invited us to settle in and join them for supper. Rex and I felt guilty as hell, but we had to put Dalipseth's food in the refrigerator for consumption later.

Next door, we took seats around a long, well-lit kitchen table. Rex and I sat across from Warren, Aaron, and Ann. Like so many ambitious residents along the Rio Grande, Warren and Aaron had taken jobs with the biggest employer on the block – the U.S. Customs and Border Protection. Both of them had retired and looked back on their careers fondly.

Warren said, "I started back in 67. We used to catch the Braceros. We would send them back, and the next night they would come back over. I wouldn't want to work for the Border Patrol today with all the issues they have to deal with ."

Warren continued, "Aaron got on after me. They had a policy back then that you were assigned a different area than where you grew up. So they sent him to California. But as soon as jobs opened up around here, those Texas boys would apply for a transfer so they could come back home."

"I went to the Virgin Islands for a while, then I came back as the Supervisor for Anti-Smuggling," Warren said. "I dealt with human smuggling and one day my boss called me in and said, 'I have an application for transfer from an Aaron Billings in California.' I told him, 'Grab him!' Aaron ended up in charge of intelligence for this sector."

A photo on the wall showed Adrian posing with a buck. Warren told us, "He killed that deer in Mexico. Back then we knew the landowner on the other side, and it wasn't a big deal to grab your rifle and cross for a few days of hunting. You can't do that today."

Warren continued, "Mom and Dad paid for Adrian's first four years of college. Then he applied to med school, and he was not accepted, so he went ahead and got his PhD studying a tick virus. He went to work for the CDC (Center for Disease Control), and then he went back to medical school. His medical schooling was paid through a National Health Corporation Scholarship that required him to work in an underserved area. This job came open in Alpine [with a clinic in Presidio] and Adrian said, 'Don't throw me in that briar patch!' He likes working so close to home, and now he is a spokesman for the program."

Although the geography was different, our upbringing had many similarities. Besides hunting deer and other game, Warren said, "We used to run traplines on the river. We trapped ringtail, raccoon, and gray fox. We didn't try to catch 'em, but we got our share of skunks."

They still enjoyed fishing on the Rio Grande. "Mostly we catch yellow cats, channel cats, flatheads, and some white bass," Warren said.

I grew up on the banks of the Mussel Fork, a creek that runs through the middle of our farm. The memory of fried flathead fillets still makes my mouth water. We didn't hesitate to eat catfish from the Mussel Fork. But flatheads are the pinnacle of the food chain in freshwater rivers and streams. If the water is polluted, flatheads are going to accumulate more toxins than any other fish.

I asked Warren, "Do you still eat the flatheads?"

"You betcha!" He smiled.

Aaron filled the table with food: *enchiladas, frijoles*, French fries, and a blueberry cobbler. I cleared my plate, repeatedly.

Between mouthfuls I asked about their new house. "Your house is built from the same stone I saw on exposed cuts along US 90. Are there still stonemasons who build with this rock?"

Warren answered, "There are. It's expensive, but it's also a popular material to build with in the Hill Country around Austin."

Langtry didn't appear to have taken quite as hard a hit as most of the small communities east of El Paso, but it sure wasn't thriving. I mentioned Marfa, and Warren's wife, Ann, jumped in, "What a dump! All those artists and whatever have settled there!"

Count Langtry's problems as consistent with the opinions expressed in Redford, Lajitas, and other small communities around Marfa.

While I was preparing for the trek back in Alabama, friends that watched too much *Fox News* made sure to warn me about Islamic State/ISIS cells that were operating on the U.S.-Mexico border. Now that I was here, the real threat had been exposed—artists migrating to town.

Everyone else had eaten their fill, but I stayed with it until the table was clear. After supper, Rex and I were walking out the door when Warren cautioned, "There's a cold front coming in tomorrow. The temperature is going to drop quite a bit."

I assured him, "I like it cold. That's the best walking weather."

The next morning Rex dropped me west of Palma Canyon at 6:45 a.m. It would be a good many miles back to Langtry.

The temperature was still relatively mild, but a light fog steadily thickened. An eastbound car emerged and the driver honked her horn and waved. Ann Billings was on her way to visit friends farther west.

A heavy mist covered my glasses and dampened my clothes, while the wind picked up and the temperature plummeted.

Walking as fast as possible didn't generate enough heat to ward off the chill, so I donned every stitch of clothing from my pack, and it still wasn't enough.

I recalled Warren's words from the night before. His family had lived in this country for generations, yet I had blithely ignored his warning about the approaching cold front. Now I was on the verge of shivering even while walking faster than three miles per hour.

For the first time on the trip, hypothermia became a concern.

My cell phone was useless with zero bars. Despite repeated attempts, my text messages went undelivered.

Multiple canyons and arroyos lined the route. If my condition deteriorated, a bridge or culvert could provide shelter. My backpack was filled with emergency supplies, including a lightweight reflective blanket that was supposed to conserve body heat. I had fat lighter and matches, so a fire was possible, even with moist fuels and numb fingers.

As a last resort, I could flag down a Border Patrol agent. They had been consistently professional and helpful.

Yes, it was cold, but the situation wasn't critical. Rex would check on me around noon. I could take shelter if needed, but I had to be visible when he drove by.

A sign identified the western edge of Val Verde County. Terrell County was still within sight when the next Border Patrol Agent pulled over and informed me that I had just entered the Comstock Unit. Correctly diagnosing my chilled countenance, he offered a ride to Langtry. When I declined, he offered a piece of his clothing that went around the neck and beneath a shirt or coat to conserve body heat.

I told him while crossing my fingers, "That is very kind of you. But my friend Rex will be here soon. I'll get some more clothing from him."

Earlier that morning Warren had handed me a brown paper bag as I walked out the door. It contained two oranges, an apple, a peanut butter sandwich, two Powerbars, and some captain's wafers. My appetite had left an impression upon them.

Most of this food was consumed during the morning's walk. Stopping was impractical because the wind chilled my body so rapidly.

The quickened pace proved unsustainable, so I located a culvert at the bottom of a protected draw, took a seat, and finished Warren's contribution while the cold, damp wind whistled above. When the shivers returned, I hit the road.

The temperature didn't rise and the wind didn't let up, but Rex finally arrived. I said, "Man, am I glad to see you." Rex lent me his windbreaker, providing just enough layers protection between my skin and the environment.

Rex immediately chilled in the wind. He wished me well and left to interview the Billings: Warren, Aaron, and their father, Pete, who had been driven up from Del Rio. After that, Rex would look for me along the highway, just before dark. Further communication was unlikely since neither of our cell phones had any reception.

Jimmy and Sierra were due to arrive later in the day, but there was no way to reach them either. We last talked when I had called from the Sanderson Budget Inn the day before. I told Jimmy, "Try to get here before dark and look for me along US 90, somewhere in the neighborhood of Langtry."

I rolled into Langtry mid-afternoon. An old combination convenience store and motel stood on the southwest corner of an intersection of US 90 and the main street running through town. A young hunter stood outside his room, watching my approach. I asked him, "Have you done any good?"

"Not much luck so far. We shot some type of a desert goat yesterday."

"Was it an aoudad?"

"No, it was something else."

The Texas landscape supports a veritable menagerie.

I needed a break from the wind, so I ventured inside for coffee and a twenty-minute rest before continuing past Langtry.

There was still an hour or more of light when Rex found me along US 90. I returned his jacket and he aimed for Langtry. A Subaru with an Alabama plate passed us, entered our lane, and slowed down. Rex said, "Alabama drivers!" as he swerved into the far lane to pass them in turn.

I recognized the Subaru. "It's them! It's Jimmy and Sierra."

Everyone was relieved to have found each other. Two minutes later, and they would have been knocking on doors and asking directions until they located the Billings residence.

Back in Langtry, we parked the truck and walked to the Billings' overlook in the fading light. I yearned to explore the valley below, with a fishing pole in hand, but we just snapped some photos before wandering back for supper.

Jimmy and Sierra moved their luggage in while I joined the Billings. It had been a long cold day, but the temperature had spurred my pace, with 25.5 miles covered.

Pete Billings sat in a chair by large picture windows offering a view of the Rio Grande valley and opposing cliffs in Mexico.

I introduced myself and pulled a chair up close, so I could hear his soft, cheerful, 98-year old voice. Pete had heard about my trek, and he filled me in on his good friend Keith Bowden's recent adventures (author of *The Tecate Journals*).

Keith had been the victim of extremely bad timing. He was floating the Rio Grande by himself, during the rain events that coincided with my walk through and east of Van Horn.

"Keith told me the river kept rising," Pete said. "And it was raining so much that all he could do was pull his canoe up on the cliffs and climb in with all his clothing. Later that night he felt the boat rocking. The water had risen and he was floating down the river in the dark."

"He found another place to pull out. He dragged his canoe as far up as he could. He got back in the boat. When he woke up he was several miles downstream. He must have done this several times that night. He couldn't get out of the channel because of the cliffs on both sides. Keith told me, 'I've never been so cold in all my life.'"

After the description of Keith's harrowing float down the Rio Grande, Pete described his early years around Langtry. "When they first settled here, my parents lived in a cave by the river. It was so cold that year that all the stock froze to death. I was born the year after that."

Pete became a railroader and worked thirty-six years for the Southern Pacific. He was in good shape as a retiree until a recent accident. "I was lifting a boat and cracked three vertebrae. I ruined my back. Now I stay with my daughter in Del Rio."

It was time for supper. Seated around the table were the Billings: Aaron, Warren, and Pete; my friends—Jimmy and Sierra, then Rex and I. We feasted on venison steaks, French fries, jalopeños, and apple cobbler.

It was the type of meal that sticks in one's memory: the food, the company, the warm comfortable environment contrasting with the brutally cold, wet, winds that had pummeled me throughout the day's walk.

The next day, Jimmy dropped me off before returning to Langtry for a tour of the Billings property and a walk down to the river. Rex was scheduled to meet a neighbor of the Billings who had accumulated thousands of Native American artifacts. The tyranny of a schedule forced me to walk while they had all the fun.

The morning's walk was fairly uneventful. But for the first time on my trip, a big truck pulled over. The driver opened a door with a rebel flag on it and asked me, "Do you want a ride?"

"No thanks, I'm walking to the Gulf of Mexico."

He saluted and drove down the road.

Scores of game feeders dotted the landscape. I expected to hear rifle shots, but there was not a single report.

A Union Pacific (UP) train line paralleled US 90 and dozens of UP trucks drove back and forth on US 90, delivering hundreds of linemen to a major track project. Thousands of brand new railroad ties lay stacked beside the tracks. At times, the smell of creosote was overpowering.

Like Pete, my father and my Grandpa Baker had spent their working lives on the railroad. It was encouraging to see railroads investing in their lines, because they carry the commerce of America. Based on the number of trains using this line, America was booming.

Around 11:30 a.m., I arrived at the Pecos River Bridge, and a breath-taking view. Hundreds of feet below, the canyon was filled with clear, still, backwater from a dam on the Rio Grande. A few fish-eating ducks swam through dead trees, long submerged. Downstream, Mexican cliffs marked the junction of the Pecos and the Rio Grande.

Traffic was minimal on US 90 so I took my time crossing, stepping around two road-killed black vultures lying on the bridge. On the other side, I dropped my pack and ate lunch while soaking in the view.

Boom! An explosion reverberated up the canyon. Downstream, geysers of water shot in the air, moments before the sound of additional booms and splashes reached the bridge. Boulders as big as cars rolled and bounced off the cliff, splashing into the river just in front of a ramp and boat launch. Had an unlucky boater attempted an ill-timed launch that coincided with the rockslide, nothing would have remained except fiberglass splinters.

It only lasted for a few seconds, but it was absolutely spectacular, and the timing impeccable. Appropriately, silence reigned for the remainder of my meal, and not a single car intruded upon my contemplation.

A few miles down the road, tractors pulled bush-hogs over the rocky terrain on the shoulders of US 90, shredding cacti, mesquite, yucca, and acacia. This littered the ground with millions of thorny twigs. The mesquite and acacia were particularly bad about sticking to the bottom of my boots. The acacia thorns were smaller and didn't penetrate as much. But the mesquite burrowed deep. Dozens of thorns broke off in the soles of my shoes. When I stepped on a rock at just the right angle it pushed the embedded thorns into the bottom of my feet. Pebbles were okay, and large rocks were not problematic, but I had to adapt my gait to avoid marble-to golf ball sized rocks.

The next town on US 90 was Comstock, and it was up to Rex and the Compadres to find suitable lodging in the vicinity. I walked up a hill and into town. The Comstock Unit of the Border Patrol occupied a large building adjacent to an older motel. The Border Patrol office was humming with activity as agents came and went.

Jimmy and Sierra had parked their Subaru and my truck by the motel. "Is this where we are staying?" I asked.

"No, they only had one room," Jimmy said. "So we made reservations at the Motel 6 in Del Rio. Do you want to call it quits for the day or keep walking?"

"This is far enough. I made good time. It should be over twenty-five miles for the second day in a row."

Rex and I moved into one room of the Motel 6, and Jimmy and Sierra secured another. After unloading gear, we drove to the Blue Oasis Bar and Grill on the north side of Del Rio. The food was good. The beer was cold. The price was right. Rex and I approved of the talented waitresses.

Jimmy and Sierra wanted to walk with me the next day, December 3rd. They planned to leave on December 4th when they would drive west to visit the Sonoran Desert. I told them, "You have to visit Chinati Hot Springs. You'll love it."

Rex seconded my opinion.

"We're all about hot springs," Jimmy said.

Jimmy & Sierra made their reservations with Dianna later that night.

At the High Sierra Bar and Grill in Terlingua

Rex at the Budget Inn in Sanderson

16

COMSTOCK TO DEL RIO

"About a year later, I got around to asking him what the people of the United States really were, and he said, "Spoiled children who are begging for a frightening but just Daddy to tell them exactly what to do."

Kurt Vonnegut. *Bluebeard*. 1987

Texas Spiny Lizard: Drawn by Ava Bailey

December 3–4

JIMMY drove north from Del Rio, passing through a Border Patrol checkpoint before dropping me in front of their Comstock station. I started walking at 7:22 a.m. Jimmy would join me later.

It took about an hour to make it back to the Border Patrol checkpoint. Westbound traffic was required to stop, but I was walking east. Three agents and a dog stood outside. One of the agents was a young Hispanic female who had slowed to a near stop beside me the day before on US 90.

Female agents are a decided minority in their workforce so she was easy to identify.

They nodded as I walked past and didn't bother with questioning.

A monstrous facility was under construction just past the checkpoint. It would serve as the base of operations for a much-expanded Comstock Unit of the Border Patrol. Most of the folks back home were unaware that the federal government was pouring billions into border security.

Jimmy and Sierra returned mid-morning, bringing a warm biscuit for my second breakfast on the hood of their Subaru. After I dispatched the biscuit, Sierra left Jimmy and me walking US 90 east and south.

The traffic was nonstop. Union Pacific trucks and Border Patrol vehicles comprised about half the vehicles, and the rest were mostly semi-trailers, of both American and Mexican origin.

In a previous life, Jimmy had maintained trails at Oak Mountain State Park, near Birmingham, Alabama, where he hiked many miles a day. His well-worn walking stick had already covered thousands of miles.

The road shoulders were covered with deer carcasses in all stages of decomposition, and thousands of bleached bones littered our path. Antlers were also scattered across the ground; some were sheds, others were broken off during collisions. We ignored the bones but collected antlers as we walked.

Another complication arose from the recent mowing. Just when some of the carcasses were at their peak ripeness, the bush-hogs had ground them into road kill hamburger yielding an aroma sufficiently putrid to gag a maggot.

We were more interested in animals killed in the mowing operation, stopping to examine a large lizard that neither of us had seen before. Jimmy is a herpetologist by education and profession. With his knowledge and the first cell phone reception in a hundred miles, it didn't take him long to ID the specimen as a Texas spiny lizard.

I found an antler in velvet, a relatively rare find.

The miles flew by, and fingers from Lake Amistad appeared on our left. In *The Tecate Journals*, Keith Bowden describes ferocious winds and waves threatening to swamp his canoe, during this portion of his trip down the Rio Grande. The famous Texas winds also blew for us, but they did not hinder our progress across land.

Too soon, Sierra came to retrieve Jimmy. He had walked eight miles, and he didn't want to injure himself, as Bob had west of Sanderson. This time, Jimmy took the car and Sierra joined me for a stroll.

The walking conditions were quite variable. A decent dirt trail paralleled the highway on some portions. At other times, we were forced directly onto the road shoulder by steep banks, boulders, or other difficult conditions.

Sierra and I were walking the road shoulder beside a guardrail as a semi-trailer roared past. Turbulence following the trailer lifted my cowboy hat into the air and deposited it just over the rail about twenty feet behind me.

"Dang, that's the first time I lost my hat in nearly six hundred miles of walking." I stepped over the railing, and noticed a tree covered in dark fruit, about one inch in diameter. "Well, I'll be," I said to Sierra. "That's my first Texas persimmon." My hat had landed at the base of a female *Diospyros texana*. Engrossed in conversation, we had walked right past it without noticing the fruit-laden tree.

Sierra laughed. "Your hat was meant to blow off at that precise moment."

"It surely was."

We approached the shore of Lake Amistad. Small green trees spotted the shoreline. Sierra asked, "Are those red cedar?"

"No, the habitat isn't right. I think those are salt cedar. It's another invasive Asian tree." When we got close enough to see the foliage, my assumption proved correct.

Sierra warned, "The bridge over Lake Amistad is very scary. There's no shoulder and lots of traffic. We'll carry you across, and we promise not to tell anyone."

Sierra had a good read on the bridge. It was a scary and unavoidable obstacle. I considered her potentially life-saving offer, but quickly rejected it. "No. I appreciate it, but I have to walk it."

"Okay." She shook her head. "But you need to have your knife out and ready if you are knocked from the bridge, to quickly cut yourself free from your boots and clothing."

It was good advice. I compiled a mental checklist of clips, belts, and shoelaces to cut or unbuckle if I were knocked over the side. Truth be told, I was probably a goner if I hit the water. If the collision didn't kill me, and I didn't drown, hypothermia would almost certainly end my existence before making the long swim to shore. It was important to stay on the bridge.

Jimmy picked up Sierra, and they drove to the far side, while I watched for a break in the traffic.

This bridge over Lake Amistad presented a short and very dangerous test. The next eight-tenths of a mile would be one of the most perilous sections I had faced. A semi-trailer came off the structure, and for the moment, the coast was clear. I started range walking across the bridge.

The wind whipped both my clothing and the water below. Amistad's waters were clear and blue in the shallows, while white-capped waves rolled across unprotected coves. I pulled my hat down and pushed hard.

I walked facing traffic on the left side of the bridge. There was no shoulder, but there was a narrow ledge about one foot in width. When cars approached from either direction, I checked to make sure they would not meet a vehicle coming from the other direction, trusting oncoming traffic to move over. Most vehicles accommodated by hugging the middle or crossing into the opposing lane. Everything clicked until the middle of the bridge.

Semi-trailers were coming from both directions at seventy-five miles per hour and they would meet beside me. I stepped onto the ledge and held my breath as a big truck passed at arm's length. The trailing winds buffeted me. Releasing my breath, I stepped down and kept walking.

There had been plenty of scary sections and situations along the border, but this mile offered the most ridiculously dangerous ground traveled thus far.

Automobiles crossed the bridge in seconds, but it took ten minutes of hard walking and two more balancing acts on the ledge before I completed the crossing.

There is a myriad of ways to die when walking the border, but getting hit by an automobile was far and away the greatest risk I had faced thus far. I'd much rather cross paths with a group of undocumented border crossers than a speeding F-150.

Sierra rejoined me on the other side, and we continued our advance on the Amistad community.

Jimmy and I had seen our fair share of road-killed deer. East of the bridge, the numbers reached epic proportions. There was a deer carcass every thirty yards or so, just on our side of the road! Many were reduced to bones and hair, but hundreds, perhaps thousands, of carcasses were in various stages of decay.

Even sadder, dead monarchs also littered the road shoulders. Some of the butterflies might have been road kill, but more likely most perished during the same, sudden cold front that caught me near Langtry. Had the temperature dropped one week later, the migrating monarchs may have survived, having migrated a bit farther south.

Sierra had had enough. We had covered several miles and I hated to lose another roadside companion, but Jimmy arrived to pick her up. He asked me, "How far or long do you want to go?"

"I know this sounds crazy, but I am going to try and make it to the motel. If my legs don't give out, this could be my record day."

Jimmy and Sierra left to explore surrounding parks and landings on Lake Amistad, while I continued walking through the largest concentration of people since Alpine.

Where hunters drove much of the economy between El Paso and Comstock, fishing looked like the big dog around Amistad. I picked up rubber worms and salamanders from the road shoulder. Some of these lures were my preferred brand for catching largemouth bass in the beaver ponds and oxbows of south Alabama and north Florida. These bodies of water are called "resacas" on the border.

A column of billowing black smoke climbed to my front. The prevailing wind was in my face, and soon, charred pieces of paper fell from the sky. What was this?

The black column stood for a few minutes, and then it disappeared. The mystery was resolved a mile up the road in the form of a burned-out shell of a trailer/camper in an RV lot. Several law enforcement personnel and firefighters stood around the smoldering ruin.

The highway turned south into Del Rio and the sun dipped toward the horizon on my right. My path followed an elevated bank on the approach to Del Rio. Jimmy slowly drove past and Sierra snapped photos of my profile against the horizon.

I shouted down, "Let's meet at the Blue Oasis."

My physical conditioning promised record mileage, if the pace held. The day's walk had started well before sunrise, and the sun was down by the time I entered the restaurant's parking lot in Del Rio. Jimmy and Sierra joined me at a table where the waitress remembered us from the night before.

We celebrated a wonderful day on the road with cold draft beer. I had covered just short of one hundred miles in the four days prior, but this day's distance made that average look puny. Plus, I'd add a mile and a half walking to the hotel from the Blue Oasis.

I asked Jimmy and Sierra, "Do you want to eat here?"

Sierra said, "The Hot Pit is a barbeque place in town with excellent reviews. Why don't we meet you at the motel with a plate?"

"Sounds good to me!"

It was dark outside the Blue Oasis, but streetlights illuminated part of the road. At times, there was just enough ambient light to see curbs and other obstacles. I walked south until Rex pulled into a parking lot to my front. He was on his way back from filming in Langtry. "Why are you still walking?"

"Because it is over thirty miles from Comstock to the motel! We just had a beer at the Blue Oasis. I should be at the room in ten minutes. Do you want me to call Jimmy and Sierra and have them pick you up some barbeque?"

"No, thanks. I've already eaten. I'll see you at the hotel."

At the Motel 6, I plotted the day's coordinates while doing laundry in a small room adjacent to the motel office. My mapping program measured the walk at 30.5 miles. Rex was ecstatic. If I kept it up, we would be home for Christmas.

After laundry, I joined Jimmy and Sierra in their room to share experiences and impressions over beer and some of the best brisket on the border. My friends were leaving for Chinati Hot Springs in the morning, and the Saguaro National Park from there.

With thirty miles and a pile of beef under my belt, sixteen hours of sleep would not have been too much. Even so, by this point in the trek, an alarm clock was unnecessary. Somewhere in the gray matter an internal switch was thrown, synapses fired, and my eyes opened at 5:00 a.m.

I worked through my typical routine. A cup of coffee. Consume calories from food that was too heavy or perishable to carry on the trail. There was plenty of granola and jerky for the road. In the early morning hours, it was doughnuts, fruit, and whatever else the hotel offered at no additional cost. More coffee. Tape the toes. More coffee. Dump some coffee. Hit the road.

It was December 4th, and the spirit was willing but the body was weak. Thirty miles had taken its toll, and everything seemed to move in slow motion.

Del Rio was the first sizable town with a newspaper since Alpine and the *Alpine Avalanche*. Conveniently, the *Del Rio News Herald* operated out of a building just a few hundred yards from our motel.

I stepped through their front door and explained myself to the receptionist. Shortly, the Managing Editor led me to his desk.

Brian Argabright had been with the *News Herald* for eighteen years. He grew up in Del Rio and we shared familiar connections to the railroad. "My Grandpa and Uncle retired from the Southern Pacific," said Brian.

I replied, "My dad and my mom's dad retired from the Santa Fe."

Once Brian understood the purpose of my walk, he provided a fifteen-minute rundown of the city and the newspaper. The *News Herald* was founded in 1929, and Del Rio's biggest local story was eerily similar to Sanderson's unwanted entry in the history books. The flood of 1998 had wrecked much of the south side of town, when San Felipe Creek overflowed its banks and carried away houses. Nine Del Rio residents lost their lives. Brian handed me a copy of the *News Herald* that ran the day after the Del Rio floods.

Folklore is rife with Texas tornadoes, but from Presidio to Sanderson to Del Rio it was floodwaters that wrecked or threatened havoc.

Brian asked about my experiences thus far.

"I was thoroughly impressed with El Paso. It was a clean and orderly town. I didn't feel the least bit threatened there or in any other urban environment that I've walked through. I didn't know exactly what to expect before my walk. I can assure you that the perception for most Southerners and Midwesterners couldn't be further from the truth. They think it's a warzone out here, but I'd rather walk through El Paso than any big city in the South."

I had made this or a very similar statement several times by this point in the walk. Later, my sister told her black coworkers about my impressions of the border. They told her, "The media does the same thing here in Missouri, sensationalizing violence in black neighborhoods." This had me wondering, was I selling our Midwestern and Southern cities short?

Brian said, "The spillover [violence] has been minimal. There was a city councilman from Ciudad Acuña who was trying to fight corruption. He crossed over when it got too hot, but they came across and assassinated him. That's the only killing we've had that was linked to the cartels."

"Our biggest criminal problem at this time is in the older sections of town, down by the river. When the water is low, teens will swim across the Rio Grande and raid houses. The Border Patrol is well aware of the problem and they are very active down there."

Brian continued, "We have part of the 'Great Fence' along Pepper Lane. You can go see what all the hoopla was about."

"We have the oldest winery in the state of Texas. The Qualia family makes great wines. Their tawny port is very good. They also make olive oil now."

Brian asked, "Where have you eaten in town?"

"I had a fun meal at the Blue Oasis. And we're pretty picky about our barbeque in the Deep South, but my friends, Jimmy and Sierra Stiles brought me some of the flat out best barbeque I've eaten. They picked it up at the Hot Pit. It was outstanding."

"The Suday family owns Hot Pit. They used to have a restaurant in Ciudad Acuña. When things got too violent on the other side, they and many other families with the financial wherewithal moved across to Del Rio. The Sudays also operate Sugar and Spice, where they make cakes and cater weddings."

"You should try Memo's. Ray Price's piano player's wife owns it. It was under water in the flood, but they have fixed it up. Blondie Calderón was the piano player. He has since passed away."

I brought up the incredible number of road-killed deer around Lake Amistad. Brian nodded. "Lake Amistad is our baby. We consider it part of Del Rio. About the deer, I hit one here in town. It's tough for people who have to drive in from the county to work. That's why we have so many insurance places in town."

From the *News Herald* it was only a short walk to US 90. I turned south and covered a few blocks before Jimmy and Sierra surprised me by showing up in their car. Jimmy said, "You haven't made it very far!"

"No. I had a good interview with the *Del Rio News Herald*. I'm just hitting the road."

Sierra said, "We wanted to bring you some breakfast burritos before we left."

"Dang, I am going to miss you all."

We ate our burritos and they squeezed back into their jam-packed Subaru for the ride west, while I turned south. Residual fatigue and a full belly slowed me down.

I was walking a sidewalk through town when a pecan landed on the road nearby. The nut had fallen far enough to crack on impact. I glanced around, but there were no pecan trees in sight.

The mystery was solved when a great-tailed grackle landed beside the cracked pecan, picked it up, and flew away. The grackle had just used the road as a nutcracker, dropping the nut from altitude. It wasn't the first time I had seen a great-tailed grackle exhibit a high degree of intelligence.

I spent the summer of 1988 with Uncle Sam at Fort Sam Houston in San Antonio, Texas. One Saturday, I ambled along the River Walk in downtown San Antonio, pausing to watch a mixed flock of grackles and English house sparrows hopping through the grass. A great-tailed grackle used its bill to grab an unsuspecting adult house sparrow by the neck. The sparrow fluttered furiously, but the fix was in. The grackle flew away with the sparrow held firmly in its bill.

US 90 joined 277 in Del Rio. Both roads turned left (east) on the south side of town. I walked a few more blocks and then 277 turned right (south) while US 90 continued east. From Van Horn to downtown Del Rio, I had covered over three hundred miles on US 90 and was not sorry to leave it behind.

The road led to a bridge over a clear, fast-flowing stream. San Felipe Creek originated from springs a few hundred yards north, still within the city limits of Del Rio. Below me, the creek ran through a small idyllic city park where a paved path for pedestrians and bicyclists paralleled the water, painting one of the prettier urban scenes of the trek.

US 277 curved south and east leading toward Eagle Pass, gaining elevation on the way out of town. Large trees lined Del Rio's streets, but east of town the vegetation decreased in height, transitioning to desert scrub in the hills.

New subdivisions had sprouted on the high ground east of Del Rio. Perhaps some of these residents had relocated from houses damaged in the flood of 1998.

An amazing number of law enforcement vehicles traveled 277. There was the ubiquitous Border Patrol, along with sheriff's deputies from Maverick and Val Verde counties, city police from Del Rio and Eagle Pass, and the Texas State Patrol. This show of force begged the question: how many times would I be stopped and questioned along this stretch? The first stop occurred mid-day, when a Border Patrol agent pulled over and told me, "We had a report of someone walking beside the road and someone lying by a bridge."

"That was me in both cases. I took a nap by a bridge a few miles back, and I've been walking since El Paso."

He must have shared the story with his coworkers, because there were no more checks that day.

Rex picked me up about dark, asking, "Where do you want to eat?"

"The editor of the newspaper told me about a place called Memo's. Why don't we give it a try?"

We were the first customers to arrive, but it didn't take long for locals to fill the tables. The waitress seated us by a window overlooking San Felipe Creek, just a few yards away.

Our table was next to a stage filled with musical instruments. Before long, the proprietor approached. Dolly had been the wife of Blondie Calderón, the bandleader for a famous country music singer named Ray Price.

Dolly said, "My in-laws started the restaurant in 1936, or was it 1946? They bought this property and moved to this location in 1959. They offered the restaurant to their children, but they weren't interested, with the exception of Blondie. He asked his parents, 'Can I put music in there?' He was only nineteen years old, but he was able to obtain a special permit to serve alcohol. He was a self-made musician, and they've held dances here every Friday and Saturday night since 1959."

"We married in 1963 and had five children. In 1966 Blondie got a call from Ray Price's bandleader. They needed a vibraphone player. Blondie asked me if he could tour with the band and I said, 'No!'"

"Ray Price called back and asked to talk to me. He said, 'I'll give your husband twenty-eight to twenty-nine jobs a month at $50.00 a job.' I did the math and changed my mind."

"Blondie's older brother loaned him $20.00. Someone else gave him a car, and I packed a suitcase for him. He met them on the road and eventually Blondie became Ray's bandleader."

Our food arrived and Dolly wandered off to talk with some of the other patrons. Through the window, Rex and I watched a cat stalking along the creek, its intended prey indiscernible.

Rex drove us to the motel after supper. He went to the room while I did a grocery run to the HEB, a chain grocery store, mainly in Texas. A newspaper rack caught my eye as I crossed the parking lot. The front page featured Sierra's profile picture of me with the headline, "Texas Trek."

There would be many more headlines to come.

17

QUEMADO TO EAGLE PASS

"The trail I've been followin' for so many years was twisted an' tangled, but it's straightenin' out now."

Zane Grey. *Riders of the Purple Sage*. 1912

Great-Tailed Grackle: Drawn by Ava Bailey

December 5–7

THE next two days entailed more complicated logistics. Rex and his friend were on their way to San Antonio for a weekend of revelry, and I would be on my own.

It was pitch black as Rex and I drove our vehicles from Del Rio to Eagle. The first hotel on the west side of Eagle Pass was the Country Hill Inn. I turned into an empty parking lot before entering the office and rang a bell on the front desk. A sleepy woman of East Asian descent emerged from an adjacent room. She quoted an affordable price and agreed to let me check in at that early hour, so I reserved a room for the next three days.

With my supplies and luggage in the room, we drove back toward Del Rio, where I parked my truck at an intersection with an empty lot across from a house. It looked like a reasonably safe place to leave my truck, although "safe" was hard to gauge in an area like this. Why were hundreds of law enforcement vehicles traveling this road on a daily basis?

A man walked his dog across the road from us, and the rapid popping of semi-automatic weapons rolled across the hills, advertising a nearby firing range and a potential explanation for the profusion of police.

Rex said, "Why don't you ask that guy to keep an eye on your truck?"

"Okay." I walked across the street while thinking, *If he's a good guy, this makes sense. If he's a bad guy, he'll know that my truck will be unattended for the next ten hours.*

I explained the situation to the man with the dog, and he replied, "You know, I may want to write a book someday."

There wasn't time to discuss his literary ambitions, but I thanked him for agreeing to keep watch on the truck.

Rex dropped me on the side of 277 and left for San Antonio.

Much of the landscape was high-fenced on both sides of the road. Because large animals could not move freely across this landscape, there were no road-killed deer.

Inside the fence, the desert scrub included more cenizo or sagebrush than the vegetation farther west. Cenizo, translated from Spanish to English is "ash," accurately describing the color of the waist-high shrub.

Outside the fence, the road shoulders were covered with dense stands of grass, and an occasional mesquite tree had been left on the side of the road. Perhaps reduced competition allowed extra moisture and nutrients, because they had grown to epic proportions. From a distance these mesquite could easily be mistaken for live oaks. The diameters of the boles were close to twenty inches and the heights reached forty feet. The spreading crowns were as wide as the trees were tall.

My endurance had yet to recover from the thirty-mile push into Del Rio. Miles passed but not rapidly.

A communications tower stood opposite the fence on my side of the road. A truck was parked beside it and a man worked at the base of the tower.

In a few minutes the same truck pulled up beside me, still on the opposite side of the fence. A man with a goatee and a street-smart air exited the truck and approached the wire. He offered me a bottle of water, which I accepted through the fence.

"Where you headed?" he asked.

"To the Gulf of Mexico. I just made it through Del Rio, and I hope to make Eagle Pass tomorrow."

Juan was upgrading towers for AT&T. He was born and raised in Crystal City, Texas, and he knew all the surrounding towns and cities.

"What's it like down here?" I asked. "I've heard it gets hotter the farther south you go."

"I've been in Laredo, and you have to really be careful down there," Juan replied. "Everything comes down to money. If you have it, they may kidnap you and take you to Mexico. If your people don't have money to give them, then you are normally not found again."

"Is it the Zetas?"

"At this point it's kind of a tossup. The Zetas are involved." He continued, "Six months ago, I was in Del Rio. American businessmen should not cross over unless it's just a short trip during the daytime."

"Where's the worst?"

"Zapata or Roma. I've been staying there the last six months, and there are fifty to sixty state troopers at the hotels. If you are driving a vehicle, you will be stopped. I didn't know why we were continuously getting stopped. I think they were just logging us in. I was in Zapata yesterday for a delivery, and people told me, 'If you don't have business over across the border, don't go over there.'"

"I want my fiancée to visit from Oklahoma, but I told her, 'I'm scared that people might watch you, and you might get kidnapped.' This has been going on for a while."

"Me and some friends were at a bar," Juan said. "Some people walked up to us and asked, 'Who do you represent?' We told them, 'Nobody, we're just here to work.' They told us they were with "Golfo" or the Gulf Cartel. There are also street gangs, mainly into trafficking – humans and drugs."

"Gangs?"

"The Mexican Mafia runs this area. They call the shots. They are in the prisons and on the streets."

"Do you see many illegals in this area?" I asked, "The terrain looks awfully harsh to me."

"I picked up people around Schulenberg – near La Grange, Texas. I left a jobsite and there was a man, a woman, and their son. They needed water and they told me the boy had an epileptic attack. They had been in the woods going in circles for two days. They had Indiana IDs, but they were probably fake. I took them to a motel and paid for their room. The boy's shirt was torn up, so I gave him some socks and pants. He told me his goal was to be a baker. He was maybe nineteen years old. There is an immigration checkpoint near there and they had been hiding from farmers and ranchers. Everything's changed to the point where we don't know what to do. The level of danger is way up, but we have adjusted to it."

I took notes as he talked. After half an hour, I told him, "This is great stuff, but I have to get moving. It's another twenty miles to my truck."

What to make of his stories? On one hand, there was Brian—the newspaper editor—telling me that spillover violence was rare and targeted. On the other, was Juan, who suggested that everyone was a potential target: I could be kidnapped at any minute!

I've known people who would not walk across an unmown yard for fear of snakes. Their fear is real. The risk, less so.

Whether a product of an honest phobia or too much testosterone, these stories left me unmoved—with one exception – picking up the family near Schulenburg. Juan came across as a decent person who made a practice of helping those in need. He'd given me a bottle of water and offered a ride, despite his perception of danger all around.

All the same I made a mental note, *Next call home, ask Katia if my life insurance policy is up to date.*

At times, a decent trail allowed me to walk alongside high fences on the east side of the road. Elsewhere, thick grass forced me to the road shoulder. I tried to slog through the unmown, knee-high grass, but it wrapped around my ankles, doubling energy expenditures. It may have worked as a workout technique, but it killed forward progress.

US 277 was a 2-lane highway where most of the cars or trucks traveled seventy miles per hour or faster.

Unfortunately, many vehicles treated the wide road shoulders as another driving lane. On flatter portions of 277, vehicles would come over the horizon driving on the shoulder, and disappear behind me, still driving the shoulder. They owned that shoulder. I mistakenly assumed they would see me and move over to the real driving lane. After cars repeatedly forced me off the road shoulder, I accepted the reality: they were prepared to run me down rather than drive in a legal lane. I considered putting a rock through their windshields, but I doubted it would improve the situation, so I dove for the ditch.

I spotted a vehicle parked on the opposite side of the road. Drawing closer, I realized it had a flat tire; a recurring theme. An elderly man stepped out and asked, "Do you know how to change a tire? I can't figure out where the tools are."

"We can give it a shot. Can you get me the owner's manual?"

Bill Perry was from Quemado, a small town between my truck and me. He was eighty-eight years old and owned a pecan orchard and processing operation in Quemado.

In short order, we had the jack and wrenches out. Bill had called his handyman before my arrival, and a Hispanic gentleman showed up as we tried to figure out how to insert a metal rod through the bumper and lower the spare. Progress halted, because the rod was incompatible with the receiver, no matter how many times and ways we tried to insert it. Eventually, I gave up and wished them well.

Mr. Perry said, "I guess giving you a ride would defeat the purpose of your walk."

I laughed. "Thanks anyway. Good luck with the tire."

Mr. Perry had a ride, and I had lost another hour.

At my suggestion, Rex had dropped me twenty-five miles west of my truck. Given my rate of forward progress, I was looking at a good two hours of walking in the dark beside a very dangerous highway.

A license plate lay just off the shoulder of the road. I removed my pack and bent over to pick it up. Out of the blue, a truck appeared on the shoulder, nearly decapitating me. He continued west, driving out of sight, still on the road shoulder.

I was shaken. This was the closest I had come to being killed on the trip. It happened because I took my attention off the road, and another irresponsible asshole was using the shoulder for a driving lane. US 90 had been an interminably long walk, but US 277 had the worst drivers. US 90 was boring, but US 277 was terrifying.

A sign for Maverick County marked the end of Kinney County, which was sandwiched between Maverick to my front and Val Verde to the west. I had traversed ten Texas counties, and seven lay ahead.

The road descended from the cenizo dotted scrub of the high desert to the floodplain of the Rio Grande.

A bridge crossed an irrigation canal, and this wasn't like the ditches around El Paso, which could be jumped or waded. Here, the water flowed deep and fast. Undocumented immigrants or smugglers would only cross these waters on manmade structures, or risk death by drowning. More than likely, the Border Patrol monitored crossings with detection devices.

Later, I discovered that almost the entire flow of the Rio Grande was diverted through this irrigation channel. The Rio Grande had been a river below La Junta. Near Eagle Pass, it was once again reduced to a trickle. It's hard to imagine a more abused river in the United States: perhaps the Cuyahoga River of the 1960s?

Just past the irrigation canal I crossed another bridge over Moras Creek. Its waters were sedentary, in contrast to the near whitewater status of the irrigation canal.

The landscape completely transformed from desert scrub to pecan plantations and agricultural fields. Flocks of great-tailed grackles rested on branches, while orange fox squirrels collected pecans on the ground beneath the trees.

For the first time since Chispa, significant rooting along the road pointed to feral hog activity. A road-killed red pig with black spots confirmed the infestation.

Back in Alabama I had called Oscar Galindo, the Texas A & M Extension Agent for Maverick County, to explain my upcoming trip. He had responded enthusiastically, so on my next break along US 277, I called again, to update Mr. Galindo on my progress. Oscar was busy but he promised to get back in touch the next day.

I trudged along until a car pulled over beside me. It was the same guy who had been walking his dog that morning. It was nice to see him driving a car and not my F-150. He asked, "Do you need a ride? It's a long way to your truck. I won't tell anyone."

It was tempting, but I hadn't covered enough miles to quit that early in the day. I sighed and shook my head. "Thanks, man. But I've got to walk it."

"Okay. We'll see you down the road."

I immediately regretted passing on the ride. What was I thinking? I was asking to get run over on this damn road.

I finally entered Quemado, passing Mr. Perry's orchards and sheds. I approached a building on the west side of the road with the sign: "Daguer's Farm Equipment."

At the same time, a vehicle turned into Daguer's entrance and a man exited his truck. He approached and introduced himself. "Hello! I am Oscar Galindo. I had to see this man who is walking the border!"

I told Oscar about my experiences along the road, with a particular emphasis on the dangerous drivers of US 277.

Oscar asked. "Do you want a ride to your truck?"

"Yes. Yes, I do."

We loaded my stuff in his truck and Oscar toured me around the small settlement.

Oscar said, "I don't know why this is called 'Quemado'. In Spanish that means 'burned out.'"

Oscar drove us to another nearby community named "Normandy." He said, "After WW II, German refugees settled here. Several of the older houses have bomb shelters. They moved here because it was close to the border. They believed the close proximity to Mexico allowed an escape route if things turned bad in the United States."

"That is fascinating! I had no idea."

On the short ride to my vehicle Oscar said, "Our 4-H chapter is meeting tomorrow. Would you be interested in talking to them?"

"I'd love to. I was in 4-H back on the farm."

"Do you need a ride back out in the morning?"

"That would be awesome." Oscar was my most fortuitous connection since the Billings family in Langtry.

I got busy at the hotel: plotting coordinates, journaling, phone calls, and emails. This trek was conceived as a means of escaping: the phone, email, and in general, too much communication with too many people, and that goal was met during the western half of the trek. There had been no phone reception for days at a time between El Paso and Eagle Pass. When the route included urban areas with cell phone towers, I turned off the ringer and focused on the environment.

Now, the tech stuff intruded again, but I finished with sunlight and time to scout a path through Eagle Pass. My best friend from back in Missouri, Mike, was driving down from Kansas City, and we needed a plan for Old Mines Road.

Rex called to check in. He had to clear a Border Patrol checkpoint on his way to San Antonio, where the agents asked, "Why were you on the border?" Rex explained that he was taking a break from our trek, while I walked toward Eagle Pass and Old Mines Road.

The checkpoint was well inland, but these guys had already heard about us. Rex relayed his conversation. "The agents told me, 'I'm law enforcement and I don't go down there. He might be okay during the day but I wouldn't be there at night.' Another agent said, 'There's a lot of stuff going on down there that doesn't get on TV. He better have an armed escort.'"

Rex told me, "I know you are a big boy, but you might want to consider skipping Old Mines. You could turn north to Carrizo Springs and follow 83 to Laredo. We have to survive this trip."

Another sobering conversation.

I called Mike to relay the address for the hotel in Eagle Pass.

Mike asked, "How's it going?"

"Pretty good, except for all the shitheads trying to run over me. We should have an exciting stretch of road on the other side of Eagle Pass. On a positive note, Old Mines doesn't get much traffic, so we won't need to dodge many vehicles."

"Are you carrying?"

"I will be."

Oscar and his family arrived the next morning. A relative had passed away in Mexico, so they would drop me in Quemado before crossing the border to attend the funeral. Later in the day, Oscar planned to pick me up at the hotel and take me to the 4-H meeting.

Oscar's wife and kids quizzed me during the ride to Quemado. With his family in the truck, I mainly focused on the positive aspects, which far outweighed the negatives.

We stopped in Quemado and I posed for a photo with Oscar, and another photo with his family. Oscar said, "If we don't get hung up in traffic I will come to get you so we can tour Maverick County."

"I'd enjoy that very much."

Open irrigation canals flooded nearby fields. A man pulled up in a truck and rolled down his window. "Where are you going, brother?" A placard on his door indicated that he worked for the water authority that monitored and controlled the irrigation canals.

I explained and asked him about Old Mines Road.

"It used to be that you would run into cartel people with AK-47s down there. But it's more controlled now."

I wondered, "Does this mean fewer people with AK-47s? Or are they just carrying pistols now?"

The highway passed through more floodplains and eventually climbed back into scrubland. It took an hour or two to reach the intersection where I left my truck the previous day. A man (we'll call him Rhett) was sitting in his yard with a can of beer. When he saw me he stood up and yelled, "David!"

I paused as Rhett walked to the fence surrounding his yard. I recognized him from our two conversations the day before.

Rhett said, "It's not David, is it?"

"No, but that's okay. My name is Mark."

"Mark! You know, I'm drunk off my ass."

I could tell.

"Come around and grab a seat."

I thought, *Oh boy,* but I reluctantly acceded to his request, while thinking, *It takes some doing to be wasted before lunch.*

A small dog yapped continuously. Rhett said, "He's a cross between a miniature Doberman and a Chihuahua." He looked over at me. "You're a *vagabondo* aren't you?"

"That's not a bad description."

Cars steadily rolled by, just fifty yards away. Rhett said, "The traffic never stops. This is the river highway, and it's the main route for everything. We are only two miles from the river here."

Rhett shared his philosophy. "Look, I'm a mess. But when I get down I say 'Jesus! Jesus! Jesus!' There is power in his name. Say it to yourself. 'Jesus, Jesus, Jesus!' It will power you up."

"Oh, Jesus," I whispered.

"What woods are your walking sticks made from?"

"Longleaf pine and sweetgum. They are the Yin and Yang of trees in the southeastern US."

"Do you have a thermos? I can make you some tea."

"No, I don't have a thermos, but I'd be happy to share a cup of tea with you."

Rhett went inside to boil some water while I wrote in my journal.

Rhett exited the house. "What type of trees are those walking sticks made from?"

I explained again, that they were longleaf pine and sweetgum.

Rhett had lived all over, but was basically a Midwesterner that ended up two miles from Mexico, isolated from most of the world. He said, "This is not my home. It's not bad here, but I need to move on sooner or later."

He went back inside to retrieve hot tea that he poured into a plastic bottle. He also gave me a small New Testament in Spanish, a CD of Gregorian chants, and a bag of pomegranates from a tree in his yard.

I thanked him for his generosity and said, "I have to hit the road. I've got miles to go."

"I understand. What were those walking sticks made from? I'm sorry I keep forgetting."

"Sweetgum and longleaf."

"All right. Good luck, Mark."

The miles went somewhat faster. There was extra incentive to hump it since my alma mater, Missouri, was playing Alabama for the Southeastern Conference Football Championship at 3:00 p.m.

An hour after my afternoon tea with Rhett, a familiar sedan drove past. I shook my head as Rhett did a wobbly U turn and slowed to a stop on my side of the road. He wasn't wearing a seat belt and he was still drunk off his ass, but he had brought a hot, greasy, scrambled egg sandwich on toast. I thanked him again and ate the sandwich while pushing for Eagle Pass.

Eagle Pass spreads out for several miles along 277. The egg sandwich was long gone and a restaurant named La Parrilla was a welcome sight. I wandered in and knocked down a *platillo mixto con una coca cola* while checking the football game on my phone. It was halftime and Alabama was only up by seven over Missouri. There was still hope.

I made it to the hotel, popped a beer, and watched the second half as Mizzou went down in flames with a final score of 42-13. It was the second consecutive week that the Tide beat my Tigers: first Auburn, then Missouri.

After the game, I showered and donned my cleanest shirt while waiting for Oscar. They got held up in traffic on the way back from Mexico, so Oscar drove me directly to a livestock arena for the 4-H meeting.

In my youth, our 4-H club met at Bill's School House on Highway D, in rural Chariton County, Missouri. My dad had attended Bill's until he graduated from 8th grade and switched to Marceline High School. The old building was a one-room schoolhouse with no indoor plumbing, and I remembered 4-H as a quintessentially white program for farm boys and girls.

As the meeting time approached, the room filled with about eighty kids and their parents. Maybe five or six of those in attendance could have passed as Anglos, but they probably weren't. Witnessing these Latino youth, with their attendance and enthusiasm for a program aimed at educating rural youth, I thought, "Maybe the family farm isn't dead. There's still hope."

The meeting started with everyone standing and reciting the Pledge of Allegiance to the American flag. Then a pledge to the Texas flag. And then the 4-H pledge:

I pledge:
My Head to clearer thinking,
My Heart to greater loyalty,
My Hands to larger service and
My Health to better living for my club, my community, my country, and my world.

Minutes and old business were followed by new business, including upcoming events such as: a food drive, a toy drive, a 4-H Council Meeting, and the 2015 Maverick County Junior Livestock Show. With that, Oscar Galindo provided an introduction and asked if I could describe my walk for the young audience.

"Thank you for this opportunity. My name is Mark Hainds and I was raised as the sixth generation on our small, diversified family farm in Missouri. I left the farm and went to college where I achieved a Bachelor of Science in Forestry Resource Management and a Master's of Science in Forest Biology. I worked for about two decades in dual positions as a Research Associate for Auburn University and Research Coordinator for a nonprofit organization called The Longleaf Alliance.

"This fall, I resigned those positions and traveled to El Paso where I started walking at International Mile Marker #1 on October 27th, 2014. I am following the road or trail that is closest to the border between Texas and Mexico, and my ultimate goal is Boca Chica Beach on the Gulf of Mexico, just past Brownsville.

"I am an author, and this walk will provide the material for my second book. As pitched to my publisher, the manuscript will contain, more or less in equal parts: a description of the environment from the Chihuahua Desert to the Rio Grande Valley, and my experiences along the way: the people, the foods, and the culture of the border area.

"I can tell you that in the Midwest and the South, where I grew up and where I live, the perceptions about the border could not be further from the truth. They think this is a war zone, but the people of El Paso were courteous, their streets were clean, and the statistics bear out my impressions, that El Paso is one of the safest cities in North America.

"Mr. Galindo mentioned that I was in 4-H during my youth. Thinking back to those days, I realized that my first speeches were in 4-H. I remember being a shy kid who was terrified to give those presentations, but 4-H provided my first opportunities to speak in front of groups of people.

"For the last two decades, I worked from Texas to Virginia, teaching landowners and professionals how to restore and manage the longleaf forests of the Southeastern US. I give hundreds of presentations annually, and I trace my education and speaking ability to my membership in 4-H. It helped me get past the shyness. It furthered my knowledge on many topics and left me wanting to learn more. I encourage you to stay involved in 4-H, to learn as much as possible, and to develop your speaking abilities. It will serve you well."

"I'll be glad to answer any questions."

"Can you explain a typical day?"

"I generally get up around 5:00 a.m., to tape and bandage my toes and feet. I fill my backpack with food and water, and eat some breakfast. Around 6:30-7:00 a.m., either Rex or the Tex-Mex Compadres drop me at the endpoint of the previous day's walk. I aim for a little over twenty miles per day. This typically requires walking from before sunrise to around 4:00 or 5:00 in the afternoon. The Compadres pick me up if I am staying in a hotel. Or, I pitch a tent in remote areas. In the late afternoon or evening, I meet with and interview people along the way: botanists, farmers, ranchers, historians, etc."

"What has inspired you along the way?"

"The people have been so kind. I've been offered rides. People let us stay in their house. They have fed us. My faith in humanity has been elevated."

"How are you going to pay them back?"

"I was walking through the town of Presidio and I met some people with the city government. One of them asked me, 'Will you be able to come back and look us in the eye, after you have written this book?'"

"I answered, 'Yes. I will tell the truth about my experiences along the border.' So far, my experiences with the people have been uniformly positive. The cities have been safe. The people have been great. The rest of the country is wrong. This is not a war zone, and that story must be told. And with my book in hand, I will retrace my steps along the border, and I will be able to look them in the eye."

After the presentation we shared a wonderful meal of home-cooked tamales, rice, beans, and many other Mexican-American dishes.

Oscar asked, "Would you be willing to be interviewed for a local cable news program?"

"Sure. No problem."

I ate supper beside Mrs. Molina, who lived on a farm a few miles past El Indio, the last community east of Eagle Pass, on Old Mines Road. Her husband worked for the Customs and Border Patrol at a station where a blimp/aerostat was tethered on Old Mines. Mrs. Molina explained that the blimp outside Eagle Pass, like the one between Marfa and Van Horn, scanned for low flying aircraft trying to evade conventional, ground-based systems. The Federal Government described these blimps as "tethered aerostats that deploy radar." She invited us to visit her farm if time allowed.

Oscar made some phone calls and shortly after supper a young Anglo showed up with a video camera. I delivered a shorter version of my earlier speech and answered a few follow-up questions.

After the interview, Oscar and I walked to the parking lot, where we heard drums beating in town. Oscar said, "Let's go look for the drum-lines. They start at the Catholic Church and walk through town in the week before Christmas. It's a tradition in many Latin Communities."

This was my second visit to Eagle Pass. The previous New Year's Eve found me at the Eagle Pass Inn, during a scouting drive along the border.

That night, I was on the phone with Katia and Joseph when the fireworks started, early in the evening of December 31. At midnight, I watched from the balcony as explosions reached a crescendo and the sky lit up in every direction. The booms continued until two or three in the morning. Eagle Pass's fireworks display is unmatched in North American cities where Anglos are the majority. In my experience, the only compa-rable New Year's festivities were from Lima, Peru, but it is probably the same across Latin America.

On that New Year's Day, I continued west for my scouting drive. Just outside Eagle Pass, a road-killed javelina lay on the right shoulder. Javelina (or collared peccary) are similar in appearance to pigs and are native to several countries in North and South America.

At the top of the next hill I did a U-turn and circled past the carcass. After another quick U-turn I steered onto the shoulder. It only took a moment to photograph the carcass and return to the Saturn, long enough for a Texas State Trooper driving east to do his own U-turn and pull behind me with lights flashing. I turned off the Saturn, rolled down my window, and extracted my driver's license as he approached. He was a young, rather cheerful looking Hispanic trooper wearing a bulletproof vest. At the car window, he inquired, "Is everything all right?"

"Yes, sir. I know it sounds silly, but I stopped to take a picture of the road-killed javelina." All the while thinking, *How do I get myself in these situations?* and *Is photographing road-kill considered abnormal behavior in this jurisdiction?*

He smiled, which did not imply that he believed the story. "Where are you headed?"

"El Paso."

"What's in El Paso?"

I sighed and answered, "This is a scouting run. I am choosing a route because this time next year I intend to walk from El Paso to Brownville."

"Why?"

I pictured myself back at the office: the emails, the phone calls, and the messages that stacked up while I was still on the phone talking with the last person to get through. My train of thought had become so easily derailed that it was nearly impossible to complete significant projects. Of necessity, I left the building for short strolls through the forest surrounding our headquarters. For a few minutes, flowers, insects, the breeze, and bird songs facilitated an escape from a harried existence behind the desk.

On one of those strolls, someone asked, "Who are you?"

I looked around, but no one was there. The voice came from a man whose life, happiness, and mental health were being consumed by a two-decade career. It was not the future he imagined as an undergraduate in forestry school.

A recent introduction to the literature of Cormac McCarthy had stirred my interest in west Texas. Back in the office, I examined maps of cellular coverage of the southwest. Vast areas of the Chihuahuan desert were beyond the reach of existing cell towers… and the destination was set.

I did not mention this line of thought to the Texas State Trooper. It was sufficient to say, "The walk will provide material for my second book."

He didn't bother with my driver's license. While walking back to his car he tossed back the bemused admonition, "Be safe!"

My best friend was driving down from Missouri for one of the toughest sections of the border walk. Mike had left Kansas City that morning at 4:00 a.m. Fourteen hours and one thousand and seven miles later, he arrived at the Country Hill Inn. Partway down, he had attempted to fill his car, and the credit card company blocked his card, forcing him to call his wife, who wired $200.00 to an HEB Grocery Store in Eagle Pass.

We moved Mike's stuff into the hotel room. As always, his gear was organized and packed efficiently. Mike once told me, "How you arrange your things is a reflection of your mind."

Picturing my desk and office I replied, "I'm so screwed."

Mike and I had known each other since childhood, growing up in rural, white, conservative, north-central Missouri. We survived the carnage of our teenage years, losing numerous classmates and good friends along the way. In big cities like Chicago and St. Louis, kids may die in gangs or from random violence. In the country, drinking and driving rural roads at break-neck speeds exacts an equally fearsome toll.

Both of us aspired to more than the poverty-level factory or farm jobs of rural Chariton County, so we joined the military and took advantage of the GI Bill.

I ended up in forestry, while Mike majored in accounting before becoming a Special Agent for the Federal Government.

We both counted the years till retirement, after which we would hunt, fish, forage mushrooms and berries, and enjoy the scores of activities that country boys daydream of while their careers grind them into the ground.

Mike started parenting earlier than I did. The youngest of his three children was the same age as Joseph. And now that Mike had arrived, it was time to let him in on the secret.

"Well, Mike, I have something to tell you. Katia is pregnant."

"Congratulations! That's going to keep you working for a few more years!"

"We've pretty much kept it under wraps. It took so long to get a second one on the way, I've been scared to jinx things by spreading the news. Now it looks like we are reasonably safe. The doctor says there is little risk of losing it at this stage."

The next morning, Sunday, December 7, we ate a quick breakfast downstairs and headed out the door. Mike wanted to walk with me, but Rex was still in San Antonio. We needed to shuttle vehicles.

We drove both vehicles past El Indio where we parked Mike's van on the side of Old Mines Road. Then we drove my truck back to the hotel. Mike reassured me his van was insured and its loss wouldn't cost him any sleep. I was spared a day of high anxiety, not worrying about my truck on Old Mines Road.

Mike and I were still walking through town when a man stopped his car and asked, "Are you the guy walking from El Paso to Brownsville?"

I said, "Yes, that's us."

Mike clarified, "He is walking to the Gulf. I am just with him for one week."

"I just wanted to wish you 'Good luck!'"

"Thank you very much." As he pulled away I told Mike, "He must have heard about me from someone with kids in 4-H."

Partway through Eagle Pass we picked up FM1021, or "El Indio Highway." It angled out of town heading southeast. Mike was in good shape, setting a fast pace that was hard to keep up with. But how long he could maintain it?

One of the big draws for Eagle Pass was an Indian casino. We passed several hotels that were out of our price range. The occupants were probably in town to deliver their hard-earned dollars to the Kickapoo Lucky Eagle. Casino traffic was heavy on 1021, with customers and employees traveling back and forth on El Indio Road. We both breathed a sigh of relief after passing the turnoff to the casino, about eight miles out of town.

Mike and I kept walking east on El Indio. Traffic was reduced to a vehicle every few minutes, where most of the automobiles were Border Patrol or oil and gas trucks. The driver of an unmarked Border Patrol truck stopped to chat with us. He had a K-9 in the back seat, and he appeared to know about my trek. He said, "If you need water or any assistance, let us know."

The day was going well. Neither of us felt threatened by the conditions around us, though the earlier, heavy traffic had been hazardous.

There were still several miles to El Indio when we spotted and smelled an enormous dead sow lying on the side of the road. It had a rope around its neck, a rather curious road kill specimen.

A few miles farther and we walked into a road-kill massacre. Someone lost a bag of corn along the highway. The corn attracted a group of javelina, and a passing vehicle had intersected with the herd, scattering three carcasses around the corn.

While we walked, we discussed a plan of action should pedestrians appear on the road.

Mike carried his firearm, and as a cop, he was more practiced with a sidearm. I elected to leave my pistol in the room until we were farther down Old Mines. I would do the talking since Mike only knew a few basic Spanish commands like "Manos arriba!" while I could carry on simple conversations.

Mike would stand farther back and to the side, allowing a field of fire if things went downhill. I had to be prepared to get out of the way.

A large abandoned feedlot covered several acres on our left, with a recessed gate in the surrounding fence. A black pig nosed through grass in front of the gate. I said, "Lookie there. A feral pig. If he were near the truck, we could shoot and cook him at our campsite. But that's probably a bad idea here. I'll get some pictures."

I eased forward with my cell phone, taking photos as I advanced. The pig detected me and froze in place.

Mike said, "He's got a bad front leg." Three legs were extended and steady while the fourth leg was folded at the first joint, giving the pig an off-balance stance.

I kept slipping forward, taking photos as I went. The pig was trapped between the fence and me, and he knew it.

In the blink of an eye the pig charged straight toward me. Reflexively, I kicked with my right leg, smacking the pig square on the snout and knocking it down. It must have been a painful blow because it took the pig a moment to regain its feet and limp into the grass. Now I felt sorry for the animal.

Mike was laughing.

I turned to Mike. "Wow. He has spunk."

Mike said, "I've only walked with you part of one day and I've already seen you survive a charging wild boar. You dominated him."

We were still chuckling at the top of the hill when another truck slowed and pulled over in front of us. I told Mike, "It's Oscar Galindo."

After the introduction, Oscar handed us some burritos. "My wife made them for you."

"You made Eagle Pass a highlight of my trip. Thank you and your family for everything you have done."

We quizzed Oscar about the road ahead. He said, "My brother drives it about once a week for the county (Maverick). You have to go slow because it is very rough, but it can be driven."

An hour later, Mike and I stopped to eat the burritos, about six miles west of the community of El Indio. Mike was holding up well and we were making good progress. Considering the one hundred miles between Eagle Pass and Laredo, we had significant ground to cover. And each time a Compadre walked with me, the day went faster. It was especially fortuitous to have a witness for the great boar attack.

We made El Indio in the late afternoon. Like many communities along the route, it was equal parts inhabited and abandoned buildings. El Indio did support a small store across from an abandoned post office. We bought some cold drinks and sat outside for a brief rest.

Mike took a picture of the hollowed-out post office, saying, "I'll send this to Amy." His wife worked for the U.S. Postal Service.

There was an intersection in town, where FM 2644 teed into FM 1021. We were walking south on FM 1021, which was still identified as "El Indio Road" on this section, but it would be identified on most maps as "Old Mines." The road that Rex hoped we would take, FM 2644, ran west to Carrizo Springs.

I told Mike, "That's our last exit. From here on it's the road our mommas warned us about: drug runners, cutthroats, Pancho Villa's descendants, and other assorted desperados. Are you up for it?"

"That's why I'm here. To keep your dumbass alive."

18

OLD MINES ROAD

"With few exceptions, everyone tried to discourage me from taking the trip. I was accused of everything from having a death wish to being ignorant of border realities."

Keith Bowden. *The Tecate Journals: Seventy Days on The Rio Grande.* 2007

Javelina: Drawn by Ava Bailey

December 8–10

MIKE'S van was a welcome sight in the gathering dusk. Our first day on the fringe of Old Mines Road had proven uneventful, save the charge of the wild boar. We relaxed on the ride to Eagle Pass, wondering if the perils of Old Mines Road were overrated.

Rex was waiting at the hotel, having returned from San Antonio. He asked Mike, "Are you up for two days in a row?"

Mike answered, "I've always been better than Mark at pretty much everything, so I have to try."

It had taken an hour's drive just to get back to the hotel. The next day, we would have to drive twenty-five miles past our ending point. Leave a vehicle. Then drive back to just east of El Indio. That was seventy-five miles on roads where we might average thirty-to-forty miles per hour.

We left the hotel at 6:00 a.m. on December 8th. I drove my truck and Rex drove his. By the time we staged my truck and Rex dropped us off near El Indio, it was 8:15 a.m.

Any vehicle parked along El Indio/Old Mines Road was bound to draw attention, so Mike placed a note in the windshield:

December 9, 2014

Vehicle belongs to Mark Hainds.

He and Mike Powell are part

of a team hiking from El Paso

to the Gulf of Mexico

MP

The road was paved and lined with high fences that took a beating; the wire had been pulled down on almost every post. Over the years, vast numbers of people had crawled up and over the woven wire. The signs of so much human passage lent an ominous feel to the surroundings.

We walked past a gate and a side road that led to buildings and a tethered blimp. A couple of young Border Patrol agents pulled up, so we solicited their experiences along Old Mines.

Mike said, "We see where a lot of people have been going over these fences."

The agent riding shotgun said, "The ranchers put up ladders, hoping they will use them instead of climbing over the fence."

"Do you see much wildlife out here?" I asked.

The same agent replied, "We see shackled coyotes and sometimes we'll be driving along with our head out the window looking down for tracks, and a bobcat will lunge out at us because it is caught in a trap. It scares the hell out of us!"

It would scare the hell out of me too.

They had heard about my trip and, based upon how far I had already come—making it through Quitman Pass and Chispa Road—they thought we had a decent chance at making it through Old Mines.

After they left Mike told me, "Experiences like this have convinced me that if I ever write a book, it will either be fiction or about drinking. It sure as fuck won't be about walking twelve hundred miles."

I questioned Mike about a subject that had been troubling me for quite some time. "You remember how the little town of El Indio looked like it was on its last leg?"

"Yes."

"Since I started walking, El Indio has been the rule rather than the exception. Outside El Paso, the country is depopulating. They're moving to the cities, or at least somewhere else. Little communities like Fort Hancock, Esperanza, Sierra Blanca, virtually everything in Hudspeth County. And if you do a search on the internet for "Hudspeth County," the highest profile webpages will be the Sheriff telling his population to 'arm themselves' against the drug runners. I didn't see and I can't find any evidence that things are more dangerous today in Hudspeth County than they were fifty years ago. But the population is hightailing it, and the Sheriff is basically telling the world, 'This is a dangerous shithole of a county to live in.' He seems to be doing his part to scare away anyone who might want to move there. Why?"

"Well, it gets him resources. Extra firearms, extra personnel, more attention."

"But he is benefiting the Sheriff's Department at the expense of the civilian population."

At the same time, unbeknownst to me, the Sherriff for the largest county in Texas (Brewster) was thinking and saying the same things I had just told Mike. In a March 1st article by the *Texas Observer*, Sheriff Dodson was describing Texas political candidates when he said, "A lot of politicians are running on securing the border. One's got a six-point plan, and one's got a nine-point plan. They're throwing tons of money at this border. I wish they'd just shut up about it."

Sheriff Dodson explained in the same article, "I think they're just throwing money at the border for nothing. I think people on the interior see all these shows about the border where there's violence," he says. "That's a problem for places like Brewster County, the home of Terlingua, Lajitas and Marathon, where tourism comprises a large part of the local economy."

If small communities in other west Texas counties hoped to persist for another generation, they needed to tap into those same tourist dollars that Brewster County relied on, but it wouldn't happen if tourists got their information from the Hudspeth County Sheriff's office.

I explored the bright side of fearmongering on the border. "After my book has sold a million copies, I'll finally have the money to buy some serious acreage. As long as these rural sheriffs keep scaring people off the border, it should depress land values and I'll be able to buy twice as much ground!"

Mike was all for it. We have, I believe, a pact whereupon we'll both get rich, buy thousands of acres, and hunt any and every critter in North America at our whim.

Another Border Patrol agent stopped in front of us. He exited the vehicle and approached. There were Captain's bars on his lapel. "Do you know where you are?" Unspoken but implied in his tone, "You dumbasses."

Mike and I laughed, but he was having none of it.

"We just had an oil/gas employee and an electrical contractor assaulted out here. This is a very active area." His radio went off in his truck. "Excuse me they are calling." He returned to his truck.

Mike and I looked at each other. I said, "We aren't camping here tonight."

"Nope."

The Captain returned and pointed ahead, "The pavement ends and past that is no-man's land. You won't have a signal. We can't even use our radios out there. If you get in trouble you can't call for help. We find an average of fourteen bodies a year down here, and we save countless more. Sometimes their kidneys are shutting down, but we save most of them. The middle of Old Mines is between our sectors. We pretty much don't go there. I just want you to be aware of the situation."

This was the Old Mines Road we'd heard about.

The pavement ended and our diligence heightened. If one side of the road was fenced and the other side was not, we hugged the fenced side. Anyone with bad intentions would have to cross the road or climb the fence to accost us. I scanned the ground like the Border Patrol, looking for signs of recent human passage.

A truck approached from our front with a crew of roughnecks. The driver stopped beside us. He wasn't smiling. "Do you know where you are?"

We didn't laugh the second time.

"We're starting to figure it out," I answered.

"You don't need to be out here after dark."

"We have a truck down the road. We'll haul ass when we get there."

They shook their heads and drove toward Eagle Pass.

I told Mike, "I only remember being asked that question twice in my life and both times were today."

The road was a straightaway and there were three dark dots head. Mike said, "We have pedestrians."

Mike dropped his pack. He pulled his pistol and chambered a bullet. He placed the pistol in the belt behind his back and shouldered his pack.

They were about two hundred yards out. I pulled out my phone and snapped a quick picture in their direction. My phone recorded the time of the photo as 1:22 p.m. I put the phone in my pocket and said, "I'll go in front."

Because the previous day had been uneventful, I left my pistol at the hotel. If needed, I would employ my walking stick or roll to the side giving Mike a free field of fire. If they were just undocumented crossers, things would almost certainly turn out well. If they were with the cartels, we couldn't know how it would play out.

Mike had experienced his share of tough situations. In his early career, he worked undercover, buying serious quantities of drugs in the toughest Midwest projects. He once bought two loaded assault weapons whose barrels had just cooled down from a shooting, and Mike was as serious as I'd ever seen him.

We converged in the middle of the road.

Two young men looked between seventeen to nineteen years old. The third guy was a little older, stocky, and inked with ominous prison/gang tattoos. The two young guys were silent. The elder of the trio spoke in English. "Our ride didn't show. Do you know where we are?"

I choked a little while biting my tongue.

I paused to compose myself, while keeping eye contact with the tough guy. He spoke English without an accent. Mike was positioned to my rear right. The man facing me looked and sounded like he was out of a big city street gang. He may have been deported and just crossed back in. He was probably acting as a coyote for the two young guys, and they didn't have a backup plan when their ride didn't show.

"You are in the middle of Old Mines Road between Laredo and Eagle Pass. It's forty or more miles to anything from here."

"We've been walking for two weeks. Do you have something we can start a fire with?"

They had no packs. No water. No food. And relatively clean street clothes. There was no way in hell they'd been walking for two weeks. If that had been the case, their clothes would be shredded and filthy.

I maintained eye contact while my hands went to the water bottles on the outside of my pack. They accepted the water and granola bars from my exterior mesh pockets. There were matches and a lighter buried in my pack, but it was too risky to look for them. I answered indirectly, "We're not camping here."

One of the young guys drank half his bottle and offered it back to me. I motioned for him to keep it.

The tough guy asked, "How far is it to the highway?" while pointing to the desert scrub east of us.

"About thirty miles. You won't make it. You need to stay on this road. Someone will come along."

"Okay. Please don't tell anyone you saw us."

"I won't."

They walked toward Eagle Pass, and we aimed for the truck.

As soon as they were out of sight, I turned to Mike. "Holy shit!"

"This place is crazy," Mike replied.

"Did you keep the pistol in your belt?"

"I kept my hand on it the whole time. They knew what I had. If there had been more of them I would have held it in the open."

We talked it out while covering ground as fast as possible, or about three miles per hour. At the top of a hill, fresh sign caught my eye. "Wow. Check this out. It looks like a dozen or so just crossed the road. These tracks are smoking hot."

Mike pointed to a dark spot. "One of them pissed in the road right here. It's still wet. They could be watching us."

"Most of these tracks look like they came from street shoes." Many of the tracks had smooth soles or minimal tread. "They weren't wearing boots. I don't know what that means."

Later, I realized that shoes without tread would be harder to track, leaving more shallow indentations on the soil.

I was tired. Mike's ass was dragging. And it was still several miles to the truck. We saw more fresh human sign, including another crossing point where someone else had urinated in the road.

We tried to recall landmarks that would give some indication as to how much farther we had to walk.

"It was dark this morning, but there was light glinting off some type of a reservoir to the right," I commented.

"We haven't passed any big bodies of water," Mike said.

"And I remember a wooden bridge."

"No bridges yet."

We reached a plateau with visibility of at least a mile. "We were coming off high ground and the water was to the right. Maybe over the next horizon, on the right," I said hopefully.

We reached the next horizon, and no body of water.

We walked through a dip in the road and climbed to another long plateau. Mike said, "It all looks the same. But this kind of feels right." We walked another one to two miles to the end of the plateau: still no water.

"We are taking breaks, but at this pace we should make it to the truck before dark," I said. "I don't think we can miss that reservoir."

Another long plateau stretched out before us. We stopped for a break and took a seat on three tractor tires that were chained together for a Border Patrol drag.

I observed, "They have a drag here but we haven't seen a vehicle since Captain Silva this morning. This is still no man's land."

I thought back to our encounter with the three border crossers a few hours earlier. "I hope they don't try to make the highway. They won't make it. They aren't cut out for that ground. They didn't even have water! On that subject, I'm down to about a liter. I wish I had more to give them, but I wasn't about to bend over and rummage through my pack."

"They walked into this fix," Mike said. "They can blame themselves for their predicament."

"There have been some puddles along the road. If it comes down to it, we can filter some water." My filter was in my backpack. "But I'll have to be pretty thirsty before I drink that nasty looking stuff."

The road traveled another long plateau. No choices in the matter, just one step after another. Eventually, we approached the southern end of the high ground, and a reservoir appeared on the right.

"Thank God!" said Mike.

"That's it! That's what I saw this morning. Now we have to cross a bridge. Then we should be getting close."

It was several more minutes of walking before we made it to the bottom of the slope…. and a wooden bridge. Our spirits lifted further. But we weren't there yet. We walked uphill while brush closed in from both sides. The road curved back and forth so it wasn't possible to see very far down the road. Near the top of the hill we rounded a bend and found the truck.

"Hallelujah!" I jogged to the truck, dropped the tailgate, dumped my backpack in the truck bed, and retrieved two ice-cold Tecates from the cooler. Mike took a seat on the tailgate and removed his boots as I popped the top and handed him a beer.

I told Mike, "Dude, that was epic."

"I was slowing you down."

"No. You sped me up. All my best days on distance and speed have been when people walked with me. This is two consecutive days over twenty-five miles. That's killing it."

I secured the coordinates for the truck and flagged some brush alongside the road. We turned the truck around and started the two-hour drive back to the hotel over the washboard road. There was no sign of the three border-crossers. We still hadn't seen another vehicle, so it's doubtful their ride picked them up. They either hid at our approach, or they were attempting to make the highway to the north. There was a glimpse of black moving east of Old Mines, but it was just a sounder of feral pigs moving through the brush.

It was dark when we arrived at the hotel. Mike told Rex about our run-in with the border crossers, describing the encounter play by play.

"I like your strategy of sending Mark in first," Rex said.

I resolved to find a higher class of associates upon the completion of the walk.

It would be our last night in Eagle Pass. Just getting to and from the Old Mines had required four hours of driving on December 9th. The following day, Rex would go ahead to secure a hotel in Laredo on the other end of Old Mines Road.

Mike and I decided to try something different; we would leapfrog. Mike would drive the truck five miles ahead, park it, and walk back to meet me mid-way. We would walk together for the remaining distance to the truck, repeating the process until we'd had enough.

Old Mines was surreal in the early morning hours. Miles upon miles of deserted countryside, then a glow appeared in the distance, where a generator powered a light tower, typically illuminating a gate and a guard shack. Behind the gate lay private lands and a road to an active work site, where oil and gas people installed wells to extract petrochemicals. This limited activity was on the ends of the road, with no illumination in the center of the hundred-mile stretch.

At 7:45 a.m. Mike let me out along Old Mines, before driving the truck five miles ahead.

I would spend half the day walking by myself, in an area where fences still bore witness to heavy human traffic. This time, my pistol was in the bib pocket of my overalls.

The landscape had been fairly open for our first two days along Old Mines, with the brush pushed back behind Border Patrol drag-lines and fences. Now shrubs and trees encroached upon the road, creating a tunnel of green. This effect was especially pronounced along lower wetter portions of the landscape.

Still, I stopped worrying about people after encountering a multitude of wildlife species. A cottontail rabbit hopped a few times and froze a mere fifteen feet away. A doe and a buck ran away to my left. Then three more deer ran away toward to the Rio Grande. Another doe and a mature buck stopped broadside at one hundred yards. As a lifelong hunter, I reflexively calculated yardage for each game species.

Before I knew it, Mike appeared in front. He turned around and we covered the remaining distance to the truck: the first five miles gone in a flash. Knowing the truck's location relieved anxiety and sped the pace.

Mike leapfrogged ahead as the surrounding lands offered up a menagerie: a javelina, fifteen ducks, three coyotes, a roadrunner, two bobcats, and a caracara.

I finally came across a Border Patrol agent, the first in forty miles. And there were more gates with light fixtures and guard shacks. In the distance a semi-trailer pulled off Old Mines and turned onto a side road. The guard remained on the road shoulder as I approached. He asked, "Where are you going?"

After I explained, he said, "I floated part of the Rio Grande when I got back from a tour in Iraq. I'd like to see more of it."

"Do you see many border crossers here?"

"They see the lights and come to us at night to ask for food and water. At that point they have already given up, and they ask us to call the Border Patrol."

"How much farther would they have to go to catch their ride?"

"From this post, it's 19.5 miles to the highway east of here (US 83) and fourteen miles to the pavement on Old Mines. The Rio Grande isn't any distance. We're very close to the river."

A steady stream of semi-trailers hauled material for erecting oil or gas wells. Frequently, the drivers held a water bottle out the window as they slowly drove past on the wash-boarded road.

I topped a hill and found Mike parked on the side of the road. This was not good. Based upon my pace, he had only moved the truck two miles down the road. Mike placed the jack and tools back in the truck and I asked the obvious, "Flat?"

"Two tires. I changed one and another is leaking."

"What happened?"

"I must have run over something in the road. I heard the hissing and one tire went flat immediately. Then I heard another one leaking air. I thought, "What the hell do I do now?" I looked around and found a screw that I stuck in the hole. I'll drive in and try to get them fixed before this one goes all the way flat."

"I'll ride with you." I quickly flagged the location on the roadside and recorded the coordinates. This part of Old Mines was still outside the range of any cell towers.

Tons of oil and gas traffic rolled down the eastern end of Old Mines Road. I told Mike, "We might be able to hitch a ride if necessary. And we won't run out of water. Several trucks have given me bottles."

Mike pointed out, "Some of these work trucks have air compressors, and they might give us enough air to make it into town."

Mike drove as fast as the wash-boarded road would allow. I told Mike,

"The guard over the last hill told me that it's fourteen miles to the pavement. These flats are wearing me out."

My cell phone picked up a signal as we approached Laredo, and the map function identified a tire place on the west side of town. The tire was low, but we made it before the tire came off the rim. They fixed both flats and we drove back to Old Mines.

Mike dropped me off and leapfrogged the truck forward. We ended the day before dark and began the long process of retrieving Mike's van. We then drove through Laredo to a Holiday Inn Express on the east side of town, where Rex had already moved in.

It had been a very long day, complicated with two flat tires, but we still finished with twenty-two miles. And, we had successfully traversed the imposing, lawless, central section of Old Mines Road. Some residents of Eagle Pass had informed me that property owners along Old Mines were resisting efforts to improve the road. I don't know their reasoning, but I agreed with the sentiment.

There's just enough outlaw in me that I'm partial to some portions of our country exceeding the reach of law enforcement and government entities. Nothing prevents the Border Patrol and the Drug Enforcement Administration from flying over Quitman Pass, Chispa Road, and Old Mines, but they generally keep their personnel on the fringes of these remote border areas. To walk these roads is to step back in time, to something resembling the frontier days when Oklahoma and lands west were still territories, and the average traveler was as likely to meet Native Americans or a band of ruffians as they were to come across pilgrims in a horse-drawn wagon.

In the wild west of today, the Native Americans are the Spanish-speaking cowboys from Pilares and Candelaria.

Instead of bank robbers and cattle rustlers, outlaws on the border carry marijuana by the bale.

Modern pilgrims in search of a better life do not speak Victorian English and travel west in a Conestoga wagons; they walk north and speak Spanish.

Some people may desire a border fence along the south and west edges of their property, manned with government employees twenty-four hours a day. They should be mindful that they just might get what they ask for.

Putting up a border fence, manning it with thousands of additional Border Patrol agents, and building the roads to support this infrastructure essentially means the pacification of some of the wildest and remotest lands remaining in North America. It means the expansion of the government's reach into the most remote borderlands. Isn't that anathema to libertarians?

It's even more preposterous to consider erecting a wall along the privately held, mountainous stretches east of Big Bend National Park. It would take a skilled mountaineer to make it through many of those stretches, making the wall superfluous. And for every landowner who wants the fence, there are multitudes that want nothing to do with it. For the government to erect a continuous wall would require invoking eminent domain on a grand scale.

In short, the pro-wall position is untenable in a world bounded and based in logic, geography, and reality.

From the day's ending point forward, Old Mines Road was paved, and most of it was high-fenced. The wire was still pulled down by most of the fence posts, and articles of clothing, especially shirts and gloves, hung from the upper-most strands.

Toward the center of Old Mines Road, there had been virtually no Border Patrol presence, so people who got tangled in the fence had time to work their clothing free from the barbed wire. But the ends of Old Mines were heavily patrolled. If their clothing got wrapped up, they left it behind in their hurry to get to the other side.

Some border-crossers climbed the wire between fence posts. Having grown up on a cattle-farm, this was an inexcusable fence-crossing faux pas for two reasons. First, the greater the distance from the fence posts the less support for the wire and the fence crosser. Climbing the wire between posts is difficult because the fence is wobbly. Second, crossing between posts tends to pull the wire farther down the post, damaging the fence.

I shared an idea with Mike. "After this trip, I am going to Mexico and set up 'Mark's Border Crossing School.' We'll instruct students about: fence crossing etiquette, reading a compass, proper hydration, water filtration, and proper footwear. I may provide gear at reasonable prices."

"They will post your picture at every Border Patrol office from here to California with the caption, "Bring him in bleeding or crying, we don't care which."

"You don't think they'd appreciate my humanitarian efforts?"

"No."

Later that morning, a Border Patrol agent topped a hill and pulled over to check me out. While we talked in front of his truck, Rex pulled up, and then Mike. I pointed to the fence and a glove hanging from the top wire. "There's lots of evidence of past crossings. Is it still active here?"

"Oh yeah. Some of these guys can scale these fences in the blink of an eye. If they get hung up they just leave clothing like shirts and gloves and hit the ground running."

With all the oil and gas traffic, one may have expected more refuse along the roads, but these truck drivers and roughnecks were surprisingly good about not tossing trash. The road shoulders were no more littered with debris than those of the previous counties. One exception was on Old Mines Road; the shoulders were covered with work gloves. I kept the cleanest and newest and handed them to Mike every few miles.

Old Mines intersected with highway 255 on the edge of Laredo. Semi-trailers loaded with freight plied the roads to the left (east), to the front (south) and to the right. If one turned right, they would follow 255 west to the Laredo-Columbia Solidarity International Bridge. Texas DOT says this crossing is known as the "Columbia Bridge" on the American side.

This intersection marked the end of Old Mines Road. On the opposite side, "Old" was dropped and the road was simply "Mines Road," as the four lanes continued south into Laredo.

Old Mines had lived up to its reputation. It was one of the most challenging portions of the trip. A few hundred miles remained, and the equally notorious Old Military Road was still ahead, but it felt like the worst was behind us.

19

LAREDO TO SAN YGNACIO

"I think life would be much better if the speed limit were three miles-per-hour."

Jennifer Pharr Davis. *Becoming Odyssa*. 2010

December 11–13

ADRIAN Billings, the young doctor from Alpine, tracked down Keith Bowden's phone number for me. I hoped to catch the author of *Tecate Journals* before Keith dropped off the grid. He was retiring from Laredo Community College and planning a move to Langtry.

Keith returned my call and we scheduled an interview for the afternoon of December 11th.

"How do we find you?" I asked.

"I used to tell people 'Go downtown and look or ask for the white guy.' There may be another white guy or two down here now, so come to 1704 Iturbide."

Rex was laid out with a bad sinus headache on the evening of December 10th. Mike and I walked from the Motel 6, crossed some parking lots, and took the only available seats at a bar in the restaurant El Capataz. The food was outstanding, and the barkeep mixed us the best drinks of the trip. After covering twenty-seven miles that day, we had healthy appetites.

The next day's walk started with Mike dropping me well before first light, in front of a gravel quarry. At the end of the previous day's walk we had watched front-end loaders dump rock into large machines that noisily vibrated it through grates, sizing the gravel before hauling it away on trucks.

There was minimal traffic before sunrise. Mines Road was a divided highway with two northbound and two southbound lanes. Dirt trails provided decent walking along much of the route, and Mike planned to continue leapfrogging the truck as we moved through Laredo.

Sections of the dirt trail terminated in ditches full of water, or walls of mesquite and huisache, forcing me back to the shoulder on the west side of the southbound lanes.

The road shoulders were covered with a treasure trove of license plates, gloves, and reflectors. After accumulating a load of junk every few miles, I'd dump my collection in the back of the pickup, take a seat on the tailgate, and drink something cold from the cooler.

Both the east and the west sides of Mines Road were lined with gigantic terminals for major truck-lines, while thousands of semi-trailers plied the road. The traffic became more congested with big trucks as the day progressed and we moved south.

I became increasingly nervous about my truck. If the wrong person saw it parked on the side of the road, a crooked tow-truck driver could wench it onto a flatbed, cross the border, and my F-150 would be in Mexico before lunch.

Mike harbored the same concern. He parked the truck at the junction of Mines Road (FM 1472) and US 83, where our route would turn south. Rather than walking back to join me, he stayed to organize all the junk we had collected along the road.

When I arrived at the truck, he said, "I had just finished in the back of the truck, and I was standing by the rear passenger door cleaning up the back seat. I saw this guy on a cell phone across the road, but he didn't see me. He crossed the highway and came straight for the truck. When he came around the back of the truck he was still talking on the cell phone. I asked him, 'Can I help you?' He spun around and took off. He was planning to break in or steal it outright."

"Damn. I'm glad you stayed this time." I told Mike, "I'm going to angle south here on Santa Maria Avenue. It's one of the closest roads to the border and I want to see as much of the town as possible."

Mike drove ahead while I walked through a rundown industrial district with more big truck terminals, before entering a blue-collar residential neighborhood. It was approaching midday and I was hungry. The first neighborhood restaurant along Santa Maria was Las Cuatas. The waitress brought me a menu and I texted the location (4403 Santa Maria Avenue) to Mike.

My order consisted of three tacos: picadillo, chicharrones, and frijoles con queso. Mike arrived and I helped him navigate the menu and place an order. We were the only Anglos in the restaurant. Counting employees there were about ten Hispanic people in view. Excepting Mike and me, everyone in the restaurant was obese. Maybe this said something about the food at *Las Cuatas*, but it also spoke volumes to the habits of low-income working class Latinos in Laredo. The weather was fine outside, but people were not walking from point A to point B. They drove, they worked, and they ate.

The two countries I am most familiar with in Latin America are Peru and Brazil. When traveling the streets of Lima, Peru or Santos, Brazil, it's obvious that the majority of the populace still walk several miles a day. The sidewalks are full, and a tiny portion of the population on the streets is obese.

In Texas, Alabama, or Georgia, citizens will spend five minutes circling a parking lot in their SUV, to save ten yards of footwork.

When I do make a winter trip to the Midwest, Christmas holidays in rural Missouri inevitably entail a trip to Wal-Mart, the behemoth that vanquished most of the small-town stores of my youth. And it never ceases to shock and sadden me, witnessing the bloated population of today, and comparing it to the people I knew thirty or forty years ago.

Either we learn to walk, or the consequences will be cataclysmic. The real sign of the apocalypse reads, "All U Can Eat Buffet," accompanied by a photo of a 44-ounce soda, a fried vegetable, and a Moon Pie.

Mike and I finished lunch and returned to the hotel prior to the Keith Bowden interview.

That morning Keith had called the biggest newspaper in town, the *Laredo Morning Times*, and a local news station (KGNS). The *Laredo Morning Times* told us they wanted to send out a reporter and a cameraman. It wasn't clear exactly when or where we would meet. For flexibility we took two vehicles to Keith's place downtown.

We parked on the street and exited the vehicles. A tall, lean man that I recognized from his author's photo walked straight toward me and offered his hand. "I know you are Mark because you're the skinny guy!"

Keith invited us upstairs to his apartment. A trashcan outside his kitchen was filled with aluminum cans. A significant portion of the aluminum was Tecate, but there were plenty of cheap American beers in the mix.

I asked Keith about his book title, *The Tecate Journals*.

Keith told me, "Don't get me wrong, I like Tecate. But I would never have named a book after a beer. That was the publisher's idea. During editing they told me, 'Don't cut anything about the beer!'"

There was a conspicuous lack of furniture in Keith's house. Either he didn't entertain guests on a regular basis, or he had disposed of his belongings in preparation for an imminent departure.

Rex selected a back porch for the interview. The room had several windows and good light. Keith sat in one corner, while Rex stood behind his video camera in the opposite corner. Mike and I took seats on the floor and out of the frame.

Keith asked me, "Are you walking in those shoes?"

"Yeah. People have said, 'Man, those are too heavy.'"

"They don't look heavy."

"They aren't. I've put 550 miles of training on these boots. I've got two pairs and I've walked about 750 miles on this route. Between the two pair, about 1,300 miles."

"In my book I talk about a fellow that walks about 250 miles to work."

"Yes! What did you say? He carries a can of sardines?"

"A plastic grocery sack with sardines. One can per day and some limes.

When I met him he had a brand new pair of work boots. And I remember thinking, 'Lord, that would be about the last thing I would walk in.' And when I got home, the first thing I did is phone his employer. He gave me a lot of resistance, denying he knew the guy, that kind of stuff. But he finally admitted, 'Yeah, he made it all right. He always makes it, but he is never in very good shape because he doesn't sleep (on his walk from Mexico).'"

"God! Two hundred and fifty miles!"

"Through rough country. I'll show you a picture of the terrain. Anyway, his employer said, 'Did you see those boots he was wearing?' And I said, 'I sure did. I'll never forget them.'

And he said, 'You know, we had to cut those things off him because his feet were so swollen.' And he said, 'First of all, he wouldn't let us do it, because he valued the boots so much. I had to go all around Fort Stockton until I could find a pair almost identical to that pair that he had, because they were new. I bought a pair and put them on the nightstand next to his bed, and told him, 'Don't worry if we cut these boots. You are still going to have a pair of boots.'"

I said, "Holy crap!"

"He didn't read. Didn't write. Didn't add. Nothing. Finally, I said. 'Did you ever go to school?' And he said, 'Not a day in my life.' And I said, 'Why not?' And he said, 'My dad didn't want me to. He needed me at home.' As a result, he was paying all this money for his youngest daughter to be in private school to study ballet and piano. It was quite a story. Because this guy went to extraordinary length to compensate for his lack of education. He was embarrassed, and he was going to make sure none of his kids went through that."

"That's quite a story," I said. "In your book, you only mentioned the 250-mile walk, so the context is amazing."

Keith and I bantered about the editing process until Rex was finally set up.

Rex said, "Hey, Keith, before we keep going, would you mind setting it up by introducing yourself as the author of *The Tecate Journals*. Could you explain what it is about?"

"Hi! My name is Keith Bowden. I wrote a book called *The Tecate Journals: Seventy Days on the Rio Grande*. The book explores my trip from El Paso to Boca Chica, which is the end of the Rio Grande at the Gulf of Mexico. I spent seventy days traveling the river. First by mountain bike, because the early part of the river up by El Paso is not passable in a boat. Then by canoe, raft, and then canoe again for the last 635 miles. I did most of it alone. And the book is, as the title suggests, in journal form, basically my experiences along the way as well as some overview of the different towns, cities, history, and social commentary of various places along the river."

"Tell us about that!"

"There are so many things we can touch on. First of all, I think there is a very real misperception that the border is actually a border. That it divides, but it really doesn't divide. The border is what unites us. And people want to think of it as some sort of arbitrary line in which the world differs on one side vs the other. And that's, in fact, the way Border Patrol and the U.S. Government treat it. But I like to think of the border as a number of strata in this region, and these strata are within what we call the 'checkpoints.' The Border Patrol checkpoints going north, and the Mexicans have checkpoints at approximately the fifteen-mile mark going south, on all their roads. That world between the checkpoints is what I think of as the 'Border,' not a specific line delineating Mexico from the United States."

"Interestingly, to me, we've always been treated differently. This is, in fact, called a 'border zone.' And our laws have always been a little different from the rest of the United States. For instance, not too many years ago there was a lot of controversy about allowing Mexican trucks into the U.S. And people to the north were outraged, but we've always had Mexican trucks."

"Another thing is immigration law. You can go across the river and they can come over here fairly easily. But to pass the two checkpoints, a very small percentage of Mexicans can pass that checkpoint. And for us to pass the checkpoints on the Mexican side we need insurance, we need a vehicle permit, and it is quite expensive. And their immigration/customs crossing the bridge into Mexico are very lax, but when you get to what they call the 'vente-seis,' or the twenty-six, which is the checkpoint, they are just as tough as the U.S., if not tougher."

"Anyway, we've always been what they call 'twin cities.' Not just Laredo and Nuevo Laredo, but Eagle Pass and Piedras, Acuna/Del Rio and, El Paso/Juarez, all of them. We're kind of an island between San Antonio in the north and Monterrey in the south."

Keith continued, "And I think, if you're going to talk about the border, you want to understand island culture as much as anything. Because even though we are not near the sea, we have a lot in common with island culture."

"It bears mentioning that we are a really difficult place to define or categorize or put into any sort of paradigm. Because we are so much a part of two, rather than one or the other. In language, we mix languages. In culture, we are just as likely to listen to Mexican music and watch Mexican TV as we are American music and American TV. When we speak English, we use a lot of Mexican words that we translate directly to English. One of my favorites, every time I hear it I get a kick out of it. A girl will tell me, 'Sir, I turned on my cigarette.' Because that is it coming from Spanish."

"Other examples?"

"They'll say something like, '*Que hiciste Saturday en la noche?*' 'What did you do on Saturday in the night?' '*Hice mi* homework.' 'I did my homework. Aah, I am just playing!'"

"So, you can't really understand us, meaning us on the border, unless you understand not only the two languages, but the mixing of the languages, and why we use these words; the English words verses the Spanish words."

Rex asked, "What can you say about United States border policy, especially as it pertains to, basically, the militarization of the border?"

"That's not 'basically.' That's what it is, militarized." Keith shook his head. "It's a travesty, this militarization of the border."

"How so?"

"I like to tell this story: I went with a reporter down to the water plant on the river. We were just exercising on mountain bikes. And these two fellows ran on the Mexican side, from the top part of the bank down to the river shore, and they had inner tubes. And then, a moment later two women ran down, got in, and these fellows swam them across, right to our feet. That is not an unusual sight. If you hang out at the river you will see it often."

"The unusual part of the story is that after the women disappeared, one of the two guys got out of the water, came over to me, and told me in Spanish, 'You are Border Patrol, aren't you?'"

"And I said, 'No, come on.' He said, 'Yeah, you are.' And we went back and forth like that. And I finally convinced him. And he said, 'Well then, he is!' He pointed to my friend, who was also an Anglo."

"No, neither is he." He said, 'Oh, you guys are full of it. We all know the game.'" I said, "No, I don't know the game. What is the game?"

"He said, 'You are here counting.'"

I said, 'What am I counting?'"

"He said, 'You are counting how many people I bring across, so that I will have to pay per head. I came over to talk to you because I want you to understand that the other fellow and I are returning. So we are not paying for us. We are just paying for the two women.' And that is a little bit disturbing. So I started asking around. It didn't take but a few phone calls, a few conversations, and I learned at that time, about six years ago, for $1,500.00 you would be guaranteed delivery to San Antonio, via corrupt Border Patrol."

"On a personal level, I like almost all the Border Patrol guys I've ever met. But if you are going to have an agency in which it is common knowledge that people can easily circumvent these checkpoints, there really is no point, because it costs a tremendous amount of money, and it is a tremendous inconvenience for us. Besides that, it is tremendously—by design—racist. In the sense of, if you are brown, you are going to get a lot more attention than if you are not."

"My girlfriend is from Canada, and when she comes down we go to the checkpoint and they ask, 'Are you American citizens?' And she says, 'No, I am Canadian.'

'Have a nice day.' They don't even ask for an ID. In fact, the one time they did, she couldn't find her ID right away. They asked us to pull over and about three minutes into her looking through the luggage for her ID they said, 'Aah, just forget about it. Go ahead.'"

"Now, if you were Latin American and you forgot your ID, I can't imagine the nightmare you would be involved in."

"Another problem, and I can't speak if it is current, because a fellow told me it is not, is the difference in treatment on the Canadian Border versus the Mexican Border. It is night and day. They don't even have checkpoints. They have a very small Border Patrol presence. I paddled a canoe along two border rivers. There is nobody. There is free passage. Americans canoeing. Canadians canoeing. People camping on either side. No checkpoints. No Border Patrol boats. No Border Patrol vehicles. You might see one a week."

"Given that the justification for all this attention we're getting is primarily immigration, well, we have plenty of people immigrating via Canada, including at least one guy in the September 11th attacks. The last I heard, we import more marijuana from Canada, in dollar value, than we do from Mexico."

"So it seems to me there is a sort of systematic racism against Latin Americans. And unfortunately, I would say most people here on the border, the majority anyway, would consider themselves "Latin American" and experience it firsthand. Many, to my surprise, don't mind at all. There's a fair number of border residents who are quite in favor of all that Border Patrol attention."

"You go to downtown Laredo, you will probably see more law enforcement and people involved in prosecution, whether they be court people or attorneys, than you would people that are not (involved in law enforcement). I don't know the numbers, but I know it is many thousands in terms of Border Patrol, sheriffs, LPD, DEA, ICE, and all the apparatus of the local and federal courts. It's got to be the biggest part of our economy."

Rex asked, "Can you talk about building a wall around the country? What kind of message does that send?"

"The wall is the worst idea I have ever heard of. First of all, when you get down in the valley, you will see the wall. You won't see it from the main highway, except in a couple of places. But if you just detour off the highway along the road that parallels the border, there is a wall, and then there is an opening. Not a small door with a lock. You can drive vehicles in both directions. And those openings are frequent. It is not like there is one, and then you have five miles of wall. They said the purpose was to force all the people who are crossing into those openings. So instead of having to patrol, let's say, one mile, they only have to patrol six openings within the mile. Well, I don't know what kind of logic that is for the amount of money they spent on that wall."

"Before they built the wall, I thought the most cogent argument against construction was: We will basically give the river and the floodplain along the river to Mexico, because you are not allowed to go on the other side of the wall, theoretically. And you are not supposed to pass through these openings to go down to the river. Well, our best resource, if you ask me, is the river. It is the reason we are here. We would never have settled in Laredo or Eagle Pass or Roma downriver, Rio Grande City, if it weren't for that river."

"But we don't, as American citizens, seem to want to have any part of that river. If you go down the river you will see the Mexican people use it quite a bit, for anything from having a picnic, to bathe in it, swim in it, fish. You won't see anyone on the American side except the Border Patrol. I don't know if we are not there because of the Border Patrol. I don't think we were ever there. I just don't think we use the river and I can't explain why, except a lot of students I have talked to over the years believe that it is dangerous, it is filthy, that if you come in contact in with the water you will contract a disease, which is definitely false."

"We don't have much wall upriver at all. I continue to spend a lot of time on the river, probably forty to sixty to days a year, but it is all in the area upriver of Laredo where there's no wall. The only thing that's really changed, is there's just a lot more Border Patrol than there was even five years ago. A tremendous Border Patrol presence to the west of here. Places that you visited on the way, Langtry, Comstock, Del Rio. They must have made a ten-fold increase in agents because they are everywhere now. But, not at the river very often."

Rex asked, "Earlier you mentioned how border towns were much like islands. Can you explain what you meant?"

"We are so removed from everything else—like Laredo is removed from the rest of the United States, and Nuevo Laredo, from the rest of Mexico—that we have a very insular culture. In that sense, we're the insiders. And all those people from other places are tourists. We treat them with a bit of suspicion. Are they here to abuse us? To exploit us? There is a perception here in Laredo that outsiders tend to be pushy and rude."

"Outsiders believe we have an interdependency with other border places. But we are isolated from them as well. We should share a lot in common with Eagle Pass or Roma, Zapata, or you name it. But we don't go that direction. We look south to Monterrey, and we look north to San Antonio and Austin. We don't go up the border. We don't go down the border. I would guess that a very small percentage of people from Laredo have even been to Del Rio, which is three hours down the border. El Paso/Juarez may be the biggest border city in the world, and a very tiny percent of our population has been there. I don't think we are even aware of the commonalities of our experiences."

"Then with the border, there is also, boy I don't know if this going to be very popular to say this, but there is this Anglo/Latino thing that we don't experience here in Laredo, and really Eagle Pass doesn't either. But the valley and Del Rio and El Paso do. The Anglos or the whites were the landowners. They were the powerful class. They insisted on English. They very much exploited the locals. And there is still resentment about that in certain sectors of the local population. We never had that. Here in Laredo we are so overwhelmingly Latino, I believe our Anglo population is under four percent. Even then I am not so sure those people would check the box for whatever "white American." I believe many of them would check Latin American."

"You always had to assimilate into Spanish/Mexican culture. You couldn't do anything as an English speaking only (person). You were shut out. There were no business contacts. There were always ruling families from our inception, and they were always Spanish. We [Laredo] were the only city to establish itself on the north side of the river. Every other border city was first on the Mexican side, and then over the course of time, eventually a sister city developed on the American side, always smaller, and always heavily dependent upon the southern side."

"I don't know if you saw this, but we're the city of seven flags. I think we are the only one in the United States. We've been under seven different countries. In fact, we were the capitol at one point of our own short-lived Republic. That's our seventh flag. The six flags are.... I feel like I am making you write a lot there, Mark."

My hand was about ready to detach from my wrist.

Rex said, "It's almost like a plantation mentality. I sensed a little bit of Anglo/Latino tension along the way."

"A huge amount. It's huge in West Texas. I can tell you right now, because I have this conversation all the time. It's my biggest preoccupation, living as an Anglo in a Latino culture. Boy there is so much racism against Latinos. And white people aren't even aware. They would get angry if you told them, "You know, you are being perceived as racist." But the Mexicans, boy they feel it, and they feel it big, especially to the west, where there is a bigger Anglo presence."

"I don't know if you knew that long after the desegregation act, we still segregated our schools here, Mexican and Anglo, until 1970. People my age would have gone to elementary or junior high in either a 'Spanish school' or an 'American school.' The railroad in the west divides, to a pretty stark degree, the Mexican side from the Anglo side of town."

"Here it is different because we don't really have to deal with Anglos very much. I don't think people feel the same way. In the valley (Lower Rio Grande valley), you'll see that, especially with educated people. People who worked as migrant farm workers come back either really politicized and anti-white, or they love it and wish the valley were like North Dakota."

"Even though the twin cities of the border have a lot of commonalities, there are really important things, like the fact that so many people in the valley have traveled north. In Laredo, no, we don't have that. We don't have a population that is aware of much beyond San Antonio. And the Dallas Cowboys, of course, who are universally adored along the border, no matter how bad they are, or how good."

Rex asked, "Can you tell what it is like living as a gringo in a predominantly Latino culture?"

"Oh, it is wonderful. But, if you are going to live here, I don't care what you were born as, if you are going to adjust and enjoy life here, you have to become this place. I don't see myself as a gringo."

"If you remain an outsider here, you are going to be very unhappy. Because there is not a lot of community for outsiders. Everyone that I worked with at the college left as soon as they retired. They were never able to assimilate, because they didn't feel part of this."

"I had some really powerful experiences on the plus side. Unfortunately, when I came here my daughter had just died. So I saw firsthand how much warmer those people were to me in Mexico and here in Laredo than the people where I am from in Houston. People up there had a hard time consoling me. Death was something you didn't really even address. Whereas here, it was, 'We are going to take care of you.'"

"I can remember, I probably don't want to say this on tape, but I really don't care. When I first came here, I played baseball across the river for a number of years and the team I played on was sponsored by the Gulf Cartel. And they were wonderful. We would have the greatest time. They would send me a maid, anything I wanted. It really made that transition from shock and grief, to, okay, life goes on. It was an impressive and memorable experience."

"One day the manager of the team told me, 'The boss is here.' Meaning the boss of *Tejas*, or the Gulf Cartel, had arrived and, 'He would like to meet you.' They took me out beyond the fence, and there was a Mercedes with tinted windows. All of a sudden, the window came down, and there was a fellow who is infamous, or was. I think they might have killed him. And a bodyguard, and a driver. And he was just nothing like we would think of those fellows. He was soft-spoken, cultured, and very sensitive. It is hard to believe, given what has happened in the last ten years."

"And he said in Spanish, 'I just wanted to tell you that we are grateful to have you playing on my team.' And I told him, 'I am very grateful. This has been the most enriching thing I have ever done. This has almost saved my life.'"

"He said, 'They told me about your daughter. This seems highly ironic now. Who knows why God does these things, takes away our flowers, and leaves behind our shit.' But he said, 'I am deeply sorry and I hope you will continue to play with us.' And the irony, because of these experiences with these fellows, in subsequent years when it became a war between the Zetas and the Gulf Cartel, I would root for the Gulf Cartel like they were the Cowboys. 'Go! Get them!'"

"Here on the border, we can't take it as seriously as the media to the north want to portray it, because it is not. There is a lot of ugliness when people can't resolve differences. Unfortunately for us, our ugliness has gotten more attention than the rest of the world's combined. And it is sad because we are not that type of society. I don't see ugliness and violence very often. I believe we had three murders last year, and we are a city of almost 300,000 people."

"I can remember being in Houston in 1981. I remember there was in excess of seven hundred murders. I never heard anybody from the north telling me, 'Oh, you live in Houston. You better be armed.' We had three! And people think you will get shot if you walk out the door. It's not a problem in isolation. It's a problem contributed to by both countries. They are now armed because American gun interests thought it was important that every Mexican who wanted one should have access to an AK 4, 15, or 47, whatever it is. It's not that these people act independently. Everything on the border is a result of binational efforts."

Rex added, "If the violence in Memphis was sensationalized as much as it is down here, no one would go to Memphis. Why is violence sensationalized so much here?"

"Boy, it would just be a guess, but I think we have never been respected in this state. And nationally, I don't think they even know we were here. I always think back to a close friend that I taught and coached on the baseball team. He was here a couple of years, and then he went back to Chihuahua, where he was from. We were sitting in the plaza in Batopilas, at the bottom of Copper Canyon. I was there as his guest for a baseball game. He worked for the Department of Education in Chihuahua."

"He said, 'I am not sorry that I went to Laredo and the United States, but I was a little shocked by the experience.'"

"And I said, 'Why?'" He said, 'I was deeply hurt that you do not respect us at all, let alone like us. That is very difficult. Because here in Chihuahua, we're a state with a lot of pride. We've had a lot of success economically and in education. Many of our cultural icons in Mexico come from Chihuahua. Maybe I was naïve,' he said, 'but I thought I would get treated the way I was treated at home, and that wasn't the case. I am not saying you guys are racist, but you don't like us, and that was obvious to me. When we would travel north of here, we would walk as a team into a restaurant, and you could feel it.' He said, 'All these brown Spanish speaking people, and people would turn away and drop their heads. It's unfortunate, and I was not sorry to leave. I hope we don't do that to you.' Meaning, we Mexicans don't do that to you white Americans.'"

"It's hard to communicate the depth of the prejudice that people from Latin America feel in the United States."

About that time, Rex noticed the reporter and cameraman for the *Laredo Morning Times* were outside on the street, so I went down to meet them: Gabriela A. Treviño, the reporter, and Victor Strife, the cameraman.

Gabriela and Victor seemed impossibly young. Conversely, I must have appeared impossibly old. Judging by her line of questioning, she may have wondered how I got out of bed in the morning, never mind walking across town.

Gabriela asked, "Where did you start?"

"I started at International Mile Marker #1 in El Paso on October 27th."

"How did you get from there to here?"

"I walked."

"From El Paso?"

I thought, *You wouldn't have much of a story if I just drove here.* But I didn't want to be a smartass. She would write the story and that put me at her mercy.

"Yes, I walked from El Paso. I started a little slower, but now we are getting about twenty-five miles per day."

"Where do you go from here?"

"We hope to make Boca Chica Beach on the Gulf of Mexico by December 23rd."

"How will you get there?"

"I will walk." I smiled. This young lady must have found my journey bordering on unfathomable. She was either coming to the conclusion that this was a story worth telling, or she was about to write it off as science fiction. She appeared to settle on the former because she bored into the "Who, What, When, Where, and Why" of the story. Victor clicked away with his camera while Gabriela continued the interview.

After Gabriela finished with me, Victor had me pose in front of some older buildings on a corner just east of Keith's house.

Rex wrapped up his interview with Keith, and I joined them upstairs. I told Rex, "The reporter would like to interview you if you don't mind."

"Not at all." Rex went downstairs and Keith told me, "Channel 8, KGNS (NBC in Laredo) would like for you to come by for an interview."

"Excellent. It will be a short mileage day, but it has been a real honor to meet and talk with you. Can I give you a copy of my book?"

"No. Pete Billings told me you gave him a copy of your book, so I will read his." Keith handed me an old hard-back book, *The Wind That Swept Mexico.* He said, "I'm cleaning off the shelves. This is worth reading."

I had brought my copy of *The Tecate Journals* with me. Keith autographed it with the inscription:

For Mark,

I sure enjoyed our meeting

and admire your border walk. Thanks

for visiting.

Keith Bowden
Laredo, TX
11 Dec. 2014

After the Bowden interview, Mike drove me to the TV station for a fifteen-minute on camera interview, before carrying me back near *Las Cuatas*, on Santa Maria Avenue.

Laredo was reminiscent of Florida's older cities, with its Spanish heritage and downtown streets lined with orange trees, pecans, or palms. One city square was particularly attractive with towering palms and municipal buildings.

Channel 8 News sent a cameraman to film me along four or five stretches of Laredo. Light was fading at his last stop, just before an intersection with US 83 or Zapata Highway, where Mike was waiting in front of a chicken shack called *El Pollo Feliz*. We discussed the day's activities at some picnic tables outside, over grilled chicken and accompaniments.

Mike's time was drawing to a close, and the route home was pretty straightforward. "I just realized that is the terminus of I-35. I'll get on 35 and take it to within a few miles of my house. I have already done the entire north end of this interstate, so I will have driven every mile of I-35."

Back at the hotel we caught the news on Channel 8. They previewed a section with the headline, "Man sets out to find out whether the border is safe."

My walk was a bit more complicated than their simplified description, but it was interesting to see which parts of the interview were culled or included for the brief segment.

The next morning's walk started at *El Pollo Feliz*. The sun wasn't up at 6:30 a.m., and barking dogs marked my passage through a residential neighborhood along the dimly lit Texas Avenue. A dark street led to US 83, which was my route south for the next several days.

The skies had lightened as I approached Laredo Community College. A man turned in at the college before stopping and exiting with a water bottle. He walked in my direction and introduced himself as a professor named "Tito." "I saw you on the news last night, and I wanted you to know that we appreciate what you are doing."

"Thank you. By the way, do you know Keith Bowden?"

"Yes, he's with the north campus. I teach here on the south side of town."

Mike leapfrogged the truck and the miles accumulated. Another truck pulled over beside me. It was an older Anglo with white hair, a white mustache, and a cowboy hat.

He rolled down his window and said, "I saw you on TV last night. Don't fool yourself. I live right here and we have to sleep with the doors locked and a gun by the bed. You take care of yourself."

That was certainly a different take on border safety. Why the differing attitudes on safety and life along the border? From my limited experience in the border cities, where the vast majority of the population resides, reality did not match up with perceptions held by the rest of the country. The statistics simply didn't support the perceived threat.

According to a report from 2010, the FBI ranked four cities as having the lowest violent crime rates in North America: Phoenix, San Diego, El Paso, and Austin. All four cities are in border states. Since the report was issued, violent crime had trended down, and these cities were even safer.

Later, I would find an analysis of FBI statistics by the *Austin American Statesman* that revealed an uptick in some crimes among the most rural, least populated counties. While overall crime numbers trended down, there were outliers.

In rural areas along the border, some people saw a threat behind every bush. It's possible, even likely, that they reside in active smuggling corridors where the world is more dangerous.

At the same time, some portion of the white population equated the browning of the landscape with every negative stereotype that many white Southerners and Midwesterners apply to blacks.

The two-lane US 83 turned into a construction zone as they converted the road into a four-lane highway. Road graders, compactors, pavers, dozers, and backhoes operated over a ten-mile stretch of 83. Where possible, I walked the west side of the road, while most of the equipment operated on the east side. When the banks on the west side became too steep, I crossed to the east side, until heavy equipment forced me back across the road.

Mike was waiting on the west side, midway through the construction zone with another truck and a young man parked beside him. Mike introduced us. "This is Daniel Barrs. I told him about your walk."

Daniel said, "Hello, Mark. I had to meet the guy who's walked all the way from El Paso. I've been out here for four years, but I'm from Madison, Florida."

"Do you know the Blantons?" I had known and worked with these farmers/nurserymen from Madison for about fifteen years.

"Sure do."

"Are you going to stay out here or move back to Florida?"

"I married a girl from Laredo, and we just had twins. Her dad owns the concrete plants in Laredo. I told my bosses, 'If you treat me bad, I've got a place to go!'"

Daniel said, "I heard you were a pig hunter."

"Mike must have told you about my first book. I enjoy hunting pigs, but I haven't had time for it lately."

"I'm getting into the Dogo Argentinos. We run pigs down by the river. I'd be happy to take you for a hunt sometime."

Dogos Argentinos, as the name implies, are a breed of dogs originating in Argentina. Typically white in color, they are renowned for their loyalty and ability to bring down large game, like the wild boar.

"That would be great. It can't happen before I finish the walk, but I'll be back for a book tour, and I'd love to see your Dogos catch some pigs."

I added, "I picked up one of your hardhats on the road."

"I'm surprised you didn't pick up a dozen. I bring some of these guys out for their first day of work. I drop them in the morning and they are gone by lunchtime."

We discussed hunting for a while before Mike said, "Look over here." A small, two-foot long western diamondback rattlesnake was curled up beside my truck. He coiled into an S-posture and rattled at our attention.

Daniel said, "There are some giants around here. A week ago, we killed a six-footer by the lodge."

I neglected to engage on the subject of killing snakes. Mike and I took a few photos of the rattlesnake, and Daniel went back to work overseeing all the crews along this section of the road.

There were still several miles of construction ahead, and a group of workers watched my approach. One of them said, "I saw you on TV last night. How far have you got to go?"

"About two hundred miles."

"Good luck!"

I'd been on television several times over the years, and none of those appearances garnered such a response. Either my previous interviews were unremarkable (likely), or this interview had touched on a visceral topic for people along the border (also likely).

A south facing sign beside the road read, "Laredo, population 236,091."

Laredo's vehicular traffic ran around the clock. Besides law enforcement, the economy appeared to have two major drivers: trade with Mexico and the oil and gas boom. Unless NAFTA is repealed, trade and manufacturing along the border should support Laredo for some time to come.

Oil and gas operations were somewhere near a peak with the advent of fracking. Brand-new, full-sized, king-cab pickups lined up at Stripes gas stations each morning. Men filled their tanks at the pumps outside, while their coworkers lined up inside for 99-cent made-to-order burritos. Thousands of these white work trucks plied the roads around Laredo.

If oil and gas took a dive, many a Texas community would crash with it. It has happened before, and it would happen again.

There were still several miles of construction ahead when Mike picked me up for the run back to the Motel 6 in Laredo.

Each Compadre had contributed to the trek in a unique way. Mike had proven the most physically fit of my walking companions. Having Mike along inspired me to cover an average of twenty-three miles a day, and that number included a short day of interviews with Keith Bowden, the *Laredo Morning Times*, and Channel 8.

Old Mines had lived up to its reputation. I may have survived the hundred-mile stretch without Mike's assistance, but it would have entailed overnight camping, filtering nasty water, a much heavier pack, and dramatically increased risks. I was dang glad to have had him along.

Mike would have passed the baton to John Dickson, but John wasn't flying into Laredo until the evening of the 14th, so Rex would cover for the Compadres until John's arrival.

Mike drove north to Missouri and I drove south to Zapata.

A gas station on the north edge of Zapata carried *The Laredo Morning Times*. My photo was prominently displayed across the front page with the headline, "Hainds' Odyssey." Beneath the photo was a Texas map with my daily end points, as prepared by Mark Bailey, another herpetologist friend from Alabama.

The Zapata Holiday Inn Express's parking lot was full of Texas State Patrol vehicles: just as Juan described in our lengthy conversation beside a high-fence between Del Rio and Eagle Pass.

I met Rex in the parking lot, as light began to fade. He exited his truck, examined the scores of cop cars and said, "Wow."

"This is a story in itself," I said.

"You're right," Rex answered.

A uniformed State Patrolman sat by the lobby entrance watching the parking lot. Examining our small mountain of gear, he asked, "Are you staying for a while?"

Although I had interacted with virtually every other branch of law enforcement during my walk, the Texas State Patrol had yet to question me. The officer looked bored stiff, so Rex and I explained the purpose of the trek. Hopefully, he would spread the word and minimize suspicions from his fellow patrolmen.

Settling into our room, I handed Rex an extra copy of the newspaper. "I haven't had time to read it yet. Let's see what she wrote."

Five minutes later we agreed that Gabriela had nailed it. Despite our worries about the youthful reporter, she had gotten the details correct and written a great article.

After some lag time, the clock seemed to be on fast forward, and at a pace of twenty-three miles per day, we were on track to finish ahead of schedule, buoying Rex's spirits. Earlier in the trip, he sometimes appeared forlorn at our slow pace and the vast distances ahead.

Though Rex saw the light at the end of the tunnel, his sinuses were still giving him fits. There were several days when he stayed in bed with a crushing headache. Rex neglected his journal and ceased our weekly interviews, where I had shared my experiences and impressions on tape.

Despite his malady, Rex got up and dropped me off in the construction zone. I soon happened upon a massive, smashed, western diamondback rattlesnake. It was longer than either of my walking sticks and backed up Daniel's stories of giant rattlers in the area.

The road crossed a small bridge, and I paused to watch four javelina rooting in a field to the right.

Rex had driven ahead to a rest stop overlooking the Rio Grande. Here, the river lived up to its name, flowing across a wide channel in the valley below.

While the flood plain was beatific, the picnic area was littered with discarded furniture and other trash. All of Texas's tax dollars appeared to be tied up in hotel bills and per diems for the Texas State Patrol, with nothing to spare for rest stop maintenance.

At the rest stop, Rex told me, "I'd like to get you walking in front of the Christmas display in the next town. Call me when you get to San Ygnacio and we'll shoot that."

It was a foggy, grey day. The road construction was finally behind me, and a delivery truck drove by going north. The vehicle did a U-turn and stopped beside me.

Jésus, the driver, introduced himself. "I saw you on the news. We really appreciate what you are doing. Take this $5.00 and stop at *Mar y Tierra*. The cook makes a great breakfast!"

I hiked into San Ygnacio and Rex picked me up in front of the post office next to *Mar y Tierra*. We drove west to the city square, just a few hundred yards above the Rio Grande, where Santa Claus and his reindeer rode across a Gazebo in a city park surrounded with sturdy benches bearing names of local citizens. Rex staged me walking past the Christmas displays and the Catholic Church.

With filming out of the way, Rex drove us back to *Mar y Tierra* for breakfast. It was a tiny, rundown building with a handful of locals sitting around a table discussing world affairs over coffee. The *Zapata News* was stacked on a table just inside the door, and I was on the front page. Rex picked up a newspaper and asked them, "Does he look familiar?"

One man said, "I saw you on the news, and then I saw you walking!"

We met everyone in the restaurant, and the cook even came out to have her photo taken with me. Rex was okay with a coffee, but my appetite was wide awake. A plate of *huevos rancheros* went down well with several cups of coffee. Everyone was kind and informative, describing the community and the history of San Ygnacio.

Back on 83, my fifteen minutes of fame was still in effect. Another car stopped so an occupant could take my picture.

I had just passed a house when a pack of small dogs charged out of the yard, with a six or seven-year-old boy right behind them. The boy tried to call them back in Spanish, but one pup wasn't minding. The kid lost his footing and fell forward, throwing out his hands to catch his fall. As soon as he hit the ground, his demeanor reflected surprise and pain. He almost certainly had cactus spines in his hands.

He needed to cry, but he looked at me and screwed up his face, trying to hold back the tears, now slipping out the corners of his eyes. The dog ran back to the boy's side, and I felt terrible. He may not have known English, but I said, "I am sorry."

I turned to keep walking. He was at home, and Mom or Dad would soon be tending his injuries. It wouldn't do for a stranger to walk into their yard with a crying boy.

I stayed on the west side of 83. Three men were nailing up rafters on a new house as I passed. One of them called out, "*Necesita algo de beber?*"

I walked over. "*No gracias. Tengo tres botellas de agua.*"

Hearing my accent, he switched to English. "Do you need something to eat?"

"That is kind of you, but a man just gave me $5.00 to eat at *Mar y Tierra*. It was very good."

"Will you take $20?"

"No, thanks. I can't do that."

Another man on top of the building said, "You should take it."

I reconsidered. Would it be an insult to refuse the offer? "All right. But I intend to write a book about this walk. If you write your address in my journal, I will send you a book or bring you one on my book tour."

Martin H. Maldonado pointed to an old single-wide trailer. "We have lived in that trailer for twelve years and I have finally saved enough money to build a house."

I described the trek to them and explained, "I am over three-quarters of the way through my walk and my goal is to reach Boca Chica Beach by December 23rd."

"When you are going out Boca Chica Boulevard you will see some oil tanks just before you reach the beach. I was on the crew that erected those tanks."

The Latinos of the lower Rio Grande Valley were hard-working, kind, and generous. And the farther I walked, the more I wanted to tell their story.

20

ZAPATA TO RIO GRANDE CITY

"But it seems to me that life made a lot more sense in this country when we made things, built things. 'It's got to the point,' my brother Sam said, 'that the only thing we make in this country is money.'"

Rick Bragg. *The Most They Ever Had.* 2009

December 13–15

US 83 led to a large bridge over Arroyo Burro, a finger of the Falcon International Reservoir, or as it is more commonly known, "Falcon Lake." Falcon Lake was created when the Falcon Dam was dedicated in October 1953. It had been one of North America's top destinations for largemouth bass fishermen, but a high profile incident scared many of the fishermen away.

On September 30th, 2010, a young couple, David and Tiffany Hartley, were riding their jet skis on the Mexican side of Falcon Lake. According to news reports, Tiffany claimed that three boats with armed men approached and started shooting. She said her husband was shot in the head and she was forced to flee on her watercraft. His body was never recovered.

The Mexican State Police sent a man to investigate David Hartley's killing and disappearance. The lead investigator was in turn killed, and his head was delivered in a suitcase to authorities in Mexico City.

The Mexican Navy exacted retribution when they attacked a drug transfer station on an island in Falcon Lake, killing twelve members of Los Zetas and recovering large quantities of arms, ammunition, and bulletproof vests. It was speculated that David Hartley's slaying happened when the couple unwittingly approached a Zeta drug stash or transaction in progress.

The story may have been a hazy memory for me, but it was still on the minds of many Zapata residents.

After dodging vehicles on virtually every other bridge along my route, it was a pleasant surprise to find a pedestrian lane on the west side of the bridge over Arroyo Burro. I was halfway across when a car stopped just in front of me. A young muscular man parked the car, exited, and jumped the divider into the pedestrian lane with me.

In other circumstances, this could have been alarming, but kids in the backseat and his smile disarmed me. His wife stepped out of the passenger side with her phone. She took a photo of the two of us, and I waved to the kids.

A few miles went by without interruption, and a Zapata County Sheriff's Deputy pulled over. I approached his car and he stepped out to ask, "Is everything okay?"

"Yes, I'm doing pretty well."

"We had a report of a person walking down the road."

It took a real effort to not reply, *Well, I'll be damned.* Or, *Oh my God, really?* Why is walking considered sinister in Texas?

Then I remembered something Rex and Mike had mentioned. "Well, there may be two of us. Someone told me another guy is walking south."

The deputy asked me, "Is he wearing a brown shirt?"

He probably wasn't a Nazi, but again I refrained from distracting the deputy. "I haven't seen him, but they told me he was wearing all black."

The deputy continued down the road and Daniel (from the road crew) stopped by with a friend in his pickup. "I just wanted to say "Hi" and tell you to keep in touch."

"I will. I want to see those Dogos during my book tour."

The city of Zapata lay ahead and forward progress slowed. An older gentleman waited on a street corner. Bill Campbell was a Methodist

Preacher who had met another young hiker named S. Matt Read along this road a few years earlier.

While I was already hiking the border and approaching Old Mines Road, I discovered Matt's blog about hiking the entire perimeter of Texas. It was disappointing to discover that I wouldn't be the first person to walk the length of the Texas-Mexico border. But our routes diverged along various stretches, and after it sank in, I was quite impressed with his fortitude.

Reverend Campbell offered any necessary assistance, and I promised to tell Rex (also a Methodist) that his service would be at 9:30 a.m. the following morning.

A few blocks later Mr. Romeo Ramirez stopped to give me a small flashlight and his well wishes. I could use the flashlight at campsites to read my Spanish Language New Testament while listening to Gregorian chants and eating pomegranates.

A building on the east side of 83 housed the *Zapata County News*. This trip had already garnered plenty of publicity, and additional recognition could lead to more interruptions than the schedule allowed.

On the other hand, these could be beneficial contacts on a subsequent trip and book tour, so I stepped inside and talked with a woman who provided the number of their reporter, Julia.

Rex picked me up at the end of the day. Back at the hotel, Corporal Medina was still standing guard over the parking lot, so I quizzed him about their operation.

Medina said, "This reassignment started back in July and August. We had troopers getting shot at every two or three days. It's settled down some since then."

"Why do you have to watch the lot?"

"We had cars getting broke into right here. They stole rifles, shotguns, and personal protective vests. That took some real balls!"

"What about these militias we hear about? Where are they?"

"They are all over the place. They are trying to help, but they really hinder us. They are generally armed, which adds an element of complexity when you approach them in the field, because we don't know who they are. The ranchers hire the militias because they are scared to death."

Rex dropped me just south of Zapata on December 14th. Two does bounced into the brush as he turned the truck toward Zapata. As the sun rose, a pair of sandhill cranes flew over, calling as they flew south.

A grey sedan passed, circled, and stopped. My celebrity status was holding strong as a young couple approached. Juan took a photo of me with his cute bubbly girlfriend, Jenny.

Farther down the road, another car pulled over. This Mexican-American man didn't appear to know who I was, but he offered a taco, some mini-muffins, and a water bottle.

After that, I made good time until a dog growled menacingly, before barking and charging out of a yard on the east side of the road. I wheeled around and advanced toward the dog, a trick that had worked before. The dog halted his advance but held his ground. It was a big brute with the head of a bulldog and mismatched eyes. The dog bared its teeth.

What next? For want of a better idea I turned to walk away, prompting the dog to charge. I turned to face the dog and swung with my right stick as it lunged for my leg. The dog evaded the short swing and went for my leg again. I fended him off with the stick in my left hand. Now the adrenaline was pumping, and I was pissed. I wound up to swing for the fences, fully prepared to fracture his skull. At the very last second, a man stepped around the corner of the house and called the dog off. The dog backed up at his command.

A combination of relief and disappointment swept over me. My legs were intact, but I wanted to hurt that dog.

A rare, open restaurant, Vanessa's Kitchen was a few miles south of the hellhound. It would be an early lunch, but I could avoid another meal of granola and dried fruits. I was unlikely to find another restaurant along the day's route. They whipped up a plate of *Migas a la Mexicana* for my consumption at an outside table.

The next bridge south crossed Tigre Grande, and the abutments on the far side had a sizable population of large green lizards. They skittered across the concrete and disappeared into crevices at my approach.

After Tigre Grande, I approached New Falcon, Texas, and a convenience store on the east side of 83. I selected a cold can of Coca-Cola and extracted my wallet, but a young lady cashier said, "It's taken care of."

"Well, thank you. That's very kind."

"We help out walkers. A man named Michael came through a couple of days ago. He's walked through this area three years in a row." She produced a photograph. "He says he is in his sixties, so he only walks twelve miles a day. You'll probably catch up with him pretty soon."

She explained that the old town of Falcon was now at the bottom of the Falcon Reservoir. New Falcon was established when they moved the population to higher ground.

Likewise, south of the border, the village of Guerrero Viejo was submerged and rebuilt as Nueva Ciudad Guerrero.

A steady stream of Texas State Troopers cruised 83, while others parked at regular intervals along the highway. A middle-aged Latino Trooper saw me coming and exited his car on my side of the road. "How's it going?" he asked.

"Pretty good. How's business for you?"

Maybe he was bored to death prior to my arrival, because he proceeded to tell stories for the next thirty minutes. He was describing his duties checking manifests on trucks entering the United States, when he paused to ask, "Would you mind if I smoke?"

"No, not at all."

"It's a terrible habit." He chain-smoked cigarettes for the remainder of our conversation.

"Ever since NAFTA it's amazing that anything is manufactured in our country. Do you remember that guy who ran for President? I can't recall his name."

"Ross Perot?"

"That's him. He warned us about that 'giant sucking sound.' Even things that are supposed to be made in this country are really made in

Mexico. I was checking a manifest for a semi-trailer load of car batteries and they were not labeled as "hazardous cargo", so I made them open the trailer, because battery acid is hazardous. It was Interstate Batteries, which are supposed to be American made. They were complete batteries except they had not been filled with battery acid. They build them in Mexico, bring them to the U.S., fill them with battery acid, and sell them as 'American Made.'"

Another State Trooper pulled over to join us. He was an older and taller Anglo with a big smile on his face. "Did you know there is another hiker in front of you? He's only about twelve miles down the road."

"They told me about him back at the Shamrock in New Falcon. She said he had come through three years in a row."

"He had on shoes this big." He held his hands well apart. "He calls himself the 'Hiking Viking.'"

"Is his name Michael?"

"Yup. He said he was sixty-two years old."

"They showed me his picture, and he looked it."

We talked a bit longer before I continued east. The conversation with the nicotine-addicted State Trooper got me to thinking about the sources of my clothing, particularly the bib overalls that had been part of my outfit since beginning the walk.

Back on the farm, Grandpa Joe Hainds wore bib overalls most everywhere, excepting church. Dad wouldn't have been caught dead in overalls, but I started wearing these work clothes at any early age. The tag on my Key® brand overalls indicated they were "Made in Mexico." Dang.

Rex carried me to the hotel in Zapata at the end of the day's walk, where I pulled out my Liberty® overalls. How could they not make Liberty® overalls in the U.S.A? Nope. "Made in China."

Carhartt® overalls were all the rage among many of my hunting and fishing buddies. The investigation continued during my next visit to a Tractor Supply, where the tags read, "Made in Mexico." Tractor Supply also carried Liberty® overalls. and it turned out their manufacturer had shifted from China to Vietnam. Of course, nothing says "liberty" quite like Chinese and Vietnamese sweatshops. That Texas State Trooper had a point.

Later that afternoon I drove to the Laredo Airport to pick up the next Tex-Mex Compadre. My friendship with John Dickson dated to his first days working as a private lands biologist with the Alabama Forestry Commission, where we were based out of the same office at the Solon Dixon Forestry Education Center near Andalusia, Alabama.

John left that job to work as a biologist with the U.S. Fish and Wildlife Service, but we continued to get together for elk hunts in New Mexico, pig hunts all over the place, and fishing trips to south Louisiana and north Florida.

John figured prominently in several chapters from my first book, *Year of the Pig*, and he was now the refuge biologist for the Tensas National Wildlife Refuge in north Louisiana. Of my close friends, John was the sole remaining bachelor. As such, he directed a disproportionate share of his income toward pursuits where I was now constrained: hunting, fishing, drinking, and wild women.

Prior to scheduling the flight, John asked, "Which airport should I fly into?"

"I hope to be finished on December 23rd, but that is going to require a lot of miles and no major interruptions. I think Laredo is our best bet."

As it turned out, my daily totals for the latter half of the trek exceeded expectations, more than making up for shortfalls on the front half. Since we were farther ahead than anticipated, I had to backtrack to pick up John in Laredo.

With John joining the trek, the next section was guaranteed to be memorable.

John emerged from the secure area of the airport in Laredo. He looked about the same as always, with a round face, shit-eating grin, but a bit more gray in his short black hair.

John looked me over. "You don't look too bad. A little thin."

"I lost weight in my upper body and face but gained some in my legs. I weighed one hundred and fifty-two pounds when I flew home in

November. That's what I weighed as an eighteen-year old, graduating Basic Training in the Army."

On the drive to Zapata I asked John, "Can you tell me that story about the Border Patrol and the helicopter? I mentioned it to Rex the other day."

"I was working around Carrizo Springs, in the middle of this ranch along the border. I had this flatbed truck with a water tank mounted on the back. It was an unusual looking vehicle, and all of sudden, this Border Patrol helicopter just appeared out of nowhere and was hovering behind me. I couldn't resist it, so I stuck my arm out the window, gave em the bird, yelled, "*Pincha la Migra!*" and floored it. They stayed on my tail for a few minutes as I hauled ass around the ranch roads. Eventually they figured out I was screwing with them, so they peeled off. I didn't hear any more from them."

From the airport in Laredo, we drove to the hotel in Zapata for one more night.

That evening, the reporter from the *Zapata County News* returned my call, and we made plans to meet the following day around Roma.

John dropped me south of New Falcon in a heavy fog, and Rex drove ahead to secure footage in Roma, where he encountered a reporter for a Mexican newspaper. Rex called, "I don't know what will come of it, but he would like to interview you. If you are interested, I will give him your contact information and let you make arrangements."

"Lunchtime in Roma should work. This other reporter from the *Zapata County News* is going to meet me along the road before then."

Rex provided directions to an overlook on the Roma Bluffs, offering a view of the river and the Mexican city of Ciudad Miguel Alemán. "It's very third world. You'll see goats grazing, old cars, and shacks."

"I had my camera set up and this guy was standing by the Rio Grande. He watched the Border Patrol drive by and then he just waded across the river! I couldn't believe I caught it on camera."

Several hours later, the road turned southwest to downtown Roma and the reporter, Julia, from the *Zapata County News*, walked toward me. She apologized for being later than anticipated. "I didn't expect you to walk that fast. Is it okay if I join you?"

"Sure. Why don't we watch for a place to eat? Do you know any good restaurants in town?"

"No, I know it's not too far from Zapata, but I don't eat down here that often."

"Pretty much everything tastes good when you are as hungry as I am."

I slowed my pace so Julia could keep up as we entered Roma. The first restaurant was a chicken place a few blocks into town. I asked, "Will this work for you?"

"That's fine."

Rex called to ask, "Did you make it to Roma? The reporter would like to hook up for a story."

I gave Rex the address and he passed it on to Julio.

Julia asked, "Where did you get to eat while you were passing through Zapata County?"

"*Mar y Tierra* in San Ygnacio had a great breakfast and was a lot of fun. There was Johnny's Barbeque in Zapata. And Vanessa's Kitchen south of town."

I asked, "What's the story locally? It feels safe to me, but I hear this is a hot zone. The Border Patrol has been warning me about this area for the last several hundred miles."

"It's pretty safe in Zapata County. We've lived here for a long time and there just isn't that much crime. You've probably heard about the incident on Falcon Lake?"

"I seem to remember something about a man getting shot and his wife getting away."

"They never found his body. I think she had a big life insurance policy, and she is, or will be sitting pretty with him in Mexico. But that was in 2010, and there isn't much violent crime in Zapata. That crime, if it happened, was an outlier."

The Mexican reporter arrived and joined us at the table. His English was only marginally better than my Spanish, so I called my wife Katia, who hails from Peru. Julio asked Katia in Spanish, "Have people helped him along the way?" Then he handed the phone back to me. I answered Katia in English, before handing the phone back to the reporter for Katia's translation.

Julio asked Katia, "Has he had a safe trip?"

"The cities have been safer than I expected. It's the remote areas that have proven to be the most active smuggling routes." I detailed our run-in with the border-crossers on Old Mines Road.

Katia translated for me and the reporter told her, "I think he (Mark) has been lucky."

Katia, "But why? Is it dangerous there?"

"Yes."

Katia asked, "How is it dangerous? In what way?"

"You are very likely to see drug shipments here. There are lots of police and they are always catching big loads of drugs around here."

"But if he sees this are they going to do something to him?"

"No, probably not."

"Then how is it dangerous?"

"I see your point. I just think it is an unstable environment."

After fifteen minutes answering questions from both reporters, the interviews were completed and the Mexican reporter asked in English, "Would you like to visit Mexico?"

"Yes, I would love to, but I won't have my passport until my wife arrives on the eighteenth."

I had originally planned on starting the trek in Mexico, after hearing an author interview on NPR. Mr. Saenz had written a book titled after a famous bar in Ciudad Jaurez. I located the publisher and gave them a call. A female answered the phone.

"Hello, my name is Mark Hainds. I am an author in Alabama."

She interjected, "First, you need to go to our website and check our guidelines for submissions."

"This is not a submission."

"Then you need to talk to Lorene (name changed). She is on the other line. Could you call back in a few minutes?"

"Sure."

Ten minutes later, I called and Lorene answered the phone.

"Hello, I am an author in Alabama and this fall I intend to walk the length of the Texas-Mexico border. There was this great interview on NPR with Alejandro Saenz."

Lorene immediately interrupted with an exasperated tone. "Saenz," she said, which sounded like "signs."

I had mispronounced it.

"My bad. 'Saenz," I continued, "and his book, *"Everything Begins & Ends at the Kentucky Club."*

"Have you bought and read it?" It was more an accusation than a question.

"No, but I will. I try to read the pertinent literature and incorporate their thoughts and knowledge into my work. Do you have some suggestions since you specialize in border material?"

"NO! We specialize in good writing!"

I wilted. A complete stranger hadn't talked down to me like this since the summer of 1987, at Basic Training in the Army at Fort Polk, Louisiana.

I gathered myself and tried again, "Okay, would you be willing to email me a list of titles?"

"No! ..... I will give you a handful right now."

"*Drug Lord* by Terrence E. Poppa. *Everything Begins & Ends at the Kentucky Club*, by Alejandro Saenz, *Dirty Dealing* by Gary Cartwright, *Contrabando,* by Henry Ford Jr, and *Ringside Seat to a Revolution* by David Dorado Romo. We are out of *Ringside Seat to a Revolution,* so you will have to order it online."

I breathed a sigh of relief while she listed the titles. I followed up with another question. "I was thinking about visiting the Kentucky Club on my walk. Would Mr. Saenz possibly be interested in providing me with more information?"

"Just do it! People go there all the time. Just go."

My thoughts traveled back to my first and only visit to Ciudad Juarez, ten years prior. Three of us were driving back to Alabama from an elk hunt in New Mexico. We detoured to an El Paso parking lot to leave the truck and walk across the border.

As soon as we walked across the bridge a taxi pulled up. The driver didn't waste time with formalities, asking in English, "What do you want? Cocaine? Marijuana? Girls?"

Setting those thoughts aside, and after more than a moment's hesitation, I said, "All right. I'll do it. I have one more question. To date, the most relevant work I've read about the border was *The Tecate Journals* by Keith Bowden. Are you familiar with it?"

"Do you mean Charles Bowden?"

"No, I am pretty sure his name is Keith Bowden. He is an instructor at a college in Laredo."

She had not heard of the author or the book, and my question further exasperated her. She forgot the purpose of my call and reverted to her first assumption, namely that I was shopping for a publisher. "We just can't speculate. We've been burned too many times. After you finish your trip and manuscript, you can send it to us." She paused. "You know, on second thought, we may not be the right publisher for you. This might be interesting or exotic to someone in New York City, but we live this life every day."

Said the bitch.

The night before I left for Texas, my passport was nowhere to be found. After a lengthy and fruitless search, everything was in the truck except my passport. I gave up and went to bed. The drive for Texas started three hours later.

Without my passport and the ability to freely cross the border, I fell back on the original plan of starting at International Mile Marker #1, on the U.S. side of the border.

I had successfully traversed most of the Texas-Mexico border and was safely distant from Ciudad Juarez, when my wife Katia magically located my passport.

Julio said, "It's no problem. I know many of the agents who work at the crossing."

Two Border Patrol agents entered the restaurant. The reporter asked them, "He (pointing to me) would like to cross over into Mexico, but he doesn't have his passport. Is that a problem?"

"It is up to the agent in charge at the time he comes across. It may be a problem, or they may let me through with a few additional questions. There are no guarantees."

From the restaurant, we walked to the Roma Bluffs overlook that Rex had previously described. Rex was waiting on us, while John scouted hotels in the McAllen area.

We spent a few minutes looking at Roma, and Julia snapped some photos of Rex and me for the *Zapata County News*. Julio asked us, "Would you like to cross to Ciudad Miguel Alemán?"

I turned to Rex. "What do you think? I would like to cross over. Julio thinks he can get me back through."

"I don't want to cross over. I'd advise against going across, but you are a big boy."

Clearly, Rex was very uncomfortable with crossing into Mexico. His fears were amplified by my lack of proper documentation. My two companions for the coming days were polar opposites, in at least one respect. Rex consistently played it safe, while John actively pursued dicey, stimulating environments.

Without Rex, I would have taken my chances and crossed into Mexico. But I didn't want to torture the guy. Turning to Julio, I said, "I will try to come back with my wife. I would love to visit Mexico with you, but I need to wait on my family and passport."

I walked back toward 83 and Rio Grande City. The landscape urbanized as 83 tracked east, with more and more communities lining the route.

John Dickson returned with reservations at La Borde House in Rio Grande City. If I pushed hard it was possible to make La Borde House on foot. But US 83 was a busy road, and walking conditions on the road shoulder were less than ideal, with thick grass and challenging slopes. I told

John, "A dirt road south of 83 would be nice, but only if it doesn't slow us down too much."

"We are going by a wildlife refuge called Las Palomas," said John. "I'll see if I can call or meet the refuge biologist and learn more about it."

"That would be great."

The skies were overcast, and the weather alternated between a light mist and rain, while the landscape transitioned to cultivated fields. John checked in just north of Las Palomas.

"I drove to the refuge and found some greenhouses where they were growing native plants. Some technicians or hourly workers were standing around, not saying much. The roads are caliche. They could get slick with this rain."

"I'll stay on the highway and push for the hotel."

With precipitation, I donned the rain jacket. When it stopped raining I sweltered, so the jacket came off. This cycle repeated itself scores of times over the day.

A CO_2 canister lay on the road shoulder. These small silver or gray metal containers held compressed gas, and I used scores of them growing up on the farm. For years, I rained air-propelled BBs and pellets down upon English sparrows, European starlings, grasshoppers, squirrels, rabbits, and a myriad of other small, unfortunate targets.

A bit farther down the road lay another CO_2 canister. Before long, handfuls of the canisters dotted the road shoulder.

It was dusk as I entered the outskirts of Rio Grande City, the largest city in Starr County.

The U.S. Census Bureau estimated a 2013 population of just over 60,000 for Starr County, of which 96% were Hispanic/Latino with an estimated median household income of about $25,000. Wikipedia ranked Starr as the third poorest county in the United States based upon 2010 Census Data, while a *USA Today* January 10th, 2015 article ranked Starr County as one of the poorest in the country, and the poorest county in Texas.

Although Starr County ranks on the extreme end of the poverty scale, it had plenty of company. Virtually every county along the Texas-Mexico border ranks among the poorest in the nation. The exceptions were counties with the bigger cities: El Paso, Laredo, and Brownsville.

I am not a stranger to poverty-stricken landscapes, having lived two years in a small black community in Baker County, Georgia, and having trapped beavers for the highway department in Conecuh County, Alabama, just down the dirt road from my current home in Covington County. Both of these Deep South counties (Conecuh and Baker) have median household incomes barely above Starr County, Texas.

If my route was representative of the Starr County landscape, there wasn't much happening with oil/gas development there. Also absent were big ports of entry necessary to capitalize on trade infrastructure with Mexico. Much of the cross-border trade in Starr County was associated with lengthy prison sentences.

There were agricultural jobs there, but having grown up on a farm in a community that experienced extreme economical duress through the 1980s and 1990s, I knew typical agricultural wages were not a ticket out of poverty.

Some of Starr County's housing reflected the statistics found in these rankings. Collections of small travel trailers parked in lots were probably "colonias." In the United States, these are a phenomenon only found in extremely poor, Hispanic areas in Border States. The Texas Secretary of State defines a "colonia" as: "A residential area along the Texas-Mexico border that may lack some of the most basic living necessities, such as potable water and sewer systems, electricity, paved roads, and safe and sanitary housing."

Despite the abject poverty reflected in these statistics, the communities and streets were relatively clean and not the least bit threatening. I was comfortable walking the streets of Rio Grande City well after the sun had set, reaching La Borde House after dark, where John met me in the parking lot with a cold beer.

La Borde House was run something like a bed and breakfast. It was an attractive, old building with patios, verandas, and ironwork that would have blended well with historic New Orleans. I joined John for another beer on our veranda that looked out on a pool hall and another old building, long abandoned. Hundreds of bats streamed from the decrepit construction across the street.

John said, "Those are probably Brazilian free-tailed bats. They often use man-made structures."

I said, "All the overpasses down here, (along the Rio Grande Valley), have abutments built with a protected lip, and there is guano on the ground below. There must be thousands of bats using each of these overpasses. Would that be the same species?"

"Probably so."

That evening, Rex, John, and I ate at a restaurant that was fancier than our normal fare. The end of the trail was approaching, and the air was celebratory.

"How does it feel?" asked Rex.

"I am a little torn. It's exciting that we've covered so many miles and maintained a fast pace. But when I start thinking about going back to bills, debt, and the daily grind, my mood sinks."

21

OLD MILITARY ROAD

"Forty-five's not old. There are good days and bad days —a good day reminding you of how you felt when you were, say, twenty-five, and a bad day seeming like a harbinger, perhaps, of what the body might be like at fifty-five, or even sixty-five, compromised and reduced..."

Rick Bass. *A Thousand Deer: Four Generations of Hunting and the Hill Country.* 2012

December 16–17

JOHN wanted to walk with me for at least one day of his week's tenure. The best opportunity would be from La Borde House in Rio Grande City to Old Military Road and points east.

A year earlier, my scouting expedition along the border had started in a little blue Saturn sedan on Boca Chica Beach. I drove through Brownsville and picked up Old Military. Initially, the road was a paved highway running through town. Then, Old Military turned to dirt, and I was forced to turn around at water-filled potholes bigger than the car.

Over the last nine hundred miles, we had been repeatedly warned to stay off or away from several notable roads: Quitman Pass, Chispa, Old Mines, and finally, Old Military.

The main difference between the previous routes and Old Military was the relative population and degree of remoteness associated with these routes. Quitman Pass, Chispa, and Old Mines were virtually unpopulated and communications were almost impossible, barring the use of a satellite phone or other advanced equipment, not in my possession.

Old Military was never more than a mile or two from the civilized world, so communications weren't an issue. Another big difference between Old Military Road and the previous routes was the overwhelming presence of law enforcement that we expected to encounter in the coming days. The numbers of uniformed personnel had skyrocketed since Zapata.

Before the walk, John had been one of my best sources of information on the border, and he was more comforting than cautionary. He explained, "From my time working on the border, particularly around Carrizo Springs, the cartels want to be invisible. They want to move their product and have as little interaction and attention as possible. They don't want to kill someone over here, because that will bring so much heat down on them. They don't want to make someone disappear, because people will come looking for them."

John was speaking from lots of experience on both sides of the border. A couple of years earlier, he was riding in a convoy traveling through Mexico on their way to hunt the Gould's wild turkey. Gould's are one of five subspecies of the eastern wild turkey, and they are only found in Mexico and small portions of Arizona and New Mexico.

El Chapo Guzman's gunmen stopped the convoy at a roadblock. The narcos were drunk, armed, and shirtless with hand grenades pinned to their vests. They hoped to intercept and kill their archenemies, the Zetas.

One of Chapo's guys pointed a gun at a Mexican national in the convoy. The potential victim was an unlucky relative of someone that had been in a bar fight with the gunman.

Luckily, the head gunman calmed his irritated underling, and eventually they allowed the turkey hunters and Mexican federal biologists to pass unharmed.

John was pretty sure I'd see immigrants during my walk. He described some of his memories of Carrizo Springs. "We'd be working dogs out in the middle of nowhere. It was thirty miles to the nearest road, and a line of six or eight immigrants would walk past. Some of them wore white shirts.

Some carried a gallon of water and others didn't carry anything at all. It didn't seem too well thought out."

John's story had already proven prophetic. The lost border crossers on Old Mines Road fit perfectly with his description.

John and I started walking from La Borde before the sun was up, leap-frogging the truck as we traveled east and south on US 83. John preferred the opposite of Mike's system on Old Mines. John would park the truck and walk with me for thirty minutes. Then he would turn around and walk back to the vehicle. Three-quarters of an hour later, John would catch up with the truck, park, and hike another segment before repeating the shuttle.

Walking with other people had its advantages. For example, they might see things that escaped my attention. We hadn't made it out of Rio Grande City before John said, "There's a roach" (remains of marijuana cigarette).

"Dang. I've walked nearly a thousand miles and hadn't seen one until you pointed it out. In fact, the only drug paraphernalia that I've recognized was three hypodermic needles. Good eye."

More expended CO_2 cartridges littered the side of the road. "I've seen these spent cartridges for the last twenty miles. For some reason, these are painted red. What do you think they are using these for?"

John shook his head. "I don't know."

Old Military (FM 1420) split from US 83 about five miles past La Borde Hotel at a small town named "La Puerta."

Old Military was paved, but compared to US 83 vehicular traffic slowed to a trickle, making for much improved walking conditions. Small communities and their dogs lined this section. John accepted one of my walking sticks as a lap dog yipped at us from behind. John warned it, "Oh baby, you don't want a piece of this!"

The trees and shrubs were increasingly tropical in nature. This flora was out of my botanical realm, and John wasn't much help with plant identification, since most of his work had been on higher, drier ground farther north or east.

We worked our way through a small community where some small cardboard boxes on the ground caught my eye. "Oh my gosh, John, I've solved the mystery of the CO2 cartridges."

The red boxes were covered with images of two beautiful, naked women intertwined in sexual positions and covered in whipped cream. Along the bottom of the box were photos of red CO2 cartridges and the label "XXX Platinum"™ 24 Triple Refined Cream Chargers." Along the top of the box it read "XXX PLATINUM TASTES SO GOOD TO ME"™.

"This must be the most oversexed community in America. I might have to pick up a few acres around here."

"The mystery is solved," said John. "I've always liked border communities."

John turned around to head back for the truck and possibly pick up some XXX Platinum™ Cream Chargers. No matter where you dropped him, John had, or shortly would have, a girl within driving distance.

Old Military led to a Y-intersection. Unsure of my route, I took a left turn that put me back on US 83. No big deal. I wanted something hot for breakfast. Dried fruits and granola bars were tiresome, so a Stripes convenience store was my next stop. John caught up and pulled into the store as I ordered a burrito. He pointed to some tables beside the windows and said, "That guy has a big backpack."

Turning to look, I immediately recognized him from a photograph shown to me in New Falcon. "I'll be damned. It's the Hiking Viking. I have to talk to him."

The weathered old hiker was conversing with a younger man seated at an adjacent table. I approached and asked, "May I have a seat?"

The older man nodded.

The younger of the two was Chris from San Luis Obispo. Chris had cycled across the country, all the way from California. He planned to hit the Gulf Coast and turn south, bicycling though Central America to the tip of South America, crossing to the west coast and following it all the way back to California. Chris said, "It will be about 20,000 miles and two years. I am trying to find out if I am up for it."

"Don't wait until you are old like me," said the Hiking Viking. "I am dying of loneliness. It gets where I just want to catch a stray bullet." By his tone, this wasn't a joke.

I introduced myself, adding, "I've been walking from El Paso." Up to this point, it had seemed like a bit of an accomplishment. I pulled out my notebook. "If you don't mind, I'll take some notes."

The Hiking Viking's real name was Mike. He said, "You have so much to look forward to. I only have so many hours of lucidity until my brain turns to a puddle of piss. How old are you? Because forty-five is the cutoff."

"I am 43," Chris said.

"45." I said

"See?" said Mike.

"How do you stay warm at night?" I asked. "I build a campfire when it gets cold on the trail."

"I have never built a fire. I try to stay south when it gets cold."

"Have you crossed into Mexico?"

"No. It's too dangerous."

"Are you headed to Florida?"

"Never again. I don't hang anywhere. I am on the road every day, year-round."

"How much does your pack weigh?"

"Sixty pounds. I make 10-12 miles a day. I am headed to Mission, then McAllen, then Harlingen."

He was wearing gigantic tennis shoes, just as the State Patrolman described. The side was cut out of the right shoe and a large bump/growth protruded from the hole. A sock covered the protrusion.

Mike saw me look at his feet. "My feet got deformed. I have a calcium deposit on my right foot."

John took a seat beside us while Chris got up to leave. Chris said, "They don't accept food stamps here. I am going to try and find a store that will." John and I exchanged glances but remained silent.

Mike told us, "I took my first steps on March 31st, 2008, on the Big Island in Hawaii. I bought a one-way ticket to LA (the California version, not Lower Alabama), and I walked to the airport. I camped there until my flight. The next thing I knew, I was in California."

"It took sixty-eight days to make it to Seattle. I determined I was sincere. I could do it at age fifty-five. I took off for Everett, Washington, and then east to Hurley, Wisconsin. Lake Superior was right there. That's just a tiny bit of it. I have been walking for seven years."

Mike looked at John. "I don't blame anyone if they don't believe me. I don't care."

"I believe you," John said.

"People are afraid to die," Mike said. "They think if they walk, they will die."

I didn't say anything, but based upon my experience, hikers would perish regularly if they walked US 277 between Del Rio and Eagle Pass.

Mike put a forkful of rice in his mouth. His tooth count was in the single digits with one or two teeth on top, and a similar number on the bottom.

He gummed the rice for a bit, swallowed, and said, "Your feet....every day, mile after mile. Your feet take so much punishment. If you are sincere, you'll adapt. You'll cope. My feet were sort of normal when I began."

I wrote furiously while we compared experiences, and then it was time to go.

On our way out the door John turned to me. "Mark."

"Yes."

"Don't become the Hiking Viking."

I wanted to get back on Old Military after the accidental detour on US 83. My GPS showed a couple of routes through a small community to Old Military, which was a mile or less south of 83. The first two attempts at southern routes failed when the roads dead-ended at fences and private property. I circled back to 83 and continued east until a paved road inter-sected from the right. John parked beside the road and joined me for the walk. This time we made it to Old Military where we turned back east, just past a school.

Old Military turned to gravel and caliche. Much of the area to our right was marked as a U.S. Fish and Wildlife National Wildlife Refuge. The Border Patrol and the Texas State Patrol worked Old Military hard. After a mile or two on Old Military, John turned for the truck while I kept going.

For the first time on the trip, stomach issues forced me off the road at least once an hour. Sometimes, I just made it through the first wall of brush before stopping to relieve myself. On one such occasion, the Border Patrol drove by, only ten yards away. Thankfully, they didn't notice the guy in the bushes.

I stepped back on the road and walked a short distance before two Border Patrol agents pulled up on 4-wheelers. One asked, "Are you the author?"

"Yes, sir. You've heard."

"We talked to your friend back up the road. Good luck." They zoomed ahead.

The sun was burning down, but a strong breeze evaporated sweat and moderated the conditions.

Several POVs approached from my front. The drivers and passengers wore military uniforms and waved as they drove by. They were the first Texas National Guard personnel of the trip.

Moments later, a young Texas State Trooper pulled up.

I introduced myself and explained the purpose of my walk.

"It's fairly uncommon for us to have the ability to tell or show the public about our operations down here. Would you like to see it on a map?" he asked.

"Sure!"

The trooper angled his computer screen so it was visible through his window. By his accent, I guessed that he was originally an Aussie or a Kiwi.

"We get lots more action here. Our guys just busted a load of dope in Sullivan City."

"That was on the news at the Stripes store on 83," I said.

"Our guy saw a driver acting suspiciously. The driver pulled over to get some gas. Our guy also needed gas so he pulled up next to him. While the pump was running, he went over and looked into the window, and there was the marijuana!"

"Do you remember that shooting up at Falcon Lake?" he asked.

"Yes."

"It was two brothers running drugs. The guy and his wife (the Americans) pulled up to them (the Mexicans) on jet skis. They thought they were getting robbed so they started shooting. They killed him and she got away."

"This incident put a lot of pressure on the *Federales*, so they sent a detective down. The brothers killed the detective and sent his head back in a suitcase. That brought a lot more heat down on the cartel, so the Zetas grabbed the brothers. Beheaded them. Gave the heads to the Federales and said, "Problem solved.""

I had now heard two completely different versions of the shooting on Falcon Lake. A firsthand account from the survivor would likely add clarification. It wasn't easy, but several months later I finally reached Tiffany by email. We spoke by phone on a Friday afternoon in October, nearly a year after the trek. It was five years and two days since David had been killed.

"Hello, is this Tiffany?"

"Yes."

"This is Mark Hainds. I apologize for not returning your call earlier. I am terrible about checking my messages."

"Don't worry about it."

I gave Tiffany a recap of the walk, the intended book, and Rex's movie.

"What would you like from me?" she asked.

"While walking through the Falcon Lake area, the shooting was still fresh on many people's minds. I wanted to get a little more information from you if possible."

"What was your impression of the area during your walk? I haven't been back since the first anniversary of David's death. I talked with the Sherriff (of Zapata County) on the fifth anniversary, but I really don't know anyone down there."

"The law enforcement presence was overwhelming from Zapata to around Rio Grande City. We stayed in a hotel in Zapata with dozens of Texas State Patrol. One of them described regular shootouts when they first deployed to the Rio Grande valley, but things were settling down. I also talked with a local newspaperman and area residents. They seemed pretty relaxed, and it felt like a safe place to live and walk." (excepting the cross-eyed Cujo dog near Vanessa's kitchen)

Tiffany began, "We lived in Reynosa for two and a half years. We started seeing convoys of a cartel called the 'CDG' rolling through town. They were at war with the Zetas. It became unsafe so we moved to Texas. We felt pretty safe in McAllen: a lot of good that did us. But, why did you call me?"

"I heard different versions of the event. I wanted to see if there have been any developments in the intervening five years, and I thought you might want to add your perspective."

"What you find online is pretty much what happened that day. The stories in the major news outlets are fairly accurate. I don't know if I care to go back through it."

"I have read the stories, but a Texas State Trooper gave me a pretty detailed, blow by blow account with some additional information. Would you like to hear his version?"

"Yes."

I retold the story from Old Military Road.

Tiffany paused then began, "We were going to see that stupid church. We went by a boat with, I think, three guys in it. We all saw each other. They waved. We waved. We were on our way out. I don't know if there was a scout. Do you know what a scout is?"

"A person who watches for law enforcement or other trouble and calls ahead?"

"Yes. A scout could have reported from the Texas side. There have been so many accounts of how or why we were attacked. For instance, we had Reynosa plates."

"I see. The area was controlled by the Zetas, and they may have thought you were with the CDG?"

"Yes. Or, it could have been to steal our jet skis. That makes the most sense to me. They were super powerful. Super fast. There's no way I could have gotten away other than on that jet ski."

Tiffany continued, "There was a beheading of an investigator. There are two brothers named Farias in custody: one in Texas and one in Mexico. They controlled that area for the Zetas. Obviously, if they are in custody, they were not beheaded."

"We don't have enough manpower to protect the border. Nor does the rest of the country know what is going on down there. I do believe that the Governor is really working hard to protect the border."

"Do you mean Greg Abbot or Rick Perry?" I asked.

"I don't know Greg Abbot. I was speaking about Governor Perry."

"Border security is going to be a central issue in my book. I believe these checkpoints, all the law enforcement personnel, and how they interact with people who live on the border – this is a balancing act."

"When we lived in McAllen, we weren't affected by these issues until we drove sixty miles north to Border Patrol checkpoints, or if we drove south to the border. Our day-to-day lives weren't affected."

"I believe that God spared my life for a reason – not to just stay quiet about issues on the border. I've done a lot of healing over the last several years."

Tiffany said, "I'm starting to get that pull, or desire, to bring awareness. It's not just our side. The people in Mexico are scared for their lives every day. People on our side are losing farms and lives because of spillover violence. We have to wake up to what is happening on our border."

I said, "Before I let you go and start packing the truck for the market in Pensacola: I know the world will always associate you with the Falcon Lake shooting, but there's more to your life. What else can you tell me?"

"Well, I was diagnosed with MS shortly after Falcon Lake. So I also have to deal with that." Tiffany followed this up with a question. "What's it like living there? In Pensacola?"

"We live in a safe, rural, friendly area in Alabama. But we also enjoy Pensacola. They have some of the prettiest beaches in the world and a vibrant art community. There's a symphony, a hockey team, a minor league baseball team, and they draw some great concerts. I love spearfishing and surf fishing. And we've made a lot of good friends there over the years."

"David and I had planned on moving to Colorado before he was shot. I moved out here, but I don't hike. I've always been a beach girl rather than a mountain girl."

"Do you mind me asking, how old you are? I am forty-six, and if I had waited much longer, my body might not have held together for this trek."

"I am thirty-four. And kudos to you on making that walk. I wish I could walk the border, but I can't do it with these two feet."

"If you feel like visiting the Pensacola or Destin area, please let us know. We'd be happy to introduce you to our friends and favorite restaurants."

Back on Old Military, the Texas State Trooper continued to provide context for the environment I was walking through.

The State Trooper said, "Anytime we intercept a load of drugs because someone screwed up, their family in Mexico dies. The Zetas only trust first or second generation Mexican-Americans, because they still have family south of the border. That's the leverage the Zetas need."

He pointed to his computer screen. "Each of these dots represents a unit. There are several hundred dots out there. For some reason, I can't expand it right now to show you the whole area."

About fifteen dots, representing Texas State Patrol units, moved across a screen that looked like a five-mile radius.

I asked, "Can I take a photo?"

"Sure, go ahead."

John caught up a few minutes later, parked the truck and joined me for the walk. I told him, "I don't know what to think about this road. There are lots of law enforcement units, and I think it is pretty safe during the day. My guess is that security goes out the window after dark. Originally, I considered camping along stretches like this, but I keep changing my mind."

We passed the third tethered aerostat or blimp of the trek. The road was rough, with water-filled potholes as wide as the road.

John turned around to walk back for the truck. The sun had set and this would be the last leg of the day. I walked to a corral on the left side of the road. The corral was designed for dipping cattle and killing ticks. A sign posted on the corral fence read:

"DANGER

Poisonous Water

KEEP OUT"

Skull & Crossbones Symbol

"PELIGRO"

Agua venenosa

No permitimos la entrada"

Most of the land along the Rio Grande Valley was part of a tick quarantine zone. Signs to this effect were posted for hundreds of miles along the river.

During my drive to the border, I spent the night in Austin with a veterinarian friend named Richard Reinap. Richard said my route went through country that may have cattle fever ticks, capable of carrying and transmitting *Babesia*, a blood parasite deadly to cattle. This was probably the insect and disease that Dr. Adrian Billings studied before becoming a doctor.

The corral was a logical place to end the day's walk, so I dropped my backpack and recorded the coordinates. There was just enough time to journal some of the day's happenings before John's arrival.

While I loaded my gear in the truck, a school bus stopped at a house about a quarter-mile east, just past an intersection with a road that ran north to 83. John drove to the intersection, turned left (north) and drove us back to the hotel in Rio Grande City.

Back at La Borde, I took a shower and checked for ticks, before taking a seat on the front porch while John cleaned up. The evening's entertainment consisted of cold beer and watching bats emerge for their insect meals. In a few days, my brother would accompany Mom on a flight from Missouri, while Katia and Joseph would fly out from Fort Walton Beach, Florida. Most of the family would be present for the finale at Boca Chica Beach.

Months later, John and I discussed his stint as a Tex-Mex Compadre. John asked, "Did you discover the history of the La Borde House?"

"No, I didn't research it."

"It's supposed to be haunted. There's a bunch of stuff on *YouTube* about the place."

La Borde's history was described on its website. The building was designed in France in 1893, refined by San Antonio architects in 1898, and restored and reopened in 1982.

After hiking twenty-five miles, consuming a big supper, and downing several beers, La Borde House's ghosts weren't up to the task of waking me.

The next morning, we packed our stuff and left La Borde at 7:00 a.m. John pulled to a stop beside the corral on Old Military. I looked down the road and told him, "There's the school bus again." The bus was picking up kids at the same place it had dropped them the afternoon before.

John left me beside the corral and drove out of sight.

I stood in the road while adjusting the straps on my backpack and starting my stopwatch. When I looked up, a full-size gray or silver sedan was parked at the intersection just to my front. The trunk popped open. I froze in dismay, knowing full well some bad shit was about to go down.

Fate had bided its time for over nine hundred miles, hanging back, watching from a distance, but she caught up on Old Military. I was flat out exposed and right in the middle of it.

Six men carrying large packages bolted from the brush on the right side of the road. They moved so fast it was hard to follow, as cardboard boxes filled with dope flew into the trunk and backseat of the car.

Kids may dart, run, and jump, but outside of organized sporting events, it's rare to see a grown man moving at anything approaching the speed of those drug mules. When grown men move fast, they are scared: because their toddler is headed for oncoming traffic; because the tree they were felling took a bad turn; because enormous stakes are at hand. And when a man is scared, he is at his most dangerous.

My body was frozen, but my mind raced ahead unfettered. *They're too fast. I can't outrun them.* Nevertheless, my hands went to the fasteners on my backpack, in preparation to unbuckle and run for my life.

The last man unloaded his dope and slammed the trunk shut. Two of the mules ran into the bushes. The man who shut the trunk looked up – straight at me. He pointed. The other three men looked in my direction... and time stopped.

It was the worst-case scenario. It was Llewellyn blood-trailing an antelope over a hill and finding the suitcase of money that spelled his doom in the movie, *No Country for Old Men.* This was what Jesse Lee Schneider, the Presidio Extension Agent, warned me about. I had imagined and described this exact moment, when friends asked, "What are you most afraid of on this trek?"

The answer: Me, alone, exposed and identified, in the middle of a drug transfer on the border.

"I'm so fucked." Maybe I said it. Maybe it was just in my head.

But I wasn't.

As fast as they appeared, they disappeared into the brush on the south side of the road and headed back toward the Rio Grande. The spell broke. I wheeled around, grabbed my cell, and called John while walking west as fast as possible. "I was just in the middle of a drug transfer! Get me out of here!"

John had barely left the area, so he made it back almost immediately. "What happened?"

I threw my backpack in the bed of the truck and hopped in. "Let's circle back up to 83, just above here."

John drove, as I explained, "You dropped me and drove off. I was adjusting my backpack when I looked up and there was a sedan parked in front of me, at the intersection just ahead."

"I saw that car!" said John. "It was barely moving down the road, and I thought, 'That's weird.'"

"Do you remember the school bus?"

"Yes."

"I think it was the key. These guys must have prepared a rendezvous around the school bus. Almost immediately after the school bus picked up the kids and drove out of sight, the car must have pulled up and stopped. The trunk popped open, and this group of Mexicans ran out of the bushes on the right. They threw the dope in the car. Two of them ran back into the bushes, but one saw me. He pointed in my direction, and the other three looked straight at me. I thought I was totally screwed."

I continued, "I ain't telling law enforcement about this. As long as the drugs get through, they won't have anyone to blame. Right now, I am the single most easily identifiable person on the border. A person moving at a slow and predictable pace. And if someone sees me as a problem, I am a very easily removed problem."

John sought to put me at ease. "That car is gone and they are headed for Mexico. I think you'll be okay here on 83."

Several weeks later I recounted the incident to Michael Eason, the botanist who walked with me at the top of Chispa Road. I told Michael, "After it happened, I prayed that the drugs would get through successfully. I didn't want to be a scapegoat for an interdicted shipment."

Michael said, "I can just picture a drug lord drinking a cup of coffee, reading the newspaper, and receiving his morning report on shipments and activities. And the drug lord says, 'Now, tell me again. Who is responsible for that lost shipment.' And his minion points to your picture on the front-page of the newspaper. 'That guy.' The druglord says, 'Take care of that for me.'"

John dropped me off again. This time, about one mile north of the drug transfer at the tick corral. It didn't have quite the same ring as, "The Shootout at the OK Corral," but it dang sure got my heart pumping.

Dalipseth and his mother in Sanderson

Eating at the 12 Gage with Rex and Bob Larimore

22

LA JOYA TO BROWNSVILLE

"The specialists render the armed forces a service no less important than the assigned doctors, lawyers, or priests."

Mario Vargas Llosa.
Captain Pantoja and The Special Service. 1978

Ringed Kingfisher: Drawn by Edlyn Burch

December 17—20

IT took a couple of hours to reach the next town, Palmview, on US 83. Along the way, another overpass had guano at the base of its abutment, testifying to a large number of roosting bats.

A Fast Mart at the intersection provided a convenient stop for a mid-morning breakfast and a seat to record the incident while the details were still vivid.

By this time, my nerves had settled and I began to place the incident in perspective. As long as I survived shit like this, it made for great material. Even so, I had no desire to repeat the experience!

In the few seconds when the drug runners had stood in the road, staring at me, deciding what to do, my fate could have been sealed by a rash decision on their part. It's a hopeless feeling to realize you are at the mercy of another's whim.

Meanwhile, John transferred our luggage to a Holiday Inn Express in Mission, Texas. Our next two nights of lodging were free, compliments of my good friend and filmmaker in Alabama, Roger Reid. Roger and I had hoped like hell that he could make it out for a stint as a Tex-Mex Compadre, but he had just been funded for a new TV series about evolution, and he had a short time-line to finish some episodes.

Since Roger couldn't come to Texas, he donated a pile of his accumulated hotel points for two free nights in Mission, and another two nights in Brownsville. Money was tighter and tighter as the trip progressed, and his contribution was deeply appreciated.

Back on the highway, another hiker approached from the east. Aside from undocumented immigrants and the Hiking Viking, he was the only other hiker I had encountered. He was tall with a small schoolbag style pack. He wore earphones and cords that went to a Walkman type device in his hand. He was in his own world: offering a smile and an abbreviated wave while walking west.

The road led south to Business 83 before turning east through a residential area and crossing US 83 and Interstate 2 into Mission, Texas. A brief stop at a local pharmacy allowed me to restock pads and tape for my feet.

Business 83 paralleled a railroad track and skirted several big warehouses associated with the citrus industry. Some warehouses were abandoned, while others were still in use. Christmas lights and wreaths decorated Mission's palm and citrus trees.

Business 83 continued through a large urban area. The Census Bureau combined Mission, McAllen, and Edinburg into a Metropolitan Statistical Area (MSA) that counted about three-quarters of a million people in the 2010 Census. Per capita, Hidalgo County is one of the poorer counties in the nation, and some sources ranked this metropolitan area as the poorest in the United States.

Yet, the town felt very much alive. There may have been neighborhoods with different vibes, but I was comfortable in Mission.

Shary Road turned south toward the hotel. Several blocks down, the Comfort Inn's parking lot was full of Texas State Trooper vehicles. One of the cruisers pulled up beside me, and I prepared an explanation before recognizing the trooper from Old Military Road, just the day before. He smiled and asked, "How's the trip going? You are making good time."

"It has been pretty exciting. (If he only knew!) I am staying a few blocks down at the Holiday Inn Express. I'll stop by the room, and then keep going south and east."

Our hotel provided free copies of the *Monitor*, the main rag for the area. I called the newspaper and they immediately responded. A reporter, and possibly a photographer, would be in touch.

Likewise, a local TV station, KVEO Channel 23, responded immediately and said, "You will hear from one of our reporters."

A Spanish language newspaper called *El Periodico USA* was stacked beside the *Monitor*. I passed *El Periodico's* phone number to my wife so she could feel them out.

Shary Road continued south from the hotel, through towering palms with a serpentine sidewalk in front of very expensive subdivisions. It was an attractive design, but palm roots or other soil conditions had wreaked havoc on the concrete, tilting and cracking the slabs. As with Laredo, people did not appear to walk in Mission or McAllen. There was virtually no sign of recent human passage through the dirt or dust on the sidewalk.

Although the sidewalk was the worse for wear, every structure along the route looked like a million-dollar house. These subdivisions represented an outlying enclave of wealth, and I had to remind myself that Hidalgo County was supposed to be one of the poorest in North America.

Lost in thought, I followed Shary Road through an intersection and continued south. The scenery transformed to a rural setting before I realized my turn on West Military Road was about a half-mile back. After retracing my steps to West Military, I stopped at a convenience store to pick up a drink. Temperatures and perspiration increased as the border moved south.

West Military had many similarities to Mines Road in Laredo. Gigantic shipping terminals, import/export buildings, and other warehouses lined the road. Thousands of semi-trailers were coming from or going to Mexico.

West Military intersected with 115, also called International Boulevard, which ran straight south through Pharr, one city blending into another with no obvious transition.

I turned south and stayed on the west side of 115. On the opposite side of the highway, big warehouses handled fresh produce for domestic consumption, or used clothing for export to Mexico. The landscape transitioned again, from urban to rural. A cultivated field lay to my right and my phone rang. It was a reporter from the *Monitor*. She asked, "Is this a good time to talk?"

"Sure," although the traffic made it hard to hear her questions. I moved away from the road to improve acoustics. Emily Sides questioned me for the next thirty minutes as I stood beside the field watching the sun go down. John was supposed to pick me up at any minute, and sure enough, he drove by, headed south without looking to my side of the road.

"Excuse me, Emily. My ride just drove by. I'll call you right back."

I phoned John. "I am on the west side of 281, just south of a big blue building that is used for cold storage."

"Okay. I'll turn it around when I find a break in this traffic."

I called Emily again and the interview continued as John circled to pick me up on the west side of the highway. I was still on the phone with Emily as John lifted my backpack into the back of the truck. I opened the passenger door and the smell of Jim Beam hit me so hard, it almost bloodied my nose. Crazy bastard. Why hang with the likes of John and Mike? I guess the straight arrows don't appeal to me. There's too much Irish in my blood.

After an hour of questions and answers, she asked, "Would it be okay if I interviewed you during your walk tomorrow?"

"Heck yeah. I'll start on the south edge of town a half-hour before sunrise. You should find me somewhere along Military Road, east of McAllen. I make about three miles per hour."

"Great. I'll pass on your phone number to a photographer if that is okay."

I particularly enjoyed two things about the Holiday Inn Express in Mission. First, it was free, compliments of my friend and Honorary Tex-Mex Compadre, Roger Reid. And second, it offered a manager's reception with food and alcohol. My budget was on life support so I drank their free beer and took full advantage of the free hamburgers, which could best be described as "containing sufficient calories."

John joined me for the free food and beer. He said, "I think Robert Earl Keen is in town tonight." Robert Earl Keen is a native Texan, and one of John's and my favorite country singers.

"Dang. I drove two hours to watch him in Montgomery this summer. I'd love to see him play in Texas, but I would fall asleep in my chair at the concert."

"I thought there would be significant downtime with this trip," John said, "but we stay busy all day."

John informed me that he had connected online with a biologist groupie.

Had I known this phenomenon existed (biologists have groupies!) at a younger age, it's quite possible that I would have majored in wildlife rather than forestry.

"So, I was hoping to meet up with her tonight."

"Son, are you asking for the keys to the truck?"

"Yes, Dad."

"All right. As long as you are a good boy."

"You know me."

"I sure do."

John slipped back into the hotel room in the early morning hours. My sleep was so sound his return went unnoticed until 5:00 a.m., when I woke up and noticed him sitting in a chair. Despite his late-night shenanigans, John got up and dropped me off before first light, just a few miles from the hotel. The Rio Grande wasn't visible, but maps showed it within a few hundred yards of the road. Mosquitoes were problematic for the first time since Chispa Road.

The skies gradually lightened from black to gray. It was warm, humid, and eventually water exceeded the carrying capacity of the atmosphere. A dreary mist began to fall.

The next town south was Hidalgo. In appearance, Hidalgo was older and less commercial than Mission or McAllen. Students walked the sidewalks on their way to school. I became self-conscious, strolling beside the kids with their school bags. I felt like an intruder and wondered if a bearded stranger with a backpack would garner extra scrutiny from the Hidalgo Police. But the cops didn't appear concerned, and even the students didn't give me a second look. Had I become so thin as to be invisible?

I passed a public school and continued east into a city park, where the sidewalk was lined with trees and monuments memorializing dozens of Hidalgo residents who lost their lives in service to our country. As Mr. Carlos Nieto from Presidio might have said, "They fought in all them damn wars."

I exited northeast Hidalgo and continued on Military Highway. Where Old Military Road alternated between dirt and asphalt in sparsely populated brush, Military Highway was paved, more heavily traveled, and most of the landscape was cultivated. Thousands of acres of fields grew cabbage, lettuce, and other vegetables.

Cars lined the north side of US 281, and scores of people worked the fields, harvesting food bound for tables across the country.

The Texas State Patrol was out in force. A cruiser was parked on virtually every side road off 281. They had to be bored out of their minds.

Land that was not cultivated on the south side of Military Road belonged to the U.S. Fish and Wildlife Service. John finally tracked down a phone number for the refuge biologist. Tons of interesting bird species inhabited or migrated through the area, but the rain was making a mess of dirt roads to our south.

Although the road shoulder provided a reasonable trekking surface, the environmental conditions were pretty miserable. It felt like a sauna inside my raincoat, with the light rain.

A relatively large irrigation ditch ran west, perpendicular to the highway, with power lines paralleling the ditch. A bird dove from the line, into the water, before returning to its perch on the power line.

It was obviously a kingfisher, but it was easily twice as large as the belted kingfisher, the only species I was familiar with. I pulled out my phone. "John, I am looking at a gigantic kingfisher. What species would it be down here?"

"I don't know. I don't have my *Sibley* guide with me. Let me get back with you."

He called back a short time later. "It looks like you saw a ringed kingfisher. It's several inches longer than a belted kingfisher, and the range reaches into south Texas. That's a cool bird."

After the big populations around McAllen and Mission, the last community of any size had been Hidalgo. There were some tiny outposts, but very few towns or even stores. Eventually, I found a small general store, where I bought a cold Coke and took a seat on an outside bench. A white cat with different colored eyes rubbed against my leg, purring as I petted.

At the end of the day, John picked me up near a historical marker. My wife and son were due to fly into South Padre/Brownsville that evening, so we drove east toward the airport.

"What's up, man?" I asked.

"Not much. I washed your clothes."

"Were they smelling?"

"Dude."

"Sorry about that. I'm never downwind from myself."

"I'm not telling the guys at work that I came out here to drink by myself and wash clothes like your bitch."

John and I made it to the airport on time, but Katia and Joseph didn't. Their flight was delayed out of Dallas. John was impatient because he had another date with the biologist groupie in McAllen. Everything depended upon us getting out of the airport on time, so he could make it to a restaurant for his rendezvous.

Katia and Joseph finally arrived. It had been over a month since I last saw her, and the baby was finally making its presence known. Her belly was bigger, and her face was radiant. She was beautiful.

Katia had packed her and Joseph's clothing into a single checked bag. After hugs and kisses, we waited by the baggage carousel for another half hour, but the bag never showed. It took additional time to file a lost bag claim. On the drive back east, John's groupie cancelled their date and John sulked.

That night, the cameraman, Nathan Lambrecht, from the *Monitor* called. We discussed my typical itinerary and the challenges involved with walking twenty- to twenty-five miles per day. As a hiker, he was familiar with the physical toll. I told Nathan, "I am trying to keep my toenails, so I get up each morning and tape them before putting on my boots."

"Would you mind if I came over tomorrow (Dec 19th) to photograph your morning prep, including the taping of the toes?"

"Come on over about 5:30 a.m., if that is not too early."

"I'll be there."

That was devotion to the job, assuming he showed.

I asked Nathan, "I hate to impose, but since you are coming over early, would you mind dropping me off in the morning? It's just a few minutes from the hotel."

"No problem. I'll see you then."

The phone rang again. It was a reporter for *Telemundo*.

The newspaper my wife had called, *El Periodico USA*, had contacted the Spanish Language TV network and they were interested. The reporter, Daniel Tuccio, also planned to find me along Military Road.

If the coverage in Laredo had been extensive, it was about to reach a whole new level.

Nathan showed on time, finding me at breakfast before following me back up to the room, where he clicked away as I taped my messed up feet.

The nails on both big toes were black. On my left foot, the nail was barely attached to the second toe. On the right foot, a painful corn had developed where the third and fourth toe rubbed together. And, as always, the off-kilter little toe on my right foot, a shooting victim from my youth, required extra attention.

The forecast called for cloudy conditions and rain, so the cowboy hat stayed and the rain slicker went. It misted as we loaded the backpack and walking sticks into Nathan's car.

During the drive out, I quizzed Nathan about the area.

"Down here immigration really isn't an issue," Nathan said. "It's not a violent area. What violence does occur is targeted. Our murder rate is lower than Houston's. The perception is different than the reality."

"What area are you describing?"

"Hidalgo, Starr, and Cameron Counties."

Nathan continued, "I know people that are not legal, that have been living here for fifteen to twenty years. They have fake Social Security numbers and have been paying into the system all that time, but they'll never get that money back."

I said, "Since I started walking, people have told me this area is the 'Hot Zone.' How safe am I?"

"If you were hiking in Mexico I'd be a little worried. We had a family of two brothers and a sister that were killed. They got into a fight at a bar outside Progresso. Rumor has it they had an altercation with a bodyguard for the mayor of Matamoros. I'd feel safe going into most areas on this side of the border. Drug lords like to sleep in, but their guys are moving loads in the morning. They stash the loads on this side of the border and someone comes back to pick them up."

I knew more about this than Nathan realized.

"What are the big legal crops in the area?" I asked.

"Watermelon, oranges, sugarcane. It's cotton to the north. We grow corn, leeks, cabbage, and lettuce. Much of this land sees two or three crops each year. Sometimes they just plow corn under to put nutrients back in the soil. They do a lot of planting in January or February. We only get a hard freeze every three years or so."

Nathan dropped me at the historical marker, and he drove farther east on Military Road. He needed more light and suitable backgrounds/settings. The sun rose, but it was invisible in the pervasive gray, overcast conditions.

I found Nathan waiting in a patch of sunflowers on the edge of a field. The rapid-fire of his camera was audible as I passed. Nathan would take a number of photos, and then jog ahead to the next patch of sunflowers, and shoot again. After repeating this scenario several times, he drove down the road and shot me with other backgrounds. When he had enough, I thanked him for his professionalism and dedication. As a group, the journalists along the border had been impressive.

That afternoon, Emily Sides, the reporter, found me along Military Road, pulling to the side of the highway and parking her sedan on the shoulder. Like Gabriela in Laredo, she was a young Latina in professional dress with press credentials hanging from a lanyard around her neck.

Emily brought her notebook and a long list of follow-up questions. She probed deeper than the other reporters from print or TV. At the same time, she left escape routes, so she didn't come across as intrusive. Because of her professionalism, she coaxed out information that normally would have remained under wraps. For two examples, Emily revealed to the wider world, for the first time, Katia's pregnancy and my tumor surgery.

Several minutes into our interview, a Texas State Trooper drove past, turned on his lights, did a U-turn, and pulled up behind us on the road shoulder.

A Captain exited his car and walked up to us. He asked, "What's going on?"

I thought it obvious with her press credentials and notebook, but I went ahead and explained the situation.

"Do you have an ID?" he asked.

I produced my driver's license, for only the second time on the trek.

He shook his head and pronounced "Alabama" in a way that could have been translated: "What's this hick doing out here?"

Had my thoughts been audible, I would have ended up in cuffs.

The Captain didn't bother running my driver's license. He returned my ID and said, "You should understand that what I see is this professional young lady and a scruffy guy with a beard and a backpack on the side of the road. I had to check it out."

"Does this happen often?" Emily asked

"On average, I get questioned about once a day," I answered.

"Well, I hope we (Texas State Patrol) have treated you in a professional manner."

"Overall, very professional. Only one of them called me 'scruffy.'"

A few hours after my interview with Emily, Daniel Tuccio from *Telemundo* located me on the side of Military Road. Daniel was setting up his camera when yet another reporter arrived from Channel 23 -KVEO, the NBC affiliate from Brownsville. The second reporter waited for Daniel to finish his interview. In the middle of all this, John pulled up with Katia and Joseph. They had moved everything out of the hotel in Mission for relocation to a Holiday Inn (also compliments of my friend Roger Reid) in Brownsville.

Daniel interviewed me in English and everything was translated into Spanish for that evening's broadcast. When we watched it that evening, they first identified me as "Mike Hainds" and at another point as "Mark Hines."

After we finished, Daniel interviewed Katia and Joseph in Spanish. The reporter asked Joseph, "*Estas contento con lo que tu papá esta haciendo?*" – "Are you happy with what your father is doing?"

Joseph answered, "*Estoy muy feliz porque mi papa va a ser famoso.*" "I am very happy, because my father is going to be famous."

Katia sent a link for the interview to her sister and mother in Lima. After viewing Joseph's interview, they told Katia, "We laughed and laughed and laughed!"

After *Telemundo* wrapped up its interviews with my family, John drove Katia and Joseph into Brownsville where they settled into the hotel.

The second TV reporter was a young Anglo male. He asked about what I'd seen along the border. I gave him a long list of wildlife. At the mention of tarantulas, he shuddered, saying, "I can't stand spiders."

After completing the interview, he said, "I'll go ahead and film you walking past various backgrounds." He drove about a quarter mile down the road and set up his camera as I walked toward him. A recently deceased but intact tarantula lay on my side of the road. I couldn't resist the opportunity, so I picked it up and put it in my shirt pocket.

I walked past the reporter without acknowledging his presence. Once past the camera, I turned around and walked back. "Okay, I don't want to scare you, because you said you weren't that fond of spiders, but against all odds, I picked up a tarantula just now. Do you want to see it?"

"Sure. Where is it?"

"In my shirt pocket." I unbuttoned the pocket and lifted it out.

"What type of person puts a tarantula in their shirt pocket?"

"The type that walks a thousand-plus miles along the border!"

He filmed the tarantula in my hand while shaking his head.

Military Road continued through a landscape that alternated between cultivated fields and small rural communities. After a long absence, the border fence reappeared on the south side of the road.

After passing numerous openings in the border fence, on a whim, I walked through an opening near the small community of La Paloma. Construction workers were building up a road on the river side of the fence. As I walked the new road, heavy equipment operators and foremen watched my passage with questioning faces.

After a mile or two, another opening allowed entry to the Texas side. The absence of Border Patrol agents was surprising; no one had stopped or questioned me, but that doesn't mean my passage to and fro wasn't on camera.

John picked me up on his way back from Brownsville. His flight was scheduled to depart very early the following morning, two hundred miles west in Laredo. John drove while I journaled.

About halfway to Laredo, John took a rural Brooks County two-lane blacktop with high fences on both sides of the road. A Border Patrol SUV approached rapidly from the rear, trailing right off our bumper.

"What's up with this dude?" John asked.

"He's going to pull us over," I answered.

Sure enough, the Border Patrol agent's lights came on and John pulled to the side of the road.

The agent approached on the driver's side. He looked at all the gear and luggage in the back seat and made a logical but incorrect assumption. "You guys hunting?"

John explained who we were, while handing the agent his driver's license.

The agent said, "I pulled you over because you did a "Stop and Go" at the intersection back there. We get a lot of smuggling through this area. When I saw you slow down at that intersection without coming to coming to a complete stop, I just wanted to check things out. Have a good trip."

The agent returned to his truck and John rolled up his window. John said, "That's bullshit. I stopped back there."

"I know you did."

John was also a federal employee, but he didn't feel much camaraderie with this agent. He said, "I know they're just doing their job, but it feels like harassment to drive down the road and get pulled over at their whim."

The Falfurrias Border Patrol checkpoint was a few miles north. Earlier in the day, Rex had interviewed landowners with properties near the checkpoint. Human smugglers would let their clients out on these roads. The undocumented immigrants had to find their way north across the desert landscape to a rendezvous point, where they would be picked up and trafficked to destinations farther north. Large numbers did not make it. Some were intercepted. Some got lost and gave up at the first ranch house. Some died along the trails.

I questioned John, "Unlike you, I have never been to Alaska, but from what I've heard and read, it seems to draw the same type of person that you find in West and South Texas. You've worked as a fishing guide in Alaska and as a quail-hunting guide on the Border. What's your take?"

"The remote areas like Alaska draw people seeking adventure or fortune: panning for gold. Commercial fishing. All types of temporary or seasonal jobs. I met a lot of people who were running from something. They were trying to get a fresh start, but they couldn't outrun the issues that got them to Alaska. They had problems with depression, drugs, and alcohol abuse."

That night, I slept like a log. The next morning, I got up and put on a particularly ragged t-shirt. John took one look and said, "Dude, that is a rough looking shirt. It screams, 'Homeless.' It says, 'I made bad life decisions.' You'll be getting a lot of visits from the Border Patrol today."

I covered the offending rag with a collared shirt.

According to the mapping program on my computer, it would only take twenty minutes to reach the airport. We packed and jumped on the interstate with plenty of time to spare, until all lanes came to a complete stop.

"This is where it's good to have 4-wheel drive," I told John. It was still dark and there were no police in sight. A service road paralleled the Interstate so I peeled off I-35, crossed a shallow draw, and scooted down the parallel blacktop. An alternate route delivered us to the airport without further drama.

With John safely ensconced at Laredo International, I headed back to Brownsville. It was only 5:30 a.m., and, minus delays, a full day of walking was possible.

Katia and Joseph were staying at an elderly Holiday Inn in Brownsville. My brother Curtis, and my mom, Betty, had flown into South Padre the night before. Once I made it to the Holiday Inn, Curtis would take over as the last Tex-Mex Compadre of the trek.

During a fuel stop in McAllen, I glanced at the newspaper rack. The *Monitor's* lead story displayed Nathan Lambrecht's photo: me, framed by sunflowers, striding down Military Road, with two walking sticks and a backpack. Emily Side's article was titled, "Walking the line: Alabama man traversing Texas-Mexico border for book." I picked up several copies for the family.

From McAllen, it was about an hour to the hotel. I dropped a couple of bags and Curtis ran me out Military Road, while I caught him up on the walk, omitting the showdown at the tick corral. The world didn't need to know about that quite yet.

I walked the road shoulder throughout the day, eventually reaching the edge of Brownsville.

Months later, I tracked down S. Matt Read, the Texas Perimeter Hiker, and interviewed him over the phone. His walk had, by necessity, included summer months. Matt told me, "It was hot. The hottest part was coming into Brownsville. I'll never forget several days of hitting the road at two or three a.m. I came into Brownsville at four a.m. and a sign said it was eighty-eight degrees. You can't make that up. I've never experienced heat like that."

Brownsville temperatures in December were reasonable.

For the third time in two days, a local TV station sent a reporter to interview me on the side of Military Road. It was a young Latina from KGBT Action 4 News, the CBS affiliate for the Rio Grande Valley of Texas.

The young woman set up her camera to a steady stream of catcalls from passing automobiles. I asked her, "Is it always like this?"

"Yes."

She worked through a series of questions before filming me walking through town. I thanked her for her professionalism. Although I didn't apologize for the continuous catcalls, I was embarrassed for the male half of the population.

Rex checked in regularly. He had already scouted the final portion of our route along Boca Chica Boulevard. "The road meets the beach, and I found a complete set of women's clothes with no one around. There were boots, jeans, a belt, a blouse and a wig. It was pretty freaky."

"Dang. That is weird."

"What time do you think you will make it to the beach?"

"With decent mileage today, we'll have less than fifteen miles remaining for tomorrow. If I get an early start, we'll make the beach around noon."

"It's calling for rain on and off much of the day. We'll just go with it. I'll let you finish the walk with your family. You savor the moment. When you are ready, we'll have you walk the final portion and I'll shoot it from several angles. Is that okay with you?"

"Sounds great. I'll hang around as long as you need me."

Brownsville was the last urban area on the border. Like all the cities behind me, the neighborhoods along my route were clean and the people were friendly.

I had been a relatively anonymous pedestrian in El Paso, Eagle Pass, and Mission. That was no longer the case. People honked their horns and waved. One junker car, on par with the age and wear of my little blue Saturn, pulled over and three people exited. From their vehicle to their clothing, they were obviously on the lower end of the economic spectrum, yet they handed me $5.00 to help with meal expenses, explaining, they had seen me on *Telemundo* and were so appreciative.

A professor from a local college asked me to autograph a newspaper containing Emily's and Nathan's article. He gave me his phone number and insisted I call if I needed any assistance in the final miles.

I hadn't given much thought to these interviews, but I began to realize what was happening. I was just expressing my observations and gratitude for all the kindnesses that had been extended, but they were unaccustomed to a positive portrayal from outsiders. They longed for the same respect that should be afforded all Americans, and by God, they deserved it.

23

BOCA CHICA BOULEVARD

"For nineteen years my vision was bounded by forests, but today emerging from a multitude of tropical plants, I beheld the Gulf of Mexico stretching away unbounded, except by the sky."

John Muir. *A Thousand Mile Walk to the Gulf.* 1916

December 21–23

MILITARY Road became Boca Chica Boulevard in Brownsville: the final road of the trek.

My brother Curtis called and said, "Mom wants to take you out for dinner."

"That's fine. I want to make it through Brownsville so we only have half a day of walking with you and Joseph tomorrow."

I pushed farther into town before taking a seat by a Dairy Queen to drink some water and rest my legs.

Mom was still dealing with mesothelioma. The cancer was discovered about two years earlier. After the diagnosis, the walk was delayed in anticipation of the worst. Mom underwent radical surgery and chemotherapy. She beat the odds and went into remission, so planning and preparation resumed for my border trek.

The walk had started on October 27th, and it would finish the following day, with Mom there to see the completion. Where did this luck come from? It felt as if all the rules had been suspended: I wasn't supposed to survive the trek. Mom wasn't supposed to survive her cancer. Yet here we are, rendezvousing in Brownsville, with less than twenty miles remaining.

A car stopped beside me and a woman about my mother's age exited her vehicle. She had seen me on TV, probably on *Telemundo*, because she spoke exclusively in Spanish. She insisted on buying me supper. She led me into the Dairy Queen where the young lady behind the cash register accepted $10.00 from Señora Antonia.

Señora Antonia wanted to know my final destination.

"*Voy a Boca Chica Beach*," I said.

She insisted, "*Te llevo.*" (I will drive you there!")

I laughed. "*No, gracias. Yo tengo que caminar toda la distancia.*" (No, thank you, I have to walk all the way.)

She wouldn't have it. "*No. Te llevo. Para que no tengas que caminar tanto.*" (I will drive you so you won't have to walk too much.)

My Spanish wasn't good enough to convey the necessity of walking to Boca Chica Beach. The young lady behind the cash register was kind enough to translate, and I ate my first supper of the night.

Curtis called again. "Where are you?"

"I am sorry, but circumstances beyond my control led to an early supper. I am at the Dairy Queen at 3343 on Boca Chica Boulevard. Don't worry, I will be able to eat again later."

"Okay. Don't go anywhere. I am on the way with Mom."

I had just finished when Curtis and Mom arrived in their rental car. I grabbed my gear and walked out to give Mom a hug. She had recovered some weight, but her countenance had aged significantly. Mom had weathered a surgery and treatments that I may not have survived. Her frail appearance disguised a fighting spirit that kept her going, regardless of the odds.

We talked for a while and made arrangements for them to pick me at dark, on the east side of Brownsville.

Toward the edge of town, I stopped for a cold drink at a convenience store, just past an airport. The person behind the counter asked, "Where are you headed?"

"Out Boca Chica Boulevard to the Gulf of Mexico."

"You know, that's a major smuggling corridor out there."

"You don't say?"

That evening Mom took us out for dinner. Unfortunately, the seafood was the same greasy stuff that is popular across much of the South. Although the food was unremarkable, we enjoyed listening to a youth group, serenading diners with English and Spanish versions of Christmas Carols. I had almost forgotten how close we were to the holidays. On the trail, weekdays, weekends, and holidays are indistinguishable. And, Christmas hadn't been the same since we lost Dad in 2000.

Mom and Dad had three children. I was the oldest. Billie Lynette, my sister, was a year younger, and Curtis Paul was the youngest.

I was the typical rural, hunting, fishing, tobacco-chewing, kid, and Curtis was the exact opposite. Where my grades suffered from too many outdoor activities, Curtis's grades excelled, and he suffered when forced to accompany me hunting, fishing, or on the trap-line.

In her passion for deer hunting, my sister more closely resembled me.

Curtis and I started our lives distant from each other, but we grew closer as time progressed. All three of us kids graduated from the University of Missouri, but only Curtis and I bled Black and Gold. Billie Lynette was a fan, but not a fanatic.

Instead of picking up firearms and fishing poles, Curtis and I learned to seek out and share the best restaurants, bars, political wisdom, and recipes.

We were similar in height and build, but my skin was weathering and Curtis was pale. I was bearded and he was clean-shaven. In another decade, he would look twenty years younger than I, rather than the real nine-year spread.

It was raining the next morning when Curtis and I started walking from a defunct gas station on the east side of Brownsville, with sixteen and a half miles to go.

The land was flat and the air was humid. The Texas coast can harbor ferocious mosquito populations, but they didn't harass us on the final day of the walk.

A tremendous ship was anchored in the distant bay to our left. It was the decommissioned, *USS Saratoga*. They broke big ships at this port. The first decommissioned aircraft carrier to be recycled at this facility was the *U.S.S Forrestal*, which arrived in February 2014. The decommissioned and storied *U.S.S Saratoga* arrived midsummer, and the biggest ship to ever be recycled in the history of the United States was under tow. The decommissioned super carrier, *the U.S.S Constellation*, was on the way to its final port of call in Brownsville.

We walked through the humidity and a misting rain. A few houses were scattered along the way, so I passed a walking stick to Curtis. Bring on the dogs!

White pelicans flew overhead, while blue-winged teal and other waterfowl filled shallow ponds along Boca Chica Boulevard. Vehicular traffic was minimal, since Boca Chica wouldn't draw many beachcombers on a day like this.

A year earlier, it took a day and a half to drive the 975 miles between Andalusia, Alabama, and Boca Chica Beach. I picked up Boca Chica Boulevard in Brownsville and drove until the paved road ended just above the surf at the Gulf of Mexico, hitting the water on December 30th. Wind and rain had swept the beach, with nary a soul in sight at the intended terminus of my walk. It was the literal end of the road.

On that scouting trip, on the next to last day of the year, I had felt like the last man on earth. And for the first time in years, a sense of purpose took hold. I could do this.

I turned the Saturn around and drove west, past a scattering of travel-trailers dotting the north side of Boca Chica Road, their inhabitants invisible, sheltering against the inhospitable weather that accompanied the next two days of the scouting drive.

These memories were clear and relevant, so I explained to Curtis, "This is the same weather I experienced during my scouting drive last December. It's a little warmer but otherwise the same windy, rainy, gray conditions: appropriate."

We approached a fixed Border Patrol checkpoint and walked past without noticing any activity. If agents were inside, they didn't bother with people or vehicles going out to the beach, only those coming back toward the mainland.

Farther down the road, two separate Border Patrol vehicles stopped for cursory interviews.

Mom arrived to pick up Curtis. They would relocate Katia and Joseph from the Holiday Inn to their hotel on South Padre. Curtis treated the family to breakfast before driving back to Boca Chica Boulevard with my son.

Joseph livened things up considerably. Curtis tried to photograph Joseph walking beside me, but as soon as Curtis produced his phone, Joseph ran or jumped to my opposite side. My brother and my son played cat and mouse like this for the next several miles, while we all laughed at the silly game.

A truck pulled up beside us. The driver's hat identified him as a Vietnam veteran. He said, "I'll be waiting for you at the beach."

Somewhat unexpectedly, in the week leading up to Boca Chica Beach, my mood had trended downwards. Going back to Alabama meant: worries about truck and house payments, navigating health insurance for the first time in twenty years, and looking for another job.

But surrounded by family, my spirits elevated. This walk was fairly momentous, at least in my perspective. And the most important people would be there for the finale.

An hour later, the veteran's patience was spent. The finale committee evaporated as he drove west on Boca Chica Boulevard, stopping to give Joseph a large plastic dolphin. My son was appreciative, if a little puzzled by the gift. We thanked the veteran for coming, but it was a relief to have the beach to ourselves. A stranger's presence would have been awkward.

Joseph, Curtis, and I wandered off the blacktop and onto the south side of the road. The sand held animal tracks from several species, and it pleased me when Joseph identified most of them. The biggest tracks were from an enormous wild boar that had walked parallel to the road within the last few hours. Its tracks were sharply defined, not yet softened by the gentle rain.

A mature wild boar is a solitary, wandering beast that may cover ten or more miles in a night. They are not very pretty, will eat almost anything, and very few predators concern them. Were I Native American, the wild boar would be my spirit animal, and I found its passage as appropriate as the weather.

We approached a large brown tank painted with white letters: "Boca Chica Village Welcomes You." We took turns standing by or sitting on the tank for photos before starting the final stretch.

Curtis asked, "How do you feel now?"

"I am happy. I have come to terms with ending the trek. My legs are tired. I want to get back to Alabama and start writing, and I am ready to go home with the family."

The Gulf of Mexico splashed ashore in the distance. The rain stopped, and every now and then the sun would peek through the clouds before hiding again. Signs appeared on the side of the road, announcing the distance to the end of the pavement, prompting us to strike goofy poses at 200 yards, at 100 yards, and finally, at the end of the pavement.

Many had asked, "Are you going to run and jump into the sea?"

But there had already been enough discomfort, and I felt no compulsion to get wet, cold, and sandy.

At the beach, Rex, Mom, and Katia held back, while Curtis and Joseph walked to the water with me.

The waves rolled in and washed over my boots: tea colored water, covered with foam, and full of Sargasso weed.

The Gulf did not care that a man had walked a thousand miles to trod upon her shore. The waves did not alter their rhythm.

The gulls would only call and come if bread was thrown in the air.

The mullet would weave their same patterns in the shallows, lest a net was cast in their direction.

The redfish and speckled trout would continue to work the surf in search of shrimp and minnows, unless a baited hook or spoon splashed beside them.

In the grand scheme, the completion of this trek mattered not the least. It only meant something to my family, to Rex, to the Compadres, and to me. That was enough.

Shopping for scorpions and tarantulas at Prada

Curtis and Joseph on the final day's walk

24

AFTER THE WALK

"...it is because I have lived very much that now I can enjoy everything so well."

Ernest Hemingway. *The Sun Also Rises.* 1926

December 22–23

I stepped out of the surf and hugged Joseph.

Curtis and Rex took photos while Mom and Katia walked down to the beach. I glanced west and noticed a woman's blouse mixed in with the Sargasso weed on the beach. Boots and women's pants lay farther down the tide line. I asked, "Hey, Rex, are these the clothes you saw yesterday?"

Rex walked over. "That's them. The surf has moved them down the beach a little."

I observed, "There's something in the pocket." I stooped down to extract two wet $5.00 bills and an assortment of documents. Rex and Curtis watched as I timidly unfolded the soaked, fragile papers: a card for Angela's Bail Bonds, a receipt from the Cameron County Jail documenting a list of items held by a "Heather L. S.", at the time she was processed in and at the time she was released. Finally, a colorful certificate on thin paper from the *"Ministere De La Justice"* in Abidjan, **Côte d'Ivoire**, awarding "HLS" $4.4 million dollars.

"This just went from weird to downright spooky," Rex said.

"What should we do?" I asked.

"I would call the police later. I don't know if this is something you want to get involved in."

I put the papers and money in my pocket and said, "I'll make the call later. Let's finish with the photos and filming."

Curtis drove the family to South Padre while Rex shot from multiple angles. After an hour of filming, he was ready for the drive to Mississippi.

"We did it, Rex."

"You did it."

"You stuck with me. It was a long time and a lot of miles, and you didn't give up, even when I dragged ass at the beginning. That's impressive."

"You were dedicated and businesslike about getting up and covering the miles."

"Good luck with everything."

"Same to you."

A crazy mix of emotions coursed through me on the drive to South Padre: amazement – I had walked the length of the Texas -Mexico border! Disbelief – did I really walk the entire border, after dozens of people predicted my demise? Celebratory – Time to hit the bars with my brother Curtis! Melancholy – Bills, chores, and job applications waiting in Alabama. Relief- these poor feet and bones need a rest. Resolve – The manuscript must be worthy of the walk and the people who assisted me along the way. Concern – What happened to that girl on the beach?

The documents dried on the vanity while a vision formed: a distraught teenager wading into the Gulf, never to be seen again. I would take the documents to the police the following morning.

Mom treated us to pizza. Most of the family went to bed early, while Curtis and I closed down every bar within walking distance.

Despite the previous night's consumption, I arose early on December 22nd. Katia had located and brought my passport. We planned on crossing the border for a day of shopping in Nuevo Progresso, Mexico. But first, I located an address for the Brownsville Police substation closest to Boca Chica Beach.

I drove to the station and walked up to the receptionist. "I found some items on the beach that I'd like to show someone."

"Okay. Have a seat."

About twenty minutes later, a sergeant led me back to an office. He asked, "What can we do for you?"

I explained my trek, adding, "I think I was on the front page of the *Brownsville Herald* yesterday."

"I don't read the newspaper."

"Anyway… we finished the trek yesterday at Boca Chica Beach, where we found some woman's clothing with these papers in the pocket."

I handed him a plastic bag containing the two $5.00 bills, Angela's Bail Bond card, the list of items from the county jail, and the bogus certificate from the Ivory Coast.

The sergeant took the items and left for fifteen minutes before returning. He told me, "Let me tell you the truth. We are going to put these in an evidence file, and they will probably never get examined again."

He let me go, and I drove back to South Padre.

We all loaded into Curtis' rental car and drove to a parking area on the U.S. side of the border, just across from Nuevo Progresso. From there, we walked across to Mexico. It was fun, although Nuevo Progresso is a long way from authentic Mexico. Nuevo Progresso is a safe, easily accessible tourist trap. We had a good lunch at a reasonable price. The streets were lined with senior citizens loading up on discount drugs. Grandma bought enough candy to keep Joseph on a sugar high for the remainder of elementary school. Katia loaded up on spices for cooking. And, Curtis and I bought the maximum amount of tequila and rum allowed in by the U.S. Customs and Border Patrol.

Seven months later, on a whim, I searched the Internet for the missing girl from Boca Chica Beach. Bingo! Heather hadn't left the border, but she had moved west. "Heather L. S." was arrested and booked by the Maricopa County, Arizona's Sherriff's office on May 22nd, 2015. Heather was smiling in her most recent mug shot, as if she were happy to be found again. Curtis was relieved to hear of her continued existence.

The clothes on the beach had cast a shadow upon the completion of the trek. The mystery was solved, allowing for reflection.

As a whole, the experience was humbling. So many people went out of their way to provide assistance. And like Katy in El Paso, I will spend the rest of my life paying this forward.

A lot of geography was covered in this 1,010-mile trek.

The majority of my route lay through the Chihuahua Desert: big, beautiful, and overgrazed. With less cattle and more fire, it would revert from shrubs to herbaceous cover, benefitting wildlife and ranchers.

The Marfa Grasslands would benefit from prescribed fire. In the meantime, wildfires provide the same benefits, with more risk.

The Rio Grande is still one of America's most beautiful rivers. It's a crying shame that we suck it dry across so much of its length.

There are too many high fences in the lower Rio Grande Valley. These barriers are symptomatic of dying communities and a war on nature. There are more important things in life than white-tailed bucks with large antlers.

If you prefer to live in urban areas but are worried about crime, move to a border town on the American side. It will probably be safer than where you currently reside.

When confronted with the topography, people, and scale of the border-lands, one should realize that erecting a wall the length of the U.S.-Mexico border can best be described as paranoid, delusional, and grandiose.

This walk was conceived for purely selfish reasons: to test myself; to get away; to change my life's direction; to tell a story that has not been told. All these goals were met. But in telling this story, perhaps the pages herein reveal the amazing character and humanity of those who call the border their home. And in telling their story, perhaps I will have accomplished something bigger than I ever intended.

My appetite for adventure was not sated. The relief felt on Boca Chica Beach was temporary.

The trail is calling.

25

ACKNOWLEDGEMENTS

MY wife Katia handled Joseph, school, the house, and the Palafox Market while I was away for almost two months. Several months after my return, she delivered Marissa Kay, our second child and first daughter. With a near decade-long gap between our children, we had about given up on Joseph's sibling. Then, with the able assistance of fertility specialist Dr. George Inge in Mobile, Alabama, the pregnancy test came back positive.

Out of superstition, I told almost no one. Most friends and family weren't notified until late in the walk, when Katia had just started showing. Marissa Kay was our little miracle.

Shortly after we made it back to Alabama, I was off again. This time, the destination wasn't quite so remote. The Escape to Create Foundation provided a month-long artist's residency at Seaside, Florida. Fellow artists in residence exhibited an array of talent: Tyler Capp, Heather Robb, Donna Ruff, and Janet Satz. But it was most fortuitous to have another author, Bobbie Pyron, as a fellow author in residence. Bobbie's assistance and experience were inspirational.

Thanks to everyone that reviewed all or parts of the manuscript, including but not limited to: Gabriela A. Treviño, Sarah Jane Howland, Bobbie Pyron, Roger Reid, Shon Scott, Ghislain Rompré, Mark and Karan Bailey, Curtis (the comma Nazi) Hainds, Rex Jones, Keith Bowden, Mike Powell, Bob Larimore, Nathan Lambrecht, Tiffany Hartley, Oscar Galindo,

Wynn Anderson, John Sproul, Lane and Priscilla Holmes, Christian Wagner, and Susan Feathers.

My head rested at a multitude of residences, motels, hotels, and campsites during the trek. Apologies to anyone neglected. To start off, the Hilton Garden Inn at the University of Texas El Paso provided a reduced rate, a great location, and fantastic facilities for the kickoff. Others who provided lodging and or meals include: Richard Reinap for lodging and food on the drive out, Simons Hane and Ronnie Vehorn in Presidio, Bob Larimore, Dalipseth and his mother at the Budget Inn in Sanderson, Debbie and Tim for the food, drink, and lodging at the Lajitas Golf Resort, the Billings Family in Langtry, Rex Jones, who split the cost with me on many a room, Roger Reid who provided rooms in Mission & Brownsville, and Mom, who set us up right on South Padre.

The Tex-Mex Compadres were amazing. In order of service: the Right Honorable Jack, Dr. Simons Hane and Mfundisi Ronnie, Bob Larimore, Jimmy and Sierra Stiles, Mike Powell, John Dickson, and Curtis Hainds. Their service is recognized here and in the body of this work.

Thanks to Rex Jones who followed and filmed me along the border. While we didn't call him a Tex-Mex Compadre, his assistance and contributions were essential to the success of this trek. I can't wait to see *La Frontera!*

Besides editing portions of my manuscript, Mark Bailey constructed maps that friends and family used to track my progress on Facebook, and these maps were utilized on the front page or as content in several newspapers. Great job, Mark!

Thank you, Joseph, for the wonderful walking stick. And thank you for walking the final miles with me.

Thanks to Decie and the Brosnan Forest staff for my other two walking sticks.

Thanks to Sandie for her contribution at the Palafox Market.

Thanks to the retired nurseryman, Robert Cross, for his contribution at our regional conference in Mobile.

Thanks to Martin H. Maldonado for the contribution on Highway 83.

Thanks to Earnie Dillard, Mom's significant other, for the money he sent. Curtis and I put those dollars to work right away on South Padre!

Thank you, Mom, for being there at the finale and for being there all my life.

Thanks to Keith Bowden, Cynta, Tiffany Hartley, Jesus "Chuy" Calderon, and S. Matt Read for allowing me to interview you and include your perspectives in this book.

Thanks to Darice for the wonderful tour of the Red Rock Ranch.

Thanks to everyone who lives along the border. I will never forget you.

Finally, thanks to the Escape to Create Foundation for believing in me and providing the most valuable commodities one may possess when writing a book manuscript – time and a quiet place to work. Without my idyllic month at Seaside, Florida, it is hard to imagine how I would have finished this book.

Lake Amistad in background

Del Rio Sunset (photo by Sierra Stiles)

26

RELEVANT
WORKS - LITERATURE CITED

Bass, Rick. *A Thousand Deer: Four Generations of Hunting and the Hill Country*. Austin, Texas. University of Texas Press: 187 pages. 2012.

Bass, Rick & Paul Christenson: Afterword to *Falling From Grace in Texas: A Literary Response to the Demise of Paradise*. San Antonio, Texas. Wings Press: 157 pages. 2004.

Bowden, Keith. *The Tecate Journal: 70 Days on the Rio Grande*. Seattle, Washington. The Mountaineers Books: 291 pages. 2007.

Bragg, Rick. *The Most They Ever Had*. San Francisco, CA. MacAdam/Cage: 156 pages. 2009.

Brenner, Anita and George R. Leighton. *The Wind that Swept Mexico: The History of the Mexican Revolution 1910-1942*: New York, NY. Harper and Brothers: 302 pages. 1943.

Brown, Larry. *The Rough South of Larry Brown*. Durham, NC. Written and Directed by Gary Hawkins. Center for Documentary Studies at Duke University. 2008.

Cartwright, Gary. *Dirty Dealing: Drug Smuggling on the Mexican Border and the Assassination of a Federal Judge*. El Paso, Texas. Cinco Puntos Press: 387 pages. 1998.

Davis, Jennifer Pharr. *Becoming Odyssa: Adventures on the Appalachian Trail*. New York. Beaufort Book: 306 pages. 2010.

Egan, Timothy. *The Immortal Irishman: The Irish Revolutionary Who*

Became an American Hero. Boston, MA. Houghton Mifflin Harcourt. 2016.

Finch, Bill, Beth Maynor Young, Rhett Johnson, and John C. Hall. *Longleaf, Far as the Eye Can See*. Chapel Hill, NC. University of North Carolina Press. 2012.

Flynt, Wayne. *Keeping the Faith: Ordinary People, Extraordinary Lives*. Tuscaloosa, AL. University of Alabama Press. 2011.

Ford, Don Henry and Charles Bowden. *Contrabando: Confessions of a Drug-Smuggling Texas Cowboy*. El Paso, Texas. Cinco Puntos Press: 240 pages. 2004.

Greene, A.C. *Of Green Water and Invisible History. In Falling From Grace in Texas: A Literary Response to the Demise of Paradise*. Edited by Rick Bass and Paul Christensen. San Antonio, Texas. Wings Press.172 pages. 2004.

Grey, Zane. *Riders of the Purple Sage*. Grosset & Dunlap, New York, NY. 1912.

Hainds, Mark J. *Year of the Pig*. Tuscaloosa, Alabama. University of Alabama Press: 248 pages. 2011.

Hemingway, Ernest. *The Sun Also Rises*. Charles Scribner's Sons. New York, NY. 1926.

Hooks Christopher. Border Lawman Tells Politicians to "Shut Up" About the Border. *Texas Observer*. Saturday, March 1st, 2014.

Ivins, Molly. *Molly Ivins Can't Say That, Can She?* Random House, Inc. New York, NY. 1991.

Jenkins, Peter. *A Walk Across America*. Fawcett Crest Books: 320 pages. 1979.

King, Stephen. *On Writing: A Memoir of the Craft*. New York, NY. Scribner. 291 pages. 2000.

Greg Lukianoff and Jonathan Haidt. *The Coddling of the American Mind. In* The Atlantic. Vol 316 No 2. September 2015.

Markham, Beryl. *West With the Night*. New York, NY. North Point Press, Farrar, Strauss, and Giroux. 1942.

Morgenthaler, Jefferson. *The River Has Never Divided Us: A Border History of La Junta de los Rios.* Austin, Texas. University of Texas Press: 317 pages. 2004.

Muir, John. *A Thousand-Mile Walk to the Gulf.* Boston, Massachusetts. Copyright 1916 by Houghton Mifflin. And First Mariner Books: 217 pages. 1998.

Poppa, Terrence E. *Drug Lord: The Life and Death of a Mexican Kingpin.* El Paso, Texas. Cinco Puntos Press: 346 pages. 2010.

Ray, Janise. *Drifting into Darien: A Personal and Natural History of the Altamaha River.* Athens, Georgia. University of Georgia Press. 2011.

Romo, David Dorado. *Ringside Seat to a Revolution: An Underground Cultural History of El Paso and Juarez: 1893-1923.* El Paso, Texas. Cinco Puntos Press: 293 pages. 2005.

Rusho, W.L. *Everett Ruess: A Vagabond for Beauty.* Layton, Utah. Gibbs-Smith: 240 pages. 1983.

Saenz, Benjamin Alejandro Alire. *Everything Begins and Ends at The Kentucky Club.* El Paso, Texas. Cinco Puntos Press: 222 pages. 2012.

Strayed, Cheryl. *Wild: From Lost to Found on the Pacific Coast Trail.* New York, NY. Alfred a Knopf: 315 pages. 2012.

Texas Animal Health Commission: *TAHC Releases Temporary Fever Tick Quarantine Area in Starr County.* News Release. June 23, 2015. Austin, Texas. 1 page.

Vargas Llosa, Mario. *Captain Pantoja and the Special Service.* New York, NY. Harper and Row Publishers, Inc. English Translation by Gregory Kolovakos and Ronald Christ. 1990.

Vargas Llosa, Mario. *The Storyteller.* New York, NY. Penguin Books-English Translation. 246 pages. 1989.

Vonnegut, Kurt. *Bluebeard.* New York, NY. Dell Publishing. 1987.

Welling, Tina. *Writing Wild.* Novato, California. New World Library: 231 pages. 2014.

Mike at end of day's walk on Old Mines Road

Breakfast at Mar y Tierra in San Ygnacio

Waffles and beer with John in Rio Grande City

Walking the final miles with Joseph

The family at Boca Chica Beach: Curtis, the author, Joseph, and Betty

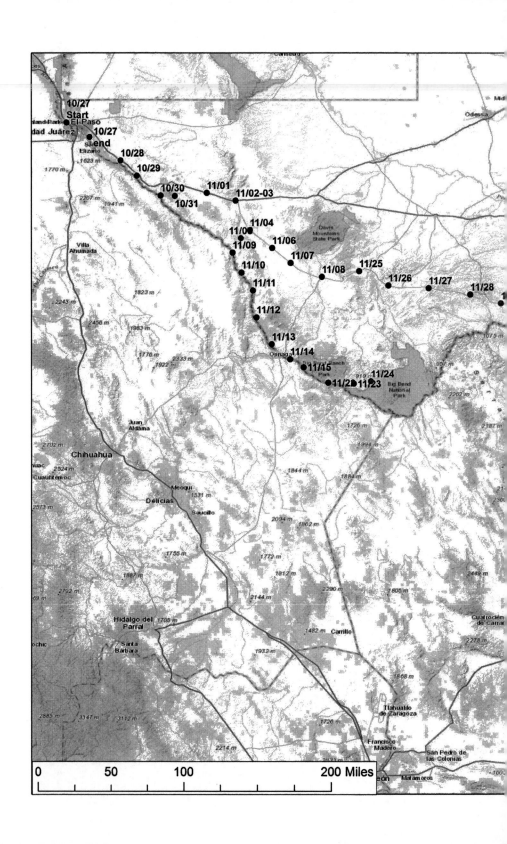

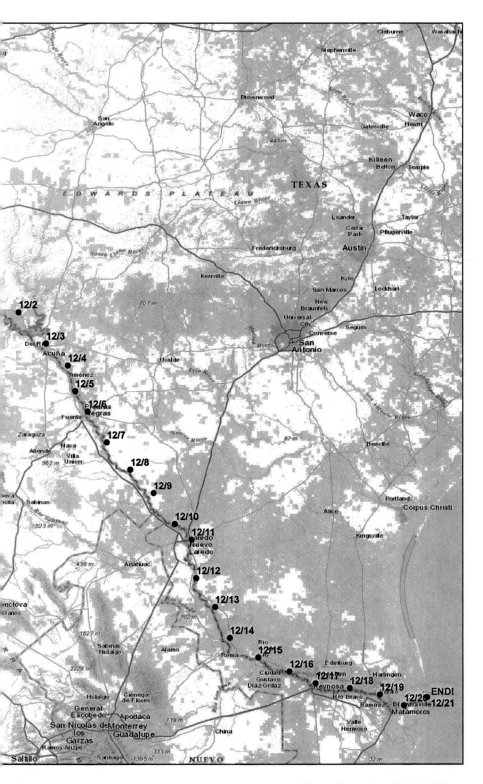

Daily coordinates plotted by Mark Bailey